SHAMANIC BREATHWORK

THE NATURE OF CHANGE

VENUS RISING

LINDA STAR WOLF PH.D.

FOREWORD BY NIKÓLAUS STAR WOLF

WALID ABOULNAGA : SARA K. ALJNEIBI : LISA ASVESTAS : LEVI BANNER : KEITH CAPLIN

KRISY CONROY & KRTI PSYSKRIT : JUDITH CORV̶̶̶̶̶̶̶̶̶̶̶̶̶̶̶̶ ̶̶̶̶̶̶̶SEPH E. DOHERTY

GAIL FOSS : NITA GAGE : MAR GUERRE

EDMUNDO & KIMBERLEE LOPEZ : CARLEY MATTI̶̶̶̶̶̶̶̶̶̶̶̶̶̶̶̶ ̶̶̶̶̶̶̶̶̶̶̶̶̶̶̶LÉH

FRANK MONDEOSE : CRYSTAL DAWN MORRIS : ̶̶̶̶̶̶̶̶̶̶̶̶̶̶̶̶ ̶̶̶̶̶̶̶̶̶̶̶̶̶̶LF

HEIDI STEFFENS : ATLANTIS WOLF : LAURA WOLF : MARIKO ̶̶̶̶̶̶̶̶̶̶̶̶̶̶̶ZBEK

SHAMANIC BREATHWORK

THE NATURE OF CHANGE

LINDA STAR WOLF PH.D

FOREWORD BY NIKÓLAUS WOLF

Featuring: Walid Ablounaga : Sara K. Aljneibi : Lisa Asvestas :
Levi Banner : Keith Caplin : Krisy Conroy and Krti Psyskrit :
Judith Corvin-Blackburn : Joseph E. Doherty : Gail Foss :
Nita Gage : Mar Guerrero : Kathy Guidi : Deb Kotz :
Edmundo and Kimberlee Lopez : Carley Mattimore & John Malan :
Freyiia Milléh : Frank Mondeose : Crystal Dawn Morris :
Judy Redhawk : Patricia Silverwolf : Heidi Steffens : Atlantis Wolf :
Laura Wolf : Mariko Heart Wolf : Zeina Yazbek

"This is a riveting read and a precious book describing journeys of transformation and discovery of inner Truth in a beautifully alive and detailed manner. So inspiring to read and I believe that many of us find ourselves in those pages. The appreciation of the ever evolving journey, blessed by the power of the Breath and the warming support of community.

Linda Star Wolf is an awe-inspiring leader with a heightened ability to access her internal resources and tune into the forces and powers outside of herself. Thank you for your dedication and leadership!"

—**Elvi Orr,** Wife and lineage keeper of the founder of Rebirthing Breathwork Leonard Orr, leader of Rebirthing Breathwork International, Rebirthing Breathwork practitioner and trainer.

"Fall in love with the vast shamanic wisdom traditions and experiences. *Shamanic Breathwork: The Nature of Change* by Linda Star Wolf, with the bold contribution by many other practitioners, is a fascinating portrayal of profound healing and deep personal transformation needed at this critical time."

—**Itzhak Beery**, Author of *The Gift of Shamanism,*
Shamanic Transformations, and *Shamanic Healing.*
Leading Shamanic teacher, healer, and speaker.
Founder and publisher of shamanportal.org

"I was astounded by the depths of Star Wolf's Shamanic Breathwork. Without psychedelics or entheogens, you can achieve similar experiences breathing. This book will inspire you to what is truly available by the blessing of breath and how it can change your life in less than an hour."

—**Maxi Cohen**, filmmaker and artist, director of Ayahuasca Diaries
and executive producer of From Shock to Awe,
a film about ayahuasca saving veterans from suicide.

"In this beautiful and heartfelt book on the transformational power of Shamanic Breathwork, Star Wolf shows that she has indeed "become a force of nature." This gathering of stories written by nearly thirty experienced practitioners describes how lives can change, how portals between the worlds can open, and how we can re-envision our relationship to death through this ecstatic healing art. There is a shaman within each of us, and when we remember that, our innate gift of multi-dimensional consciousness can be birthed."

—**Azra Bertrand**, M.D., founder of Biomancy University,
co-author of the Nautilus-award-winning *Womb Awakening*
and *Magdalene Mysteries*

"This book is a wonderful endorsement of Linda's work and of shamanic breathwork itself. This kind of work is powerful and important, because it offers the opportunity to go within to the wisdom of your deep self and the remarkable gifts of healing and transformation that Creator has placed within you. In a time when so much attention is focused outward and on someone / something else rescuing us, it is especially relevant and beneficial."

—**Brooke Medicine Eagle**, author of *Buffalo Woman Comes Singing*
and *The Last Ghost Dance*

"Powerful, inspiring, transformative, touching, awakening, healing…these are only some of the qualities of this amazing book. Read it, and I promise you will cry, recognizing yourselves in many of the stories told, and you will feel grateful for the hope those stories offer you. And possibly, after reading it, you might react like I did: going to their website and checking when the next Shamanic Breathwork workshop is offered, ready to sign up for this potentially life changing adventure!"

—**Shama Viola**, Damanhur Mystic
and creator of Bral Talej Divination Cards

"*In Shamanic Breathwork: The Nature of Change*, the reader is offered a series of personal stories, each a divine design showing that despite our resistance to change, our souls are always 'calling us awake'. Star Wolf, in sharing her shamanic breathwork teachings clearly shows a woman who has stayed her path, so others might walk theirs. Collectively they make clear, that by facing our labors in life, individually we can birth our soul's calling, that we are sovereign beings."

—**Sandra Corcoran**, author of *Shamanic Awakening*, integrative coach, international shamanic teacher, and Thoth Tarot reader

"*Shamanic Breathwork: The Nature of Change* brings together a stunning array of brave, courageous souls who have been burned to the ground and have been rebirthed like a Phoenix from the flames of transformation. I am so moved by the raw authenticity, searing vulnerability and courage these individuals share in this remarkable collection of soul stories for a new millennium. We live in a culture that has lost the understanding and importance of true soul initiation and Linda Starwolf and Venus Rising have been creating sacred, safe and fierce containers for such life altering and transformative initiations for decades. I highly recommend this moving book for those who are interested in an inside look at this unique form of transformative breathwork and how it can help you navigate so many of the current challenges we are facing individually and collectively."

—**Michael Brant DeMaria**, Ph.D., Integrative Psychologist (retired), Best Selling Author of *Ever Flowing On* and *Peace Within*, 4-time Grammy nominated recording artist

"We live in a Great Mystery in this world. For all our beliefs and knowledge, science and stories the underlying truth is our presence and opportunities in this world are expressions of a great mystery. Fact is, we do not actually know for a fact where we come from or where we go to once we leave our human bodies. That alone is all I needed to come to terms with realizing I am far more mystery than I am known, even to me. Life is the presence of this amazing mystery and Earth is the mystery school experience place. As human beings we live between the realms of form and Spirit, Wind and Light, Earth and Air. We are the weaving of the elements of life with an added spark of Spirit-fire. Lindas breathwork is a fantastic tool to guide our awareness and attention back to our self, our consciousness, and all the layers of experience and legacy imprinted within us as human beings. For us to come to know our self, as the true spirit that we really are, we must unravel the layers of legacy and beliefs, judgments and role plays that come to "define" our lives in this world. Breathwork opens us up to that opportunity to unravel, realize, release, and re-imagine our being.

Linda is a master as she has a lifetime of practice with her art of Shamanic Breathwork. Practice makes the master.

Be courageous and take advantage of the opportunity to read this book and then DO THE EXPERIENCE OF SHAMANIC BREATHWORK. The gift is in the jumping in and living YOUR experience with breathwork.

Our world needs us to WAKE UP and Shamanic Breathwork is a wonderful alarm clock."

—**Lee Mccormick**, Creator/ Director Spirit Recovery Inc.

"What a beautiful book written by Linda Star Wolf, with the bold contribution by many other practitioners. The entire book is written with love, teaching us what we need to know and understand about the way of Shamanic Breathwork. I was especially taken aback by how I was able to apply these teachings to my life. Thank you Star Wolf for bringing this incredibly needed medicine to us all!"

—**Daniel Gutierrez,** International Best-Selling Author, Mindful Leadership Expert, Master Life/Business Coach, Director/Owner of Catalina Retreat Center in Pisac, Peru

Paperback ISBN: 978-1-954047-50-1

eBook ISBN: 978-1-954047-48-8

DISCLAIMER

This book offers health and wellness information and is designed for educational purposes only. You should not rely on this information as a substitute for, nor does it replace professional medical advice, diagnosis, or treatment. If you have any concerns or questions about your health, you should always consult with a physician or other healthcare professional. Do not disregard, avoid, or delay obtaining medical or health-related advice from your healthcare professional because of something you may have read here. The use of any information provided in this book is solely at your own risk.

Developments in medical research may impact the health, fitness, and nutritional advice that appears here. No assurances can be given that the information contained in this book will always include the most relevant findings or developments with respect to the particular material.

Having said all that, know that the experts here have shared their tools, practices, and knowledge with you with a sincere and generous intent to assist you on your health and wellness journey. Please contact them with any questions you may have about the techniques or information they provided. They will be happy to assist you further!

DEDICATION

This book is dedicated to you and your steadfast dedication to walk the ongoing spiral path of shamanic death and rebirth in order to remember who you really are. You, my dear, are a powerful Force of Nature!

I want you to know, deep down, that you can change your life and make the impossible possible! Yes, I am speaking directly to you!

You can make unbelievable, radical changes in your health, profession, personal relationships, and spiritual connection with something far greater than your ego-mind. Your whole life can become your beautiful, sacred purpose so that you don't have to compartmentalize who you are.

There is a shaman within you who inherently holds the wisdom and truth of who you are and why you are here on Earth at this time. You are not here by accident, so you must be here on purpose.

I invite you to take the most important journey of all, the inner one, that will wake up your shamanic consciousness and give you the courage to step fully into your passion, power, and purpose. I know you can do this because I have traveled this road before you as my teachers walked it before me. My life is my own now and has been for a long time.

Let your wolfie nose sniff out the trail to freedom as you lift your heart and spirit with a big howl at the moon. What are you waiting for? Let's Breathe!

TABLE OF CONTENTS

FOREWORD

Nikólaus Wolf

As I am writing the foreword for *Shamanic Breathwork: The Nature of Change*, I am feeling a deep sense of pride and appreciation. I've had powerful, life-changing experiences with Shamanic Breathwork (SBW) since 2011. To properly address the gravity contained within the authors' stories and the shared transformational medicine, I must first begin at the end, as all endings are the bridge to the next great beginning.

While I am writing this foreword as the Co-Director of Venus Rising Association for Transformation and as a Shamanic Breathwork Master Practitioner, I am also writing to you as Star Wolf's faithful, ever devoted husband and direct lineage carrier of this sacred work. There are no bounds to my belief in this woman, and nowhere I would not tread to be by her side, whether that's to the edge of this world or beyond.

Spiraling back to a trying time in my life, close to my 20th birthday, I found myself walking through the local, new age bookstore in St. Charles, Missouri. I was in search of a sign from the universe to guide me towards a new way of living, as I was at a crossroads and the old way was no longer working. As fate would have it, I was drawn to read Star Wolf's original Shamanic Breathwork book, *Shamanic Breathwork: Journeying Beyond the Limits of the Self*. It was around this time that I began to experience intense, and at times quite painful, electric shocks shooting up my spine. As this continued to happen, I realized that this stimulating sensation was connected to reading Star Wolf's personal journey. It was as if something inside me began to stir and recognize my future self was calling me. Although, I would not have been able to put this into words at the time.

The sheer magic, synchronicity, shadow, and challenges of this path I've been called to walk, has led me to become a walker between the imaginal and manifest worlds, as if in a waking dream. Yet, I'm more grounded and on purpose than I have ever dared imagine.

Just as Star Wolf was supernaturally called in the Dreamtime and given the seemingly impossible task of finding Seneca Wolf Clan Grandmother Twylah Nitsch, in a pre-Google era, I have my own synchronistic tale of following the impossible star that led me to be by Star Wolf's side. As a young man struggling with addictions and the loss of attachment to this world, I was somehow miraculously guided, or rather drawn, into her life and all that that entails! After reading her book and moving to the Venus Rising mountain retreat center, I apprenticed with her late husband, Brad Collins, as my beloved mentor.

The time came when I was called to continue my vision quest back out into the world, where I had the opportunity to practice embodying shamanic consciousness in my everyday life. I traveled all across the country, explored nature, fell in love, experienced heartbreak and disillusionment, and found myself led to take a deeper dive into my family of origin patterns.

As I was making my way to Virginia to spend time with my birth father, I was meditating in the redwoods in northern California when I received the news that Brad had been diagnosed with late-stage cancer. I immediately felt the call to return home to the magical blue mountains of western North Carolina to be with Brad as he prepared to return to the stars.

Finally, this quest ended with me checking myself into a psychiatric unit in Virginia during a dark night of the soul. I was at another octave on my soul's path of seeking guidance and direction as the pressure to change built to an unmanageable level. Because the medical environment was not trained to recognize the difference between a spiritual emergency and a psychotic break, I was prescribed psychiatric medications. Fortunately, I knew enough from my time with Venus Rising to know that what my soul was in need of could not be found in a pill. I declined treatment and checked myself out.

Around this time, I received a synchronistic call from Star Wolf, who invited me to visit and attend a Soul Return workshop. After the workshop, I decided to extend my stay. Star Wolf and I were still in the wake of the devastation left by Brad's untimely death. We found ourselves processing our shared grief through lengthy late-night talks, watching old movies, working the 30 shamanic questions, and trying to put the pieces back together again.

Star Wolf and I have felt a deep soul connection with one another that transcends time and space from the first moment we reconnected in this lifetime. The nature of this loving connection has shape-shifted several times as our relationship has evolved over the years. Inevitably, the time came when we surrendered to our heart's inner knowing and to Great Mystery by acknowledging that our love and sacred purpose were deeply interwoven together, thus our sacred marriage was born.

Spiraling forward to the present time, these collective authors hold a transmission that the world seems in dire need of now more than ever. It's time to remember that we are all children of the great Neteru (also known as the nature spirits). Through embracing the elements of Water, Earth, Fire, Spirit, and Air, we can reconnect to our divine birthright. If we are to change the way we live upon this planet, we must start with the understanding of our connection to the elemental world and how to embrace the cycles of change, remembering to breathe and shape-shift as we journey through the shamanic initiations of life, death, and rebirth.

Throughout these archetypal stories, each author offers us the opportunity to take a deep breath, open to our unique connection of all that is, and to remember that these stories are a part of us. Knowing that, we too can experience this shamanic medicine of the soul as we take the time to heal and transform the wounds within.

Based on my own experience, I trust if you are reading this book, it is not by accident! You will soon discover that Shamanic Breathwork is a unique ceremony that invites folks from of all walks of life to heal themselves and heal the world. Each author shares how they answered the call to go deep within themselves, faced their wounds and traumas stored on a cellular DNA level, and reclaimed parts of their soul.

Shamanic Breathwork is an evolution of Star Wolf's life work and personal medicine. Each of the authors in this book is an integral part of this legacy as they share their own medicine. It's also important to honor and acknowledge the wise elders and ancestors whose shoulders we now stand upon in the world. A deep bow of gratitude and love to breathwork pioneers Stanislav Grof, Jacquelyn Small, and Leonard Orr. These visionary pathfinders had a profound influence on Star Wolf's early path and led to the creation of Shamanic Breathwork. And a big wolf howl to Grandmother Twylah Nitsch (Yehwehnode - *She whose voice rides upon the wind*) for the wolf clan teachings.

In my life, Shamanic Breathwork has made the impossible possible. I know this to be true for each author within this book, as they too have experienced the transformational power of the Shamanic Breathwork ceremony. My heart's desire is for you to remember who you really are and to rediscover your own magic as you journey alongside each author into their medicine stories.

Nikólaus Star Wolf, beloved of Linda Star Wolf, is the Co-Director of Venus Rising Association for Transformation. Nikó is a Shamanic Breathwork Master Practitioner, an Ordained Shamanic Priest and Shamanic Minister through Venus Rising. Nikólaus holds a Master's Degree in Shamanic Psycho-Spiritual Studies from Venus Rising University and he is the Co-Founder of the Shamanic Mystery Tours, facilitating shamanic journeys throughout the world. Nikó apprenticed under the late Brad Collins and is dedicated to serving the planet, awakening shamanic consciousness in others as he continues to follow his own souls' path.

Chapter 1

SHAMANIC BREATHWORK
Becoming a Force of Nature

Linda Star Wolf, Ph.D., DMin

*"It is not the strongest of the species that survives,
nor the most intelligent, but the one most responsive to change."*

~Charles Darwin

MY STORY

Sometimes it takes being caught up in a wild, raging thunderstorm on top of a mountain and suddenly, out of the blue, getting struck by a bolt of lightning before I'm finally ready to let go of an old ego identity that is dying.

There is definitely the me that existed prior to being struck by lightning, and the me that was reborn after being brought to my knees in Venus Rising's outdoor air temple in the summer of 2018.

A glowing red ball of fire shot across the sky, somehow sending an electrifying charge through the microphone into my hand while I was transmitting teachings to our group of students about shamanic death and rebirth.

Ironically, or perhaps synchronistically, on the night before my shamanic encounter with lightning, I intuitively placed a bronze sculpture of a Norse God with his two ravens and two wolves on the Breathwork altar. I acquired this unique piece during an adventurous journey to Iceland with my partner Nikólaus a year earlier. Initially, I thought the statue was Thor, who's known for his close association with thunder and lightning. Later, however, I realized it was actually Odin, his powerful and mysterious father. He is the elemental, wizard-king of the old Norse Gods who presides over all of nature, including storms, thunder, lightning, birth, death, and the afterlife.

On this evening, I was drawn to play an elementally themed Shamanic Breathwork music set for our group session. It included intense drumming with evocative music mixed in with the sound of lightning and thunder for the sixth initiation that I teach, called Activating Your Imaginal Cells. This final journey in the series is meant to be both evocative and integrative and always takes place towards the end of our Venus Rising intensive training program called the Shamanic Healing Initiatory Process® (SHIP).

On this particularly warm, candlelit evening, the group gathered at the air temple on top of our magical, blue mountains. We intentionally cleared our sacred temple space and each other's energy fields using my wild turkey wing (the giveaway bird) to fan the sweet, pungent smoke from the sage in the abalone shell.

Once the safe container for our sacred circle had been set, the Shamanic Breathwork session was ready to get underway. I started to softly beat the heartbeat of my drum as I gently walked past each member of our group who was lying down and ready to enter into the altered state.

The intention is always the same at the beginning of the Shamanic Breathwork ceremony. It's important to surrender to Spirit, let go of our ego's agenda, and trust our inner shaman to take us where we need to go.

Suddenly, I felt the old familiar tug in my solar plexus signaling that my inner shaman was calling me to breathe. I caught the attention of the other facilitators and let them know I was going to lie down and breathe with the group as they held space.

It's not unusual for our staff and team members to take an opportunity when it's available to join in the Shamanic Breathwork journey. By doing so, we're modeling that we are all still walking the spiral path of healing transformation and that life changes are constantly in progress.

As I laid down on my comfortable palette in the dark softness of the night, I surrounded myself with a sacred golden hoop of protection. I called in my spirit animal, the White Wolf, and Anubis, my Egyptian Wolf guide. I invited my beloved ancestors on the other side of the veils to be by my side. I humbly asked for help from all spirit keepers between the realms of heaven and earth. I then surrendered my heart into the care of the Great Spirit and Great Mystery. I had been holding back facing a big truth in my life, and it was becoming very uncomfortable and undeniable.

I began to connect to the natural rhythm of continuous deep breathing, syncing and flowing with the musical journey. As I reminded myself to "breathe until I was surprised," I felt my ego attachment to storylines fading. The healing power of the ceremony opened me up in an energetic way as I journeyed, showing me that I couldn't run from my truth any longer. I felt a growing acceptance that big changes were coming, whether I was ready or not. I remember howling and letting my energy run free, accepting whatever the future would bring.

The session came to a close with the sound of the heartbeat of the drum calling us back to this world. The facilitators encouraged us to journal or draw our experiences, messages, and symbols from the Shamanic Breathwork journey. I often think of these spontaneous symbols that appear during an altered state as our soul's hieroglyphics. They carry the transformational messages encoded in our DNA. When made conscious, they can translate into a new level of awareness. In other words, we shape-shift from caterpillars into butterflies and evolve into who we are meant to be.

Before I share more about where the spiral journey is taking me presently, let us time travel back to where many of my elemental patterns were forged.

On the day of my birth, the delivery doctor disappeared for quite some time, leaving the nurses highly concerned. They were not supposed to deliver babies without the doctor being present in the 1950s. Apparently, this resulted in me being stuck in the birth canal. Finally, after a long and exhausting labor, I was pulled out of my mother's womb with forceps, causing dangerous complications. As a result, my forehead was bruised, leaving an angry reddish spot on the center of my forehead, which still becomes activated when significant changes are occurring in my life. I later learned through a Shamanic Breathwork journey that my young, frightened momma was in the throes of labor when they "knocked her out" with heavy drugs, which meant I was unconscious as well.

I remember feeling confused and guilty as an only child when I would overhear family conversations indicating that my mother was quite ill and almost died giving birth to me. It was implied that that is why she didn't have any more children, explaining her unconscious resentment towards me.

Growing up, I spent the majority of time with my Mammy and Pappy Jones (my maternal grandparents) on their farm down the road while my parents worked at their jobs. It was often said in concerned, hushed tones that I was considered overly sensitive. I now realize I was a natural empath, deeply in touch with nature spirits, fairies, and the star beings that visited me from time to time. I had prophetic dreams about future events where I knew private things that no one had told me, which was unsettling to some adults. Sometimes I even felt like I was the parent to my young parents. Even though I was the youngest student in my class, I often found myself in the counselor role with others.

Many of my childhood days were filled with countless blessings as I walked barefoot on the Earth from spring to fall. I was surrounded by the beauty of nature, a lush garden, and a diverse collection of friendly farm animals. My tender being was held by two nature-loving grandparents who "thought I hung the moon," as we say in the south. They made me feel special instead of strange. After all, I was told I was a lot like my Mammy, who was a force to be reckoned with in all of our minds. She taught me that we shared the gift of being powerful seers who could read "signs and wonders" in the natural world and decipher dreams. I lived in this idyllic atmosphere where I felt protected and almost "normal" until my "rock" and soul mate, Mammy Jones, left this realm unexpectedly shortly after my 12th birthday. I was utterly devastated and felt a profound soul loss without her physical presence in my life for many years to come.

Fast forward to the 1960s where I came of age as a teenager. The whole world turned upside down and inside out with the arrival of technicolor, psychedelics, and electric rock n' roll right alongside civil rights, gay rights, women's rights, war protests, and new ways of perceiving the world.

The assassination of President John Kennedy shocked the world in 1963 when I was eleven. In 1968 the world was brought to its knees with the assassinations of presidential candidate Robert Kennedy and the civil rights leader the honorable Reverend Martin Luther King Jr., just a short time apart. In the wake of these tragedies arose civil unrest and protest. "Make Love Not War" became the famous hippie chant, and the "free love revolution" was in full swing.

After graduation from high school and briefly attending a local community college, I moved away from my small hometown and became fully immersed in the hippie lifestyle at a politically aware campus at the University of Kentucky. I felt at home again for the first time since my Mammy's death. I met many like-minded people who didn't see me as strange. It was a breath of fresh air to be appreciated for my natural gifts and abilities to read palms, auras, tarot cards, and interpret dreams. I vibrated to a wild combination of swirling archetypal energies that included Marilyn Monroe, Janis Joplin, the Beatles, Bob Dylan, the Rolling Stones, Ram Dass, and Mahatma Gandhi. I proceeded to embrace my lifestyle as a Hippie Queen of peace and love. I managed to rent an older two-story house a few blocks off campus that became a regular communal-style hippie hang-out. It was quite popular with many who dropped in regularly and kindred spirits who were passing through town.

Ecstatically, we experimented with alcohol, marijuana, and hallucinogens while listening to the most incredible music bubbling up from all around the globe. We frequently stayed up all night in an altered state engaged in deep philosophical discussions. Yet somehow, I managed to make passing grades with social work, creative writing, sociology, and psychology classes. It was one of the most consciousness-expanding times of my life. However, I was not grounded in my being, still very sensitive and innocent in many ways. I also had unhealed family of origin wounds and unconscious shadow pieces taking me into dangerous places in my psyche. I ended up having a near-death experience after taking some unidentified drugs during an outdoor rock concert.

In the early morning hours, I was rushed to a hospital. Before passing out, the last thing I remember was the sensation of floating above my body close to the ceiling while watching the hospital workers trying to revive me and hearing them say, "I don't think she'll make it." I wondered what all the fuss was about because from where I was, I felt just fine. I woke up a day later and had to deal with the reality that I had almost died from a drug overdose and the fact that I had innocently ingested unknown drugs without questioning it.

This experience left me anxiety-ridden, often emotionally triggered, and hyperventilating with a pervasive feeling of non-reality for more than a year. Doctors prescribed psychiatric medications that made me feel even stranger. Thankfully, my higher self knew it wasn't what I needed for my healing. Instead of pharmaceuticals, I started practicing transcendental meditation, deep yogic breathing exercises, writing poetry and short stories, and working with oracle cards. I carried a paper bag in my blue jean's pocket for more than a year to recirculate the carbon dioxide back into my bloodstream, returning my breathing to normal when I felt anxious.

Shortly after I returned to college, I fell in love and married my hippie Italian boyfriend from Pittsburgh. We decided to move back to my hometown and receive family support to start a new life together. I was still a hot mess in many ways, and my husband also suffered from drug-induced anxiety, which we medicated with alcohol. He found work in construction while I was basically homebound for almost a year. I began to self-heal through reading and practicing what I learned from a large box of esoteric books that my older psychic cousin gave me. I know it may sound a bit crazy, but I now see it all as a divine plan of perfection for my early shamanic training. This is where I learned to listen to my inner guidance instead of the advice of so-called authorities, who wanted to medicate my symptoms. The mainstream tried to return me to a state of "normal" that I had never been.

I find it interesting how the pattern of not being able to be fully myself kept resulting in traumas and dramas, creating the feeling of being too much and not being able to breathe. This pattern has been a lifelong wounding repeating itself at different octaves on my spiral path. As I have embraced the wisdom of my shamanic path, learning from both inner and outer shaman's, I can breathe more freely and take what was once mainly a wound and turn it into "good medicine" for countless others around the planet.

Those who become shamanic healers and guides for others often experienced soul loss through difficult births, premature loss of childhood, and sometimes multiple near-death experiences. Many have learned to deal with temporary insanity, traumas, and various afflictions and addictions before emerging victorious with their own healing medicine, which they learn how to share with the world.

When I experienced one of my first breathwork journeys, I was spontaneously transported back in time and relived my actual birth process. I realized just how near-death the experience was for my momma and me. We were both so drugged it made birth more difficult and life-threatening on a whole other level. Thus, I entered this world with what I believe to be a karmic shamanic imprint that has followed me throughout my entire lifetime.

Over the years, conscious breathing journeys have been beneficial with time-traveling and soul return to heal the trauma of my original birth blueprint. I can't change my original birth, nor would I want to, since I see it as a valuable part of the wounded healer archetype my soul obviously chose. However, I've created an overlay of new imprints about how to go through healthier symbolic death and rebirth experiences with Shamanic Breathwork. The good news is that I didn't die during my original birth experience, and I'm still breathing and alive after several near-death experiences with even more determination to live my life more fully and authentically and not hide from the world who I really am. "Ready or not, here I come" has become my celebratory chant and mantra!

A few decades later, during one of our Shamanic Mystery Tours to Peru, I climbed high into the Andean mountains above the village of Pisac to an abandoned settlement. It's said that wisdom keepers once watched the shifting seasons reflected and mirrored in the changing night sky from here. They could read the signs in the heavens as they sat in the ancient seer's astrological chair, which is carved out of solid stone and sits on top of these great mountains.

Our Peruvian Paqo's eyes became wide when I shared how I'd been struck by lightning earlier in the year. He explained, "In my tradition, when an initiate climbs high into the mountains, crying for a vision, and is struck by lightning and survives, they are seen as having been chosen by the spirit world to return to earth to become shamanic guides for their people." This information felt like another confirmation that I am on my path. The elemental forces of nature have always been my allies. They have been initiating me since my birth, sometimes gently and at other times shaking me to my vibrational core.

Many years ago, a beautiful teacher came into my life to help guide me on my Shamanic medicine path. Seneca Wolf Clan Grandmother, Twylah Nitsch, adopted me into the wolf clan teachings and taught me that we all have a vibrational core. This core holds the frequencies of our true essence intact, no matter what happens in our lives. It does so even in between lifetimes and always guides us as we walk between the worlds of birth, life, death, and rebirth. Gram gave me the magical spirit name Star Wolf, and told me, "As you find the courage to face your true self and destiny, your spirit name will make more sense." When I went through a divorce at 40 years old, I took a leap of faith and legally changed my name to Linda Star Wolf. Within a short period, most everyone spontaneously began to call me by my soul's name, even my mother.

Gram Twylah impressed upon me that the name Star Wolf and Wolf Star were really one and the same. She said the Dog Star, also known as Sirius, was actually a Wolf Star since all dogs evolved from wolves. She called Sirius the sacred six-pointed blue star of love and wisdom from which many of Earth's children originated. The name she had chosen for me reflected the energies of higher love and wisdom that emanate from the Blue Wolf Star. These qualities are meant to be embodied here on our beautiful Earth as we are all learning how to be "real humane beings."

At the time, I couldn't fully understand the depth of what Gram was saying to me. Today, however, I am finally beginning to step more fully into my destiny as a modern-day Shamanic Wolf Clan Grandmother for our worldwide Venus Rising Aquarian Shamanic Tribe.

I have a deep sense many of my beloved teachers and ancestors on the other side are still with me and helping guide my footsteps every step of the way. As a lifelong seeker, I've had many seminal wisdom teachers and guides, most of them on the other side of the veils. I remind myself, *they are just one breath away*. I sometimes feel them sending signs through synchronicities and always cheering me onward. Their collective wisdom contributes to the phenomenal universal explosion of consciousness and spiritual growth we are witnessing take place all around the planet.

Nature is calling to us! She is sending a wake-up call to remind everyone that these are the shamanic shape-shifting times that the old ones prophesied so that we would be prepared to do our part when the time arrived. We must own our birthright and remember who we really are. So instead of feeling alienated and separate from nature, it's time to recover our human nature, born out of the great collective of our loving ancestors of water, earth, fire, and air.

Our shamanic hearts are urging us to awaken from the collective denial and see how perilously close we are to the edge of no return due to the imbalance of nature here on Earth. It's up to us to do our part to answer the call and consciously walk through the fires of transformation.

As I approach the end of my story, I must spiral back around to the nature of the electrifying wake-up call that brought me to my knees in total surrender on the day I was struck by lightning.

After falling to my knees and being semi-conscious, I felt as if I was rising above the raging storm and being suspended in pure sunlight as I encountered shimmering beings of light that asked me one simple question, "Do you wish to drop your physical body or your old ego identity?" I don't consciously remember my response, but I know I must have chosen to surrender to love and truth because I returned to this body, opened my eyes, and knew without a doubt what I must do in order to be in integrity with myself and others.

On a daily basis for 40 years, I have consciously worked to surrender my will to the will of Great Mystery. I've walked the path of shamanic consciousness, doing my utmost best to be in right relationship with all my relations. I continue to fulfill my soul's karmic sacred purpose to be a powerful force of nature in order to birth positive change in our world.

Over the years, I've witnessed how the unconscious shadow in myself and others can cause hurt and confusion. This has made me hyper-vigilant to continue my spiritual practice with Shamanic Breathwork. The breathing helps me see myself more clearly, especially as I regularly process and stay accountable to trustworthy teachers and colleagues.

After months of a deep internal struggle, I finally faced the storm within myself and accepted the undeniable fact that I was in love again. I had fallen madly in love with Nikólaus, who had become my best friend, steadfast ally, and co-leader.

Nikólaus had become my lifeline while I was experiencing deep despair after my husband, Brad Collins, passed from this world with cancer. Nikó also deeply honored Brad, who was his beloved mentor and friend. As time went on, it became obvious beyond a shadow of a doubt that Brad's love brought us together for mutual support and a sacred purpose.

I felt I had no choice but to surrender my ego's struggle about how others might judge our relationship, especially family members and colleagues. I knew how deeply attached others were to me being with Brad, my late husband. We had been so close and taught side by side for so long. Also, because Nikólaus is considerably younger than me, I was nervous about how others would see me. I had to face some of my own fears and judgments around ageism. It was a time of surrendering on many levels, opening to humility and experiencing a deep gratitude for the beautiful love that had healed my heart and brought me back to life, inspiring me to move onward.

As our collective consciousness signals the world that it is time to enter the shamanic birthing chamber, we all have a sacred responsibility to find the courage and enthusiasm to take the necessary steps of reclaiming the best parts of ourselves while releasing the destructive dysfunction. Our individual courageous actions can become an inspiring collective catalyst for others around us.

As we begin to remember who we really are and why we are here on Earth at this time, we will find ourselves "on purpose," becoming powerful agents of change. When we awaken to shamanic consciousness through the power of our breath and our connection to Spirit, we discover the courage to trust love and become undeniable forces of nature.

SHAMANIC MEDICINE OFFERING

*"If you bring forth what is within you,
what you bring forth will save you;
If you do not bring forth what is within you,
what you do not bring forth will destroy you."*

~Jesus the Christ

In my chapter, I shared some of my personal struggles to demonstrate that spiritual growth is a never-ending, spiral journey. There's always another turn of the wheel.

Shamanic Breathwork is the most powerful medicine I've encountered to help me make it through the portals of death and rebirth.

I hope the sharing of my personal experiences with Shamanic Breathwork has encouraged you to connect with the elemental forces of nature within yourself.

Join me in an online transformational Shamanic Breathwork ceremony by clicking the link below.

Take a deep breath. Let go. We will see you on the other side, and back again.

Click on the link below to enter your name, email, and to sign the SBW release form. You will then receive an email with further instructions for the Shamanic Breathwork Ceremony offering.

Shamanic Breathwork Ceremony with Star Wolf
https://www.shamanicbreathwork.org/sbw-book-ceremony

Linda Star Wolf, Ph.D., has been a shamanic visionary teacher and guide to thousands of people over the last four decades. Starting out as a therapist in the mental health and addictions fields in the 1980's, Star Wolf was a nationally certified alcohol and drug counselor for 30+ years. She draws much of her wisdom from her personal experience of recovery and discovery from addictions.

The author of several books, Star Wolf is the creator of Shamanic Breathwork®, the Shamanic Healing Initiatory Process® (SHIP), the Founder of Venus Rising Association for Transformation (a non-profit organization), and Founding President of Venus Rising University for Shamanic Psychospiritual Studies. Star Wolf is also co-founder of the Shamanic Mystery Tours and guides spiritual seekers to travel as emissaries to sacred shamanic sites worldwide.

Dedicating her life to assisting soul seekers to release dysfunctional patterns and behaviors of all kinds to radically transform their lives, Star Wolf teaches how to embody the shaman within and step into a life of passionate soul purpose. Her commitment to sacred activism and visionary leadership led her to create the Shamanic Ministers Global Network and train Shamanic Breathwork Facilitators around the world.

Star Wolf was inspired by eastern yogis and breathwork luminaries Leonard Orr (founder of Rebirthing Breathwork), Stan Grof (founder of Holotropic Breathwork), and Jacquelyn Small (founder of Integrative Breathwork) and became a lead breathwork trainer at Eupsychia Institute.

Star Wolf has a deep connection to shamanic earth wisdom teachings originating from Indigenous elders. Twylah Nitsch, beloved Seneca Wolf Clan Grandmother, gave her the spirit name Star Wolf and adopted her as a Spiritual Granddaughter.

Star Wolf's lifelong passion and purpose is to support personal transformation to raise planetary consciousness of love and wisdom, one breath at a time.

You can connect with Star Wolf on Facebook and via email.

~ venusrising@shamanicbreathwork.org

~ https://www.facebook.com/StarWolf.VR

ONE BREATH ~ ONE TRIBE ~ ONE LOVE

CHAPTER 2

SHAMANIC DEATH
You Are The Authority Of Your Life

Atlantis Wolf

"Dying is a wild night and a new road."

~Emily Dickinson

You were born and conceived, in your original form, as naked love, in constant connection with all living beings, an embodied soul with no fears, not even death. You were swaddled, wrapped, and cloaked in invisible vestments and garments of identity, beliefs, and ideas bound to you until you became afraid of being exposed, of ego-death, comfortably encased in your unchosen persona. But death is relative. Shamanic death disrobes your identity, which can feel like standing and screaming in a fire as your clothes ignite and turn to ash, remembering your soul won't burn. Your inevitable journey is to reveal your soul to yourself, your naked center of conscious love, regaining your divine authority and moral compass, and feeling your way into the great mystery of your interior life with truth and personal integrity; like two hands feeling into the darkness, meeting one fear at a time. The journey within is inevitable. Start where you are.

MY STORY

"Where's my wolf pack?" a woman yelled as she ascended the stairs to the stage, banging her hoop drum and walking to the center. "Aroooooow!" She had shoulder-length blonde hair, flowing layers of colorful clothing, and the air of an aged hippie who kept the vibe of 1969 around her like a pink, invincible bubble that didn't acknowledge calendars. Her voice was a buttery southern biscuit dipped in Kentucky bourbon.

What kind of lunatic is this?

It was opening night at The Gathering of Shamans summit at Mago Retreat Center outside of Sedona, Arizona. Each workshop leader had a chance to introduce themselves to the 300 participants. I arrived early and sat in the center of the second row, waiting to see the great Toltec master, Don Miguel Ruiz, author of *The Four Agreements* and the keynote speaker. It took all my resources to get there. Everyone else was a passing curiosity.

She had a fruitcake kind of name, and I didn't understand what she would do at her workshop. Stephen Farmer, Heather Ash Amara, and a Hawaiian woman who built custom labyrinths on commission around the world followed her. Don Miguel arrived on stage last. I was breathless.

He began to speak; I fell asleep.

Don Miguel spoke in his low, slow, baritone voice about the nature of love, and it felt like a heavy quilt and blanket of night sky was placed over me. I struggled against gravity to open my lids with every breath, hoping he took my closed eyes as focused meditation. The universe made it clear: fruitcake for you.

On the third day of the retreat, as most of the participants attended Don Miguel's master class, I walked to the Shamanic Breathwork workshop held in a large yoga studio, joining people who were choosing a spot designated by a yoga mat, Kleenex, and a plastic bag ("In case you throw up," we were told at the introduction). I noticed that the CEO of the publishing company hosting the event was sitting two mats from me. So was Stephen Farmer.

I picked my mat, placed my crystals close to my head, put on my eye mask, and relaxed into a supine position, settling my body for meditation.

I could use a good shamanic journey. I wonder if she drums the whole time or has helpers? I saw helpers. Do they have rattles? Maybe they rattle, and she drums.

That would be great!

She passed the microphone around the room to let each person speak a word that came to mind. I sat up to speak. My word was '¡Alé!' I was happy to say it. The word had vibrations of elation and the sound of gold sparks, a crescendo of joy, like fireworks falling from the sky after a burst and a bang, but I have no idea who said it. It wasn't me. Some voice said it through me.

"Breathe until you're surprised!" she shouted to the room as we lay together for a group journey. And she added, "At Shamanic Airlines, we will definitely lose your baggage. See you on the other side."

Then the music started.

Music? Music?! She doesn't even know how to do a real shamanic journey. Come on! What a bust. Okay, okay. At least I can try her breathing thing and hope to push this whatever music away and have a nap. What can I lose?

I breathed in through my nose and out my mouth without pausing. In, nose; out, mouth. One breath, two breaths, and. . .

The blackness behind my eyes was replaced with a series of seven consecutive movies, each with its own emotions, characters, settings, and timelines. The only common thread was me. But 'me' had many forms, and none of them were what I see in the mirror when I brush my teeth.

The first movie was ecstatic dancing and shout-chanting in Africa around a fire with my tribe at night with drummers, dancers, and medicine keepers.

The second was galactic, aerial sex with my samurai guardian, who has watched over me for 800 years. At the end, as I laid on his body to rest, gazing into the small fire inside our Mongolian yurt with dark brown yak skins covering the floor, he said, "Your body is your library. Use it."

The third movie was about my past life in Atlantis. I'm walking down to the crystal vaults on the main street in Atlantis on a sunny day, tears falling down my face. *I love Atlantis; she is my whole heart.* I had sent my daughter to Lemuria, and other friends to Turtle Island, far to the north. *It will be over soon. The fifth evolution of Atlantis is the last one. The Powers won't harm another city. I'm the one who has to do this. I volunteered.*

I go down to the vault room with the red power crystals, explaining the plan. They agree. I hold the two largest red crystals in my hands and turn the generator points toward each other, tip facing tip. I never let go. My vow is to hold them in place as their power continues to build to an apex. Not long. One last minute. Tectonic trembling and loud vibrations. More tears. Salty, stinging tears. A few more seconds. Vaporized.

The music changed, and my fourth movie appeared. I'm dancing in a white, sequined ball gown on a circular, glass stage with a tall, handsome man I was dating. He wore a tuxedo and a blazing smile.

The fifth movie was darkness, the void, the silence in the multiverse between stars.

In the sixth movie, I was walking with purpose-filled, muscular legs in darkness on a land bridge toward an open door, golden light behind it, wearing gold sandals with gold ties around my calves and a short white tunic dress and gold belt, carrying an enormous sword in my right hand. I felt larger than normal around my shoulders. I glanced mid-stride to see white wings about ten feet wide outstretched from my back. As I came close to the door, I heard a voice.

You are part of Archangel Michael's army. Do you answer the call?

Yes, I said, and stepped through the door.

In the seventh movie, I was surrounded by gold light with pink and white flecks. I felt happy, weightless, and eternal, a small ball rolling, following a pattern of sacred geometry. The sensation was dissolving from being a whole body to a single cell, a droplet of liquid love floating on a cosmic sea of peace.

The music began to fade. The blonde woman started drumming the heartbeat on her drum, bringing us all back from our shamanic journey. She said something about coming back slowly, getting in small groups, and processing.

I lay on the mat, rewinding the seven film reels in my head.

I need a pen and paper to get this all down, fast. So many details! This is better than acid. And no recovery day. Screw small group processing. I'm fine. I'll process after I write my notes.

I stood up, light-headed and airy, walking on weak legs, stepping over yoga mats and other participants in a straight line across the room. They call it altered; your crown chakra is open, and your third eye is activated.

"Excuse me," I said to the blonde woman standing at her laptop connected to the speakers, "What was all of that? And, I'm sorry, what's your name?"

She turned her face to me, the Queen of the Magnolia Fairies. Her skin was velvet white, like a flower petal. Her eyes looked like jewel-blue waters in the Caribbean Sea. She smiled at me in a way that reminded me of the full moon over a quiet, country road.

"Oh, you get it," she said. "I'm Linda Star Wolf."

I gave her a summary of what I saw. She was kind and generous with her time in the wake of my rambling babble-speak. I signed up for her email list.

Six months later, I attended a Star Knowledge conference at the Amicalola Lodge north of Atlanta, Georgia. I had to convince a friend to join me to split the hotel room cost, find the cheapest flight possible, move my weekend clients, get my kids to their dad's house, rent a car, and pay for the conference. But she sent an email to her list, and I hoped to say hello and apologize for the long babble-ramble.

She wasn't attending the conference, per se. She was asked and agreed to come and hold a short Shamanic Breathwork session for us, then return home. She lived two hours away in North Carolina. She was filling in for a speaker who couldn't attend.

I found her in the vendor area outside the conference room while one of the speakers presented about sustainable something or other. It put me to sleep, so I walked out of the room, and there she was with her companion, Niko. I walked over to her, smiling, and introduced myself. I explained that I was here to see her and shared some of the details around my challenges to get there.

She took both my hands in a way that conveyed gravity. Her eyes were bluer than I remembered. Extraterrestrial. She was unexpectedly close. I'm a single mom, and I'm not used to close, continuous, connected contact with a person I don't have to feed.

I lost consciousness.

She talked without a pause for fifteen or twenty minutes, never losing contact. I didn't hear the words; I downloaded the vibration to understand the words later. It took three months to process the energy exchange. The core of the conversation was one sentence.

"You can do this," she said.

She held the Shamanic Breathwork session, starting by talking about how we came to be together in the room. She looked at me across the circle, and I felt seen as if a celestial ray of sunshine paused to illuminate and warm me as it circled over the sky.

After the breathwork, I stood and stretched, smiling and full as the sunset rays filled the west side of the room from the patio doors. I took a step in her direction, but she was already walking toward me in a straight line. She grabbed both my arms behind my elbows and pressed her left cheek into mine, her mouth close to my ear. She smelled like the woods, earth, and air.

"Your name is Atlantis," she said, "Atlantis Wolf."

"Yes," I said in a hushed, breathless voice. She stepped away, and I walked, stupefied, through the patio door into the golden evening sunlight.

Saying a sacred yes to my new teacher, Star Wolf, I made a conscious decision to step onto the spiritual, spiral path. This led to saying a sacred no and farewell to my previous teacher, my dad, who taught me about rage, silence, and resilience.

For me, shamanic death disrobing and revealing have felt like a series of goodbyes and rememberings. I grieved and dropped the ordinary, expected life I built with a husband, a city-suburb house in a family-friendly neighborhood, a desk job, two kids, four weeks of vacation, timid conversations, and a 401(k). I regained my connection to the shamanic world of spirit guides, power animals, and a perpetual line of galactic dragons. (Oh, and I kept the kids; they were too big to throw back. And the house; I picked it.)

I peeled off the fear of sharing my spiritual visions with clients when their spirit guides and ancestors asked to convey messages while drumming a cow skin drum over them. I reconnected to an Egyptian temple, a favorite healing space of mine from a previous lifetime, to hold space for my medical massage and shamanic coaching clients. By opening a prayer to Great Spirit to open a healing space for me, it appeared in my vision complete and populated with Egyptian men and women. Lately, it appears with extraterrestrials, too.

I unwrapped the debilitating grief of losing my champion, my mother, twelve years ago, so I could feel her support and guidance again from the spirit world. With no mother, grandmothers, sisters, aunts, or female cousins, I struggle to feel supported in the physical world but gladly hold the connection between my line of powerful, feminine spirits and my two daughters, one I birthed and one I adopted as my spirit-daughter. I remember previous lifetimes; life and death are both temporary.

As my starshine began to emerge, I operated my business from a place of integrity, not lack, not a place of fear of not generating enough money to pay my bills. I said no to clients who abuse their bodies and want me to erase their pain so they can continue the abuse pattern. I embraced my connection to dragon spirits, like Tatianna, a white, marbled dragon-friend, covered in miniature spheres of opalite, who channels healing energy into the vortex created by my singing bowl's spinning, elliptical tones when I play it over clients.

To my great delight, as my light and shadow came into balance and wholeness, I came into the company of an international mystic society of ladies who also work with dragon spirits. They are ancient medicine keepers of personal power and self-sovereignty, ego-less and centered in their divine, original form. I'm consciously connected to a web of unconditional love and planetary service. I anchor my Aquarian energy from the center of a medicine wheel with Metatron's cube drawn over it, surrounded by a council of dragons and angels. I no longer believe that I am small, insignificant, and unable to up-level the energy in the world.

Yes, today is a good day to die a shamanic death; no, there will never be a better time than now.

SHAMANIC MEDICINE OFFERING

If you read this far, you are what I call shamanically-curious. You hear a calling in these words and ideas. Something inside your DNA remembers drumming and dancing around a fire, living with the changing cycles of seasons bisected by sacred solar and lunar days, and feeling the spirits of your ancestors around you. You've found yourself at a crossroads, again. You'll keep coming back here until you step onto the road with no predictable destination, the one with the sharp drop, the one that holds the Great Mystery. You can do this.

We all make our way in the world without a connection to spiritual guidance and assistance until we can't. When we become broken, abandoned, or betrayed, we reach for grace. When we surrender what we think we want, we are carried into a greater purpose, a divine design. I like to say, 'There is the one thing your ego wants (a gabillion dollars in the bank, a big house, or an electric car, etc.), and there is one thing your soul wants: to be a pure vessel, an artery for supreme, divine love. One ego (in your mind) versus the support of every living being in the universe. Guess who wins in the end?" This lifetime or next. Up to you.

ONE FEAR, ONE FLAME MEDITATION

Here is a meditation to begin your spiritual journey. You can follow these instructions or use this video link and let me guide you through it with drumming and verbal cues: https://youtu.be/eIEs3YdXlpo

Take a pillar candle to a quiet, comfortable place. Hold the candle and close your eyes. Breathe in and out three times, exhaling longer each time as if you were emptying all moments in your life except this one.

Using your most powerful tool of transformation, your imagination, imagine your greatest fear. Light the candle and gaze into the flame. Let every detail of your fear fill your body, digging deep into the shadowy mine of your mind, then send it to the flame. Every terrifying detail that you don't want anyone to know - the affair, the baby, the sexual identity, the hidden truth.

Blow out the candle.

Close your eyes again and breathe three more times, this time filling your body with golden light with each inhale and sending the remaining flecks of fear out with every exhale. Light the candle again and gaze into the flame. Imagine your life without your fear. How do you feel? What is different? Does anyone notice the fear is gone? As Master Shaman Bob Marley said, "None but ourselves can free our minds." Your fear lives in your mind, meet it there.

When you are ready to take one step onto your spiral path, I'll be here. Until I'm not.

I'm Atlantis Wolf, and I believe in you.

Atlantis Wolf is a Shamanic Life Coach and workshop leader who collaborates with her spirit guides, power animals, and galactic dragons to support people seeking solutions to their chronic pain and mysterious medical conditions. Her joy is helping people discover their personal power by walking with them into their interior labyrinths, their dark castles, and their hidden stories.

Atlantis grew up on a single-lane dirt road, sure her mother was an angel in human form, whistling to birds and asking the question: What am I supposed to be doing on Earth? She continues to walk into the forest at sunrise in all weather to ask that question every day.

She holds dual degrees in Civil Engineering and English with a minor in Environmental Engineering. Atlantis has worked as a civil engineer, technical writer, business analyst, project manager, licensed massage therapist, certified Emotion Code practitioner, marketing consultant, and entrepreneur.

She is a Shamanic Breathwork Facilitator and Ordained Shamanic Minister from Venus Rising Association for Transformation. She is certified as a Reiki Master by William Lee Rand, Founder of the International Center for Reiki Training, and a certified Kinesio Tape Practitioner by Kinesio (Dr. Kenzo Kase), Corp.

She was spiritually asleep until events around her mother's death awakened her gifts to see and communicate with spiritual beings and remember her past lives as an Egyptian healer, Toltec curandera and Ayurvedic traveling shaman. She is the Dragon Medicine Woman.

Atlantis is an Aquarian and single mom to four kids and three cats. She lives on Turtle Island.

AtlantisWolf.com

DragonMedicineWoman@gmail.com

YouTube: Atlantis Wolf

Instagram: @DragonMedicineWoman

CHAPTER 3

THE RELUCTANT SHAMAN

Finding Integration of Mind, Body, and Spirit

Joseph E. Doherty, MSW, PhD

MY STORY

We all know the old saying "You can't wait for an opportunity to just come knocking on your door, you have to go out and seek it." Well, I have always prided myself on being an exception to the rules and my spiritual transformation was no different. In October of 2004 Linda Star Wolf did indeed come knocking on the door of my yoga studio! And reluctantly I let her in. I had no clue what mischief Spirit had afoot for me. The offer was "We want to rent your space for a Shamanic Breathwork weekend, we can pay you for the rental or you can come to the workshop in exchange." Being a dedicated yogi and teacher I thought, *breathwork, yoga, sounds like a good fit, I'll just go.* I had no idea what I was getting myself into that October 17 years ago!

Down the rabbit hole I went. Spirit had long been telling me, "Stop digging in your heels," and my response was always, "I'm not." Only to then dig them in firmer and deeper. Now Divine timing was set in place, and I was primed to make the shift. The teacher arrived because the student was ready, albeit still slightly reluctant. What amazed me was the ease of my first magical journey. On the cusp of turning 50, my very first Shamanic Breathwork began the unfolding of my Mind/Body/Spirit integration experience.

MIND: I started my career in mental health at age 22 after witnessing the murder of my 18 year old brother. After my testifying in two murder trials, I decided to put my double major of Psychology/Sociology to work. I found a job in a psychiatric hospital in the hopes of trying to understand the human mind and make 'sense' of my brother's murder. It was the top psychiatric facility in the country, Harvard's teaching hospital. This set my 40 year mental health career in motion.

BODY: I've studied yoga since my early 20s. I started studying both yoga and buddhism as a way of rebelling against my Irish Catholic upbringing. So after moving from Boston to the 'Left Coast' I did find a great yoga studio to attend and a wonderful teacher for instruction. Several years into my yoga classes with her, my teacher approached me and said, "I'd like to invite you to attend our teacher training. I think you are a natural yoga teacher." I had lectured at all college levels, but never in my life did I even think of teaching in my body. Reluctantly I accepted, not knowing how integral teaching yoga would become in my mind/body/spirit healing path.

SPIRIT: My early spiritual path was a heavily indoctrinated Catholic one. Then in late adolescence it took the form of studying Buddhism. But eastern spirituality was always a 'left-brained' philosophical practice for me. I continued eschewing anything that even smacked lightly of religion. Post MSW degree, I regularly attended conferences on psychotherapy and spirituality but always left feeling dissatisfied. I successfully eluded Spirit for most of my adult life.

The spiritual path was lagging far behind me, barely visible and only in the rearview mirror. Then, five years after teaching yoga and opening my own studio my reluctance was split-open by Shamanic Breathwork. By the conclusion of that first weekend, my spiritual path became clear. I definitely wanted to study further with Linda Star Wolf. And okay, I'll reluctantly study with this guy, Brad (her late husband and co-teacher). I did not know I was even looking for a sacred masculine archetype, mine had long ago been defiled and shattered by an alcoholic and abusive father. Yet now, it manifested itself fully, completely, gently, and with unconditional love in the person of Brad Collins. I was accepted into the 13 moons Shamanic Healing and Initiatory Process (SHIP). My reluctance was melting.

Divine timing being everything, things were already shifting. I was to begin SHIP that December here on the west coast. But to my disheartenment, having cancelled my birthday India trip, the training was suddenly rescheduled to February of the following year. And also now it would be held in North Carolina. *Hell no*, was my first response, being my reluctant self. My mind was reeling, I knew I should not have signed up, this is not what I agreed to do! But Star Wolf worked her Blue Star magic. I was offered to teach yoga during my stay at Isis Cove to help defray the unexpected costs of flying cross county for the six initiations. This was clearly my sacred-but-reluctant initiation to the melding of mind/body/spirit.

I clearly remember that my heightened anxiety in waiting for the first circle on opening night was physically palpable. *Who are all these strange people and why am I here? I need to leave NOW.* That was my immediate reaction. And then the magic happened. As soon as I wandered into the sanctuary I received the affirmation loud and clear: "This is where you were meant to do this work!" It felt like coming home. As we went around the circle first night with introductions and intentions I was honestly shocked with how much I shared in common with each member of this ragtag group. It did help that two members were also therapists which put my thinking mind at ease. We were affectionately, and not so affectionately at times, known as The Shadow Dancers, and *that* we most certainly were! For the next 13 months there was a whole lotta shadow going on. The bonds formed in the vulnerability of deep spiritual work as a cohesive cohort were not only healing but life-changing. I did indeed find a Spirit family, guided by two amazing spiritual teachers in Star Wolf and Brad.

And so the transformation began, the Family of Origin Initiation was first to be experienced. Cleaning out the childhood family wounds was hard work. And again divine timing came into play. My mother, who had been on hospice at the start of this experience, passed away two months later. Beautifully dove-tailing on my newfound shamanic ritual experiences from this first initiation at Venus Rising, I was called to create a shamanic ritual for my mother's soul release. I called the funeral home and arranged a time to arrive before my family. I asked the funeral director if it was okay to burn sage around her in the open casket, he replied "I don't even know what that means, but sure." He watched intently as I drummed, rattled, called in the directions, and with an obsidian blade cut away the cords connected to her body that held her to this life form. This was not a left-brained experience for me. It was created in my heart through a connection to Spirit that I had never felt before. The mind/body/spirit connection was now manifesting through me. And it just kept building through the subsequent five initiations.

At the end of the SHIP in March of 1996, I was asked by Star Wolf if I desired to join her Wolf Clan lineage. This lineage was handed down through her Grandmother, Twyla Nitch, of the Lakota Tribe. I very enthusiastically replied, "Hell Yes!" And I was baptized as JaguarWolf, my shamanic essence. The guy formerly known as "The Reluctant Shamanic Healer '' was reluctant no more. I felt SO secure on this newly awakened spiritual path, more than I ever had before.

INTEGRATION: Working in the mind and then the body had served me fine (I thought) up until then. Now, with the newly added ingredient of Spirit the lock sprang open! It revealed so many blessings, not only for me, but to those I worked with as clients, patients, students, family, and friends. The proverbial cup literally overflowed with unimagined blessings for all.

My yoga teaching shifted significantly to incorporate a much more spiritual component. I had been teaching Men's Tantric Naked yoga for years. Now Shamanic Breathwork had unlocked for me what others call the Full Kundalini Awakening! I was now fully connected to my seven chakra energy centers. The breath, the choreographed music, the container held by and through co-journeying, along with the healings offered by Star Wolf and Brad facilitated my unfolding. I incorporated this into my teaching and my yoga students felt the difference. The responses I got were, "This isn't like any other yoga class I've attended, it is *so* much more."

My psychotherapy practice deepened as well. I was now talking to patients about spiritual transformation, chakras, Shamanic Breathwork, and energy healing, something I had been trained to never do.

Living in Mexico during my shamanic initiations, I meditated and breathed daily on sacred Zapotec land. During one potent Shamanic Breathwork session, I took in the sacred breath of hot air; the condors circled in the updrafts of the blue sky; the ocean surrounded me on three sides; I listened to the power of its crashing waves; the earth supported me by the solid cool stone ancient altar; the fire raged wildly in my soul. Then and there it was revealed to me. The name "Elemental Healing" was birthed and gifted to me in that experience by Spirit. It then became the name and the focus of my new body/mind/spirit psychotherapy practice. www.elementslhealing.org

Equally potent, as a newly ordained Shamanic Minister, I was invited to officiate at weddings, memorials, births and many life transitions. I would write each ceremony as directed by Spirit. Calling in the directions, honoring the ancestors, and engaging the elements—all which I experienced as an embodied soul in my breathworks. There honestly were times in these experiences I would stop and ask myself in amazement, "Who are you?" much like I had in the ceremony at my mothers casket. My response was always a clear affirmation that I was indeed more of 'me' than I ever had been.

I continued on my sacred path with Star Wolf and Brad. I began my apprenticeship as a Shamanic Breathwork Facilitator which included amazing journeys to sacred sites in Mexico at Teotihuacan and in Peru at Machu Picchu. I was called to this work by an unseen force called 'Spirit' with whom I had been waiting for such a long, long time to meet. Never knowing that Spirit had been right there beside me my whole life long.

The shamanic path of transformation was truly that. It allowed me to really 'see' on all levels and know the truths. I continued to transform. Now it was not only my receiving the experiences that was transforming, it was actively facilitating them for others that equally activated me on all levels. As Star Wolf so wisely shares "The healing is the learning and the learning is the healing." I was healing on so many levels from a very toxic and wounding childhood with two alcoholic parents and significant physical, emotional and sexual abuse. I was healing from the trauma of witnessing my younger brother being shot to death before my eyes. I was understanding I could transform all the pain by allowing the grief to be honored, felt, and released through my breathwork experiences. It happened in ways so much deeper and more wholly than all my years of verbal insight oriented psychotherapy. That had simply laid the foundation for change. I was indeed being transformed at a cellular level. My work was not only to find my inner shaman, but facilitate helping others discover their own "shaman within".

SHAMANIC MEDICINE OFFERING

Start with your body. This is the foundation of the integration process. Sit in a chair, on a meditation cushion, or lying on the floor with towels or blankets thinly rolled under you. The key in starting is alignment. Check the three natural curves of your spine. The lumber curve in the lower back, the thoracic curve at your shoulder blades and the cervical curve behind your neck. Each should be relaxed but not hyper-curved. They should not be flat. You want them stacked upon each other in alignment. The chin should not be lifted or dropped, nor is it jutting forward. Think of a string attached to the crown of the head gently lifting your body into alignment. Make sure you will not be disturbed or interrupted—phones off, pets in another room, people know you're off limits.

Close your eyes and focus on your breath. It is a resting breath. A gentle rise and fall, no emphasis on the inhale or exhale. Just breathe as you begin to drop into your body. Quiet the mind.

Next scan your physical internal and energetic bodies. Am I holding tightly anywhere bodily? If so, breathe into that space and ask it to soften. Once the body is relaxed, gently dive deeper, into the energy body. The seven chakras running from your tailbone up your spine to your crown. First notice, can I feel my energetic body? Where do I feel it? Think of a string of Christmas lights. Are all seven bulbs glowing brightly? Are some dim, some too bright, some dark? Now think of a roll of colored lifesavers, they are whirling circles of energy. Imagine the color of each chakra wrapping around your body.

A. Start your scan:

1. Root Chakra. Located between your legs at the base of your tailbone, pubic bone and sits bones. How does it feel? What do you notice somatically?

   Issues: Stability/balance/survival, manifesting, health/home/money

   Color: Red

2. Sacral Chakra. Located below your navel. This includes your low back, your hips, your genitals. Notice the physical cues. Is my second chakra vibrating?

   Issues: Connection to self and others/sexuality/creativity.

   Color: Orange

3. Solar Plexus. Above your navel and below your ribcage, front back and sides. What do you feel?

   Issues: Personal power/fear/dread.

   Color: Yellow

4. Heart Chakra: Center of the ribcage and wrapping around the back. What feelings do you feel?

   Issues: All emotions

   Color: Green

5. Throat Chakra: The whole throat. Is your throat open/closed/tight/loose?

   Issues: Speaking your truth, things said and unsaid stuck in your throat. Connects Heart and Mind.

   Color: Turquoise

6. Third Eye: Forehead and the brain inside the whole skull.

   Issues: Seeing and perceiving the truth, intuition, perceptions. Can you quiet your mind?

   Color: Indigo blue

7. Crown Chakra: Top of your head. Can you feel it open or closed?

Issues: Connection to all spiritual support that is available to us.

Color: Amethyst

B. Engage the Mind:

What chakras speak to me? Which are flat? Which have sensations? Images? Emotions? Are they connected? Where is the disruption/blockage? What messages am I receiving?

C. Spirit:

When we open up each chakra and connect them in alignment the vibration is high.

Bring your awareness to your root chakra on the exhale. Pause the breath. Then inhale through the root and draw it slowly up the spinal column one chakra at a time. When you eventually reach the crown, pause and hold the breath for a few seconds. Then exhale back down the spine one chakra at a time all the way back to the root. Pause again. Repeat two more times. At the end of the third full-body breath return to resting breath and focus on the top of your head. Ask of Spirit "What messages do you have for me? What lessons am I meant to learn? What is in my highest good and well-being? What do I need to leave behind?" Have a notebook nearby, or a large piece of paper and some crayons/colored pencils/markers. Write down what you felt in your physical body, your energy body and your spirit body, or draw an image that represents your experience to you.

When we continue to practice the body/mind/spirit exercise we strengthen the muscle of our integration experiences. When I work with clients in person I use chakra attuned crystals and bowls, drumming, rattling, gongs and tuning forks to assist in releasing blockages and attuning the whole person experience. My inner shaman meets yours, and we walk the path together!

AHO! Mitakuye Oyasin!

(May it Be so! We are All Related!)

Joe Doherty, MSW, PhD, LCSW is a licensed clinical psychotherapist with a private psychotherapy practice in Portland, Oregon. He holds a Master's degree in Clinical Social work from Smith College and a Doctorate from Venus Rising University. He is a Certified Shamanic Breathwork Facilitator and an Ordained Shamanic Minister through Venus Rising www.shamanicbreathwork.org

He has over 40 years experience in the mental health field and specializes in working with C-PTSD as well as GLBTQI+ individuals. He trained and has presented in the arena of relational mutuality at The JMBTI Institute of The Stone Center at Wellesley College focusing on gender socialization and the treatment of Gay and Lesbian couples. www.wcwonline.org/JBMTI-Site

He is also an Iyengar Yoga Instructor specializing in Tantric Yoga for men.

His body/mind/spirit approach is detailed on his website www.elementalhealing.org and on Facebook https://www.facebook.com/Elemental-Healing-214060701939079

His doctoral dissertation: The Non-Dualism of Shamanic Psychotherapy is published in the book *Shamanic Transformations: True Stories of the Moment of Awakening* by Itzhak Beery (Editor) 2015.

He has also contributed to three books by Linda Star Wolf PhD: *Shamanic Breathwork; Visionary Shamanism; Soul Whispering*. Joe is also a Psychedelic Integration Therapist www.portlandintegrationnetwork.com

CHAPTER 4

SHAMANIC TRANSCENDENCE

From Trauma to Triumph

Krisy Conroy and Krti Psyskrit

OUR STORY

The evolution of human consciousness is an extraordinary phenomenon.

From the time we're conceived, we begin encoding cellular memory. Our neurological pathways are critically important to our development. Any trauma or shock to our systems and these pathways can be easily impaired, causing emotional, physical, or psychological damage. We have the potential to spiral downwards into low frequencies of fear, hatred, and so on, which inhibit our growth.

This damage can have a devastating impact on us as we grow. In pain and still hurting from all the turmoil, our inner child can display destructive behaviors such as self-sabotage, addiction, and failed relationships, amongst other suppressive activities, in an attempt to outrun shadows.

One of my first breathwork experiences allowed me to re-experience my actual birth—my mother's labor—on the 10th of August, 1968.

I was deep in the process, breathing as we were told to do, when all of a sudden, I was back in my mother's womb, feeling safe and comfortable, abruptly followed by an extremely intense pressure around my neck. The pain was excruciating, as though someone was squeezing my head in an attempt to pop it like the cork of a wine bottle. As I tried desperately to avoid the large forceps attempting to grab and yank at me, I remember screaming, "MUM!" uncontrollably. Tetany froze my fingers into claws. The pain was so bad that I decided to hold my breath for some time but was guided by the facilitator to continue and breathe through the pain.

I could hardly open my mouth; my jaw was clenched so tight it felt as though I was breathing through a straw. My body was in total catharsis, shaking in utter distress. I had no understanding of what was going on, and I felt tears building up as I attempted to fight yet had no control to do so.

Suddenly, I was birthed into the world, crying. I never felt something so intense. This voyage through the birth canal was utterly unforgiving. I relived my first breath of oxygen which was only after a suction tube was forced down my throat.

The experience of being born is fraught with an emotional charge. The conditions practiced in hospitals, in my view, can be downright violent. Nobody, not least of all the obstetrician with his blatant superiority complex, considered how I as a newborn baby could be feeling, or even how their dismissive behavior could profoundly and negatively influence me later in my life.

Such trauma would continue into my childhood, inflicted in particular by my father.

I grew up in Melbourne, Australia, with my parents and two older brothers. My father, Victor, was born in Poland fleeing the Nazi dictatorship and the iron rule of the communists in 1949. He was only 21 years old. He had served in the Polish Underground Movement until he was arrested by the Special Communist Secret Police and interrogated and physically assaulted. Eventually, however, he managed to escape to Australia. He had learned his parents were captured as a reprisal due to his escape, and were confined to a labor camp. Their home and business were taken away, as well as their freedom.

In the early 1950s, my father met my mother at a dance in Port Melbourne. He was charming, good-looking, a musician by way of the piano and harmonica, and he loved to make people laugh. My mother was a widow with a baby boy named Peter who had lost her first husband in a horrific work accident. She married my father a couple of years later, and they had my brother Paul.

The war had a devastating impact on my father. Around the time he and my mother began their relationship, his unresolved trauma reared its ugly head, and he started turning to alcohol in a failed attempt to quiet his inner demons. It ruined our family and provided a profoundly toxic home life for my brothers and me to grow up in.

Almost every day, in the early hours of the morning, I heard my dad's old Bedford Ford truck rattling down the street towards home. He would stumble inside and barge into our bedrooms, reeking of alcohol, yelling in a drunken rage. The slightest misnomers would trigger him to become verbally loud, aggressive, violent, and abusive. He would often say things like, "You are all lazy bastards," or "I will kill you all if any of you decide to leave," leaving a harrowing impact on our young developing minds and hearts. We lived in a hopeless situation of daily fear and despair which I emphatically resented and hated him for.

One result of this constant abuse was my total fear of speaking out of turn. I could never have friends over. My mother would not dare to invite the family into the house. My dad kept our family as hostages. On weekends, he made us work as stallholders at the markets. As a result, with all the constant heavy lifting I had to do at such a young age, I suffered acutely with dislocated hips and a hernia, all by the time I was nine years old. And, by the time I was 27, I was diagnosed with cancer to my left thyroid gland.

My mum was too scared to share our situation with authorities fearing that our father would kill us by using one of the guns he kept in the house.

Most nights in my teens, I would either sleep on top of my high school roof or break into the marina in St. Kilda and sleep there. Anything was better than being at home.

As for my mother, Winifred, I witnessed, like a slow drip, her health and life deteriorate from all the years of feeling trapped, limited, unsupported, and everything else that goes with living in an abusive relationship. Every morning I would see her take out a shopping bag and pull out a cocktail of antidepressants, anxiolytics, and pain killers. During her final years, she suffered terribly from cancer.

From the age of 20, I graduated as a Registered Nurse and went on to get a Bachelor of Psychiatric Nursing. My qualifications led me to work in all types of facilities, including drug and alcohol centers, prisons, aged care homes, schools, hospitals, and many other places in between.

Music and graffiti art became my creative outlets. I found work on a radio show once a week presenting for one of Australia's most iconic Hip Hop shows, 'Stepping 2 the A.M.', as well as DJ'ing. I was getting gigs to open up for well-known US Hip Hop artists such as Common Sense, Lord Finesse, DJ Q Bert, and Big Daddy Kane. I was incredibly dedicated to being as skillful a DJ as possible, eventually winning third place in the Australian DMC DJ Championships in 1997.

This is how I met Krti. He was one of Australia's most respected and well-loved emcees and break-dancers. Not only did we both share a passion for music, but I recall us always chatting about the mystical, spiritual, and paranormal. Something that we both connected with deeply.

Over time though, my life started feeling hard and exhausting as I attempted to juggle nursing with my passion. I loved DJ'ing but doing both was breaking me. So, perhaps inevitably, and behind closed doors, unexplainable darkness began to grip at me. My soul was screaming for help with nowhere to turn. I felt lost, alone, and in total despair with my life. I didn't know what to do.

Thus began my downward spiral to find a way through the physical, spiritual, and emotional darkness. There was no life left in me. I felt utterly numb to the magic of life. I felt stuck in a destructive loop of being overworked and unfulfilled, which led me to seek solace in overeating, excessive drinking, and numbing out with television and pharma drugs.

This cycle of destruction went on for years until, finally, one day in my 30s, I bowed down to God and asked for help. I remember this powerful, divine moment: this would be my saving grace.

My call was answered through the discovery of the Inner Peace Institute for Well Being, run by Marlyse and Michael Carroll. Here, I was introduced to spiritual healing and awakening through shamanic journeying, breathwork, and so many

other healing modalities. My soul was ignited. I couldn't get enough of these practices! I felt reconnected to myself. I was so excited to learn as much as possible that I decided to train with Leonard Orr (founder of Rebirthing/Breathwork). On completing his training and recognizing there was far more for me to unravel and heal, I was moved to a path, to a shamanic path through a training called Shamanic Healing Initiatory Process by Star Wolf and Nikolaus Wolf.

The experience helped me begin dissolving years of pain and stuck energy that kept me emotionally paralyzed for so much of my life and helped me reconnect to far deeper wisdom than I ever thought possible. I couldn't believe just how quickly we as humans can experience consciousness, all through the power of our breath!

I believe there is a force essential to our existence that is invisible to the naked eye, phenomenal "life force" energy we can feel with our heart and soul. Through working with the breath in Shamanic Breathwork, I believe we can activate for healing and transformation. I only wish I had discovered this years ago.

Krti Psyskrit:

Do you remember being four years old?

I do, and it looked like this:

In the 1950s, my mother was born into a family of 12, all abused by their father. The boys were beaten, and the girls were sexually abused. They were all, but one, finally placed into orphanages, which in those days, wasn't a haven from mistreatment, but rather just another place for the same treatment, often worse. They were beaten by the nuns that were assigned as their caretakers until they were old enough to fight back, which was usually around the age of 12. At this point, they were all sent from the orphanage into foster care, and this is where my story begins.

At the age of 12, my mother was placed into foster care with an alcoholic woman and her son. Her son, only a year or two older than my mother at the time, was just as vindictive as his mother. They used her like a slave, beating her if her chores weren't completed to their expectation. The son would bring his two friends to the house, and from the ages of 12 to 16 years, they would force themselves onto her, raping her on an almost daily basis. I was the result of one of those rapes.

My mother had nowhere to go and so was forced to stay in her current situation, pregnant and alone and continuing to withstand daily torture. When she gave birth to me, she was not even afforded the freedom to name me. By force, the son and his friends demanded their names be bequeathed to me. On my birth certificate, my first, middle, and surnames are the names of my mother's rapists.

Finally, the State could no longer hold her in the system, and a year later, she was released from the home. She set out into the world with me on her hip. However, having only known abuse her whole life continued to surround herself with what she knew. Sometime later, she married a biker from a world-renowned biker club, and the horror continued.

One of my earliest memories is at four years old. I remember watching my mother stab her husband in the head. At the time, I only knew him as my father, though later in life, at aged 21, I finally learned my true heritage. Leaving him bleeding out on the floor, with a butcher's knife she'd found in the kitchen sticking out of his head, she picked up my brother and me, stepped over his body, and walked out, never to return.

I heard that he survived, though I never saw him again.

Around 1977, I was finally placed into foster care, shortly after my mother left her husband and that harrowing event I was an unfortunate witness to. I remained in foster care until the mid-90s, where, for all that time, I endured the same terrors and traumas as my mother did.

It wasn't until I turned 40 that I began to open up, talk about, and share my story. I endured my story alone for years, bottling it up and attempting to appear 'normal' to the outside world. Even those I had known for over 20 years had never known my life story.

From a very young age, I found solace in music. The Finn brothers of Crowded House visited the different homes I was living in, helping to fuel the fire of what would become my lifelong passion. Music was my escape from my reality until I reconnected with Krisy, who I met and knew on the streets of Melbourne when I was a teenager. Through my dear friend Jenni, we began talking again, and it was through Krisy that I discovered Shamanic Breathwork.

Krisy was organizing one of her group breathwork sessions and asked me if I would put together a list of songs her clients could breathe to. I said I would go her one better and live-DJ the songs in a set as the session played out.

This is where my transformation truly began.

I was so entranced by this process and wanted to know more about the depths of this Shamanic Breathwork healing modality that Krisy was so in love with. So inspired, I undertook the same training with Star Wolf that she had done to better understand what it was she so passionately offered the world. All this without truly knowing it was about to change my life in powerful and wonderful ways.

Eventually, and together, we set out to create a business, Shamanic Transcendence. Since its inception, we've had the honor of holding space for thousands of beautiful hearts and souls. We continue honoring the practice and people we cross sacred paths with by facilitating a safe space for them to experience their realities in a way they may not have thought possible—at least not until they too were touched by Star Wolf's incredible Shamanic Breathwork process.

I have been transformed from a victim of childhood abuse to an Ordained Shamanic Minister, Shamanic Breathwork Facilitator, Shamanic DJ, and producer of Goa Trance and Medicine music. I hold a Diploma in Parapsychology and Demonology and lead a Paranormal Investigation team called Get Out Paranormal. I teach courses on this subject at Debbie Bullions' Spirit Quest School of Spiritual and Paranormal Arts on the Gold Coast, where Krisy and I live.

In all this, I continue to learn, transform and grow as time goes on.

Of course, this is only the short version of the first half of my life, though I know it will serve to portray a profound truth: that anyone can travel from trauma to triumph. It is within reach for anyone willing to face their demons and breathe through the murky depths of their Shadow and let go of that which no longer serves them.

I wholeheartedly thank Krisy for introducing me to Star Wolf and her teachings and guiding me into a life I live rather than a life I exist in.

SHAMANIC MEDICINE OFFERING

The soundjourney play's a pivotal role as the guiding light of a Shamanic Breathwork process.

This is my passion, my love, and I create these DJ sets from my heart to yours in a chakra-based workflow. The soundjourney begins on earth at the root chakra with primal/tribal rhythms, moving into the tantric, continuing upward, becoming emotional as we reach the heart, with blissful space as we reach the third eye and crown chakras, before grounding sounds abound as we approach the earth plane once again, completing another cycle upon the spiral of life we travel upon.

With that, I'd love to share with you all, the reader, this wondrous soundjourney as an example and reminder of the medicine within us all.

Blessings in love and light, now and beyond.

DJ Psyskrit aka Chakradamus presents: Shamanic Transcendence (A Shamanic Soundjourney).

https://soundcloud.com/psyskrit/dj-psyskrit-shamanic-transcendence

Krisy Conroy is a Shamanic Breathwork Facilitator, Medicine Woman, Shamanic Practitioner in Soul Retrieval and Extraction work. She is a dedicated Reiki Healer, Registered Nurse, Psychiatric Nurse, Meditation Teacher, Therapeutic Massage Therapist, and Light Trance Medium. Krisy has an extraordinary gift for making a connection with the spirit world – for healing and helping those awaken and reclaim their true essence, especially during life's challenges.

Krti Psyskrit is the Co-Founder of Shamanic Transcendence. Also, a Paranormal Investigator at Get Out Paranormal (GO Paranormal), Shamanic Breathwork Facilitator, Samurai Reiki Master/Teacher, an Ordained Shamanic Minister, Parapsychologist, Demonologist, and teacher at Spirit Quest School. Krti is a passionate shamanic DJ - creating medicine music and sound journeys for the breathwork process. He is also an electronic music producer - creating trance dance experiences through the mystical Goa Trance soundscapes under the name Chakradamus.

See: https://www.facebook.com/shamanictranscendencevarsitylakes for our upcoming events & workshops.

https://www.facebook.com/ShamanicTranscendenceVarsityLakes

https://www.meetup.com/en-AU/Shamanic-Breathwork/

https://www.instagram.com/shamanictranscendence/

https://www.facebook.com/DJPsyskrit

https://www.facebook.com/gopparanormalinvestigations

Email: dj_krisy@hotmail.com

Email: psyskrit@yahoo.com

Email: getoutparanormal@yahoo.com

CHAPTER 5

HIGHER DIMENSIONAL MAGIC

Opening the Portal to Our Multidimensional Gifts

Judith Corvin-Blackburn, LCSW, DMin.

MY STORY

With images of the Great Pyramid and the Sphinx still fresh in my mind's eye, the sound of the morning prayers seeping into our Luxor hotel room before sunrise, and my heart full of the warmth of the camaraderie between the 40-some people on our Shamanic Journey in Egypt, we gather in the hotel lobby in the early morning darkness. The air has a slight chill as we walk to board the boat, which takes us to the Temple of Isis. As with many of the sacred sites on this trip, we arrive hours before other tourists are allowed in.

It is already a week or so into this amazing three-week experience led by Nicki Sculley and co-led by Linda Star Wolf and her late husband, Brad Collins. Isis has always been important to me. As a young woman, I had a beautiful poster of her in her winged glory at the head of my bed, so I was especially excited to experience her temple. This was also the day that Brad and Star Wolf would lead us in a Shamanic Breathwork at the temple itself.

This was not my first foray into Shamanic Breathwork. I had an informal experience years before when a friend studying with Star Wolf had me try it out. But this was my first formal experience. All I remembered from the very first time was seeing the chakras line up vertically with their vibrant colors, and knowing this was an image to be used on the website I was just beginning to develop. That was in the late 90s, and it's an image I have on my website today. Now, on this Shamanic Journey in Egypt in 2005, I'm ready to experience 'the real deal.'

It's still dark as all of us set up mats on the stone floor of one of the open porticos of the temple. The air is fragrant. The guards who accompany us throughout the tour stand facing outwards, guns strapped around their shoulders. We lay down on our mats, and then the music begins, and my focus goes to my breath. Before I know it, I'm transported to a different reality. I become a kite, the hawk associated with Isis, and I'm flying over the Nile, diving in to catch a fish or two and soaring back up. I can feel what it's like to have those wings, to flap them and direct my course, to see the water below, to dive and use my beak to catch a fish as it jumps. Then I find myself being a priestess serving Isis, a memory that came to me that morning before the breathwork, but now I'm back in time, walking in my priestess robes.

A half-hour later, we are drummed back into awareness of being on our mats in our group. The sun had risen, and John Lennon's *Imagine* is playing on the recorder.

Despite all of us being in an altered state, we get on our feet and wrap our arms around each other in a large circle. Not only does this circle include those of us on the tour, but Star Wolf calls to the guards to join us. They shake their heads and say, "It's Ramadan. We are not allowed to touch women." Star Wolf replies, "Rules are made to be broken!" and miraculously, they put down their guns and join us.

We sing boisterously together, feeling our soul connections, as we envision creating a world based on love, harmony, and peace. Lennon's words seem to be activating all our cells: "*. . . Imagine all the people living life in peace. . .You may say I'm a dreamer, but I'm not the only one; I hope someday you'll join us, and the world will live as one.*"

It is over 16 years later, and I can still feel the magic of being in that circle. I realize we not only experienced our individual Shamanic Breathwork journey, but something shifted in the collective field, which allowed these traditional, religious Muslim men to break their rules by joining us to sing about the world we all longed to create no matter what our religious or cultural background. It still brings tears to my eyes. And I understood that what happened in breathwork had a far greater reach than the individual psyche. I realized the energy of going deep within, of tapping into our essence, which also holds all of creation, allows us to open dormant parts of our DNA, and from here, we can reach out into the larger world to shift consciousness and transform our planet.

My husband and I returned to the States and through a variety of synchronicities, ended up buying land next to Brad and Star Wolf in Isis Cove as part of our plan to relocate when my husband retired. After that, I did several Venus Rising programs, all of which, of course, included Shamanic Breathwork. Because I worked through most of my emotional healing before experiencing breathwork, my breathwork experiences were transpersonal rather than personal. I found that I was provided with another portal into my multidimensional nature, which significantly enriched my sacred purpose in this lifetime. I got to shapeshift, to dive through oceans, go deep into the earth and ascend on newly formed wings to the higher realms. I moved easily through other lifetimes. My awareness of reality greatly expanded.

Shortly after moving to the Cove, I came across a book called *The Alchemy of Nine Dimensions*, which took my teachings and the workshops I offered to a new level. My passion for teaching people how to access their multidimensional potential and stepping into their 5D ascended expression formed. Since I'm not a breathwork facilitator, every time I run a multidimensional workshop, I make sure to either have a co-facilitator who is, or to have someone come in to give my students this breathwork experience because I know it connects them even more strongly to their multidimensional nature, and it is from here that we heal our planet.

The magic is palpable when sitting in a circle in the Shamanic Multidimensional Mystery School that Carley Mattimore and I created.

Emily shared her journey. "Again," she said, "the panther was there to take me through the different aspects of myself—through the jungle, through the cosmos, connecting me in a way that I've never experienced before." Maura shared: "I went to the red planet again. I know now it is where I come from. They are training me for the next step I will take in my sacred work this lifetime. I feel awed at this emotional reunion. These are my tribes, the ones I was always looking for throughout my childhood." Each share from participants is more magical than the ones before, and if I had any doubt about the power and depth of Shamanic Breathwork journeys, it has fully dissolved.

SHAMANIC MEDICINE OFFERING

Like Shamanic Breathwork, which cannot be experienced through writing, the guided meditations which follow allow you to get in touch with your multidimensional wisdom and expanded consciousness by going deep within to your essence. Unlike breathwork, you are guided with specific imagery. There is no evocative music, but these meditations still give you a sense of what you might experience on your own breathwork journeys.

You can find the following meditation in my book, *Activating Your 5D Frequency: A Guidebook for the journey into higher Dimensions**, and on my YouTube channel *Wisdom Within Us*.

This meditation activates dormant DNA and connects you more deeply with your sacred purpose. Find a comfortable, private space to read them slowly and quietly, allowing yourself to experience them through the written word or listen to it here: https://www.youtube.com/watch?v=6Ma5y0jmsRc

Meditation: Connecting with Your Cosmic DNA

Allow your eyes to become soft and take several deep centering breaths. On the exhale, release any tension, concerns, or distractions - just allow all that to come out with the breath. On the inhale, imagine drawing in tiny golden spirals of light and allowing those spirals to flow to every cell in your body, feeling yourself both soothed and activated by their energy. Keep focusing on your inhale and on your exhale until you find yourself in a deep state of relaxation.

Imagine now that you are on a pristine private beach. The sky above you is a vibrant blue. The white sands below your feet are warm and shift gently as you walk.

Allow yourself to drink in all the colors and shapes, all the visual beauty in front of you. Listen to the sounds, the rhythmic crashing of the waves, the birds cawing and calling to one another. Feel the bright sun warming your skin and hair. Notice any fragrances. You might want to take a minute and walk along the water's edge, feeling its coolness and its energy. Put your palms on the ocean floor and feel its energy. If you feel called, go for a swim or wade deeper into the water. Let your body direct you and feel the rhythm and power of the sea.

Return now to shore and put a towel or blanket down on the sand where you can lie comfortably. Lie down and stretch your body out, feeling Mother Earth supporting your back. Feel her energy, her power, and her wisdom begin to seep into you. Allow this to soak into all your cells. Perhaps you will begin to feel the warmth and consciousness that is rising up from the golden pyramid in the crystal iron core at the earth's center. Drop into this feeling and notice yourself feeling more and more spacious.

Now imagine that each cell in your body has a tiny solar panel, and as you lie on this pristine beach, each and every cell in your body is becoming energized, activated by photons, by the light-filled with higher consciousness coming from the sun. You may begin to feel very big. Perhaps your energy field feels as if it is taking up the entire beach, maybe even the entire planet. This is fine. There's plenty of room. Let yourself luxuriate in this feeling. Realize that these photons and the energy waves emitted from the earth's center, which is now coursing gently through your body, have activated new areas of your DNA that have been dormant and now are ready to become awake.

You can sense that you are now experiencing the world through the eyes of your 5D self. Take a moment and send the 3D self within you, love and appreciation for just being part of you. Then tune back into every one of your cells. They are vibrating very quickly. It feels as if you are getting a cellular massage. You find yourself in a state of remarkable ease. Allow yourself to drop into this feeling. Notice your heart feels more expanded. Joy is filling each and every one of the cells in your body. Keep surrendering more to this ecstasy.

In your mind's eye, see yourself as part of our 5D global team. Send love to all your teammates, and if you are unclear about your role, go ahead and ask the wisdom in your cells what it is that you are here to do. What is your unique contribution? Listen as answers come forth quietly.

Take a few more minutes and see yourself walk through your daily life fully activated as this 5D human, spreading love and joy wherever you go as you live out your sacred purpose more and more.

Whenever this feels complete, slowly sit up and thank Mother Earth and Father Sky for all the love, support, and wisdom they are bringing your way. Thank the ocean and the sands and the birds. Then as you are ready, slowly leave the beach and bring yourself back to your room, becoming aware of any sounds, the feeling of the cushion or chair you are sitting or lying on. Slowly wiggle your fingers and toes and allow your 5-D expression to lead you throughout your day.

This next meditation gives you the awareness of the fluidity of time. As multidimensional beings, we have access to the past, present, and future. Accessing our future selves is similar to Star Wolf's teachings on the imaginal cells, and in experiencing Shamanic Breathwork, participants often find themselves experiencing different timelines of what we call "past" and "future." This meditation can also be found in my book: *Activating Your 5D Frequency* and on my YouTube channel *Wisdom Within Us,* https://www.youtube.com/watch?v=RkOcbqn1IuE

MEDITATION: CONNECTING WITH THE WISDOM OF YOUR FUTURE SELF

Before doing this meditation, I would suggest you first consciously choose what you want help with or information about. Write it down. It is important to release any attachment to the outcome, so generally people need to work with their egos before doing this. Creating and answering a few journal questions beforehand, such as: "What is the worst that can happen if I do not get the outcome I'm hoping for?" "What resistances and limiting beliefs might stand in my way of reaching this goal?" will help you free your ego from intervening.

Allow your eyes to become soft and take several deep centering breaths. On the exhale, release any tension, any concerns, or distractions—just allow that all to come out with the breath. On the inhale, imagine drawing in tiny golden spirals of light and allowing those spirals to flow to every cell in your body. Feel yourself both soothed and activated by their energy. Continue to use your breath to bring you a deeper and deeper sense of relaxation.

Imagine now that you are on the banks of a crystal-clear lake surrounded by gentle mountains. This may be somewhere you have been before, or it may be someplace you create in your imagination. Find a comfortable place to sit, perhaps leaning against a large tree or boulder, and gaze over the lake to its distant shore. Breathe deeply and luxuriate in the sense of calm and relaxation that fills you.

The sky above you is a brilliant blue. The air is crisp, and the sun beams down, warming your hair and skin. Allow yourself to drink in all the colors and shapes before you, all the visual beauty around you. Listen to the sounds, to the water lap gently against the shore, the birds chirping, and the leaves rustling in the wind. Notice any fragrances. You might want to take a minute to get up and walk around this beautiful spot, touching the cool water, the trunks of the trees, the rocks, the leaves. Allow the palms of your hands to soak in the energy of each thing you touch.

Then return once more to the place where you can sit peacefully, gazing over the water. You will start to notice from far across the lake that a horizontal beam of light is beginning to move in your direction. You get a strong sense of the loving nature of this light and so become excited when you realize that it is getting closer and closer.

As it comes almost to the shore where you are sitting, you see there is a figure in this beam of light, and when the light finally fully reaches the shore, you realize that it has delivered to you a part of yourself that is from your future. Greet this part; welcome it and offer it a seat in front of you.

This part may look older or younger. It may look like you or like an etheric version of yourself. It may not resemble you physically at all. Just allow the image to unfold in any way it wishes. Perhaps you will only have a sense of someone there.

Now focus on what you want to know. Take a moment to go into your heart and feel it filled with love so that no matter what information you receive, you can feel safe and nurtured and understand it is for your highest development. Then go ahead and ask your question to this future version of you.

Now take several deep centering breaths and wait patiently. You may hear a clear response, or perhaps you will be shown a picture or an object. Maybe you will just be given a feeling. No matter what you are presented with, know that there is important guidance for you from your future. Take a few minutes to just sit with this. Notice what this means for you.

Now become this future self, looking back at you in the present. Breathe deeply to feel more embodied in this part of you. Notice what you see when you look at yourself now. Go into your heart and beam this self with love. Then speak whatever you feel called to say.

Return now to your present self. Thank this part of your future for showing up and for being there for you. And then, whenever you are ready, slowly allow your awareness to return to wherever you are, wiggling your fingers and toes and listening to any sounds around you.

I encourage you to journal on this experience and date it.

* *Activating Your 5D Frequency* by Judith Corvin-Blackburn, LCSW, DMin, published by Inner Traditions International and Bear & Company, ©2020. All rights reserved.
http://www.Innertraditions.com Reprinted with permission of the publisher.

Judith Corvin-Blackburn, LCSW, DMin, is an award-winning author, internationally-known teacher, transpersonal psychotherapist & Shamanic Minister who has inspired people to step into joy, purpose, and inner authority for over 45 years. Her passion is to guide & empower individuals to heal their wounds and reclaim their true soul nature so that collectively we can transform our planet into the loving, conscious, and peaceful place it is meant to be.

She is the author of three books, Activating Your 5D Frequency: A Guidebook to the Journey into Higher Dimensions; Empowering the Spirit: A Process to Activate Your Soul Potential, and Journey to Wholeness: A Guide to Inner Healing.

Her current offerings include: "Connecting Star Consciousness with Earth Consciousness," a 10-week zoom class based on her newest book, Activating Your 5D Frequency. This is designed to activate our dormant DNA to more fully step into our 5D expression and to envision New Earth collectively; "The Global Shamanic Multidimensional Mystery School: Becoming a Fifth Dimensional Human on Planet Earth" – a two-year process to do just that and step more fully into bringing our unique contribution forward; and "Empowering the Spirit Online," a self-directed course based on her book Empowering the Spirit. Individual sessions are also available to clear the emotional body, transform fears and resistances to becoming the beautiful beings we truly are, and carry out our sacred work for planetary healing.

She lives in the beautiful Smoky Mountains with her husband, Dennis.

Website: https://www.empoweringthespirit.com

Instagram: https://www.instagram.com/judithcorvinblackburn/

Facebook: https://www.facebook.com/empoweringthespirit

You Tube: https://www.youtube.com/channel/UCzOOTp5tfP0T8SB1aw868tw

For a free downloadable meditation, go to https://www.empoweringthespirit.com/subscribe/ and sign up for inspiring information to support your evolutionary process and our planetary healing.

CHAPTER 6

THE ALCHEMY OF FRUSTRATION AND SOLITUDE

Intimately Co-Creating with Earth and Sky

Mar Guerrero

MY STORY

"Mar, I'm not going to make it easy for you."

The Universe seemed to be speaking to me with a British accent. The deep, almost cosmic voice pierced my heart like a rumble of seemingly distant thunder that made me tremble from my core. It belonged to one of the Shamanic Breathwork Facilitators who was walking the floor that day in Bali. I was bathed in sweat, squeezed by two people holding me tightly, pressing me to recreate my own birth. I pushed with the incipient energy of a seed that longs to sprout, opening myself up to be vulnerable. I was longing to feel the air of life on my skin, the vitality of spring palpitating in my Aries signature.

I could feel how within me the same force that enables life to flourish and to bloom was beating rhythmically despite the difficulties, or perhaps, encouraged by them. However, my strength was slowly escaping from every pore; my muscles contracted and stretched, trying to get rid of those arms that squeezed me with unbearable pressure.

The screams of the rest of the participants echoed in my ears and my blood as if they were ancestral drums initiating me, marking me with the phrase:

"It is really hard to be born."

And, finally, I understood.

That was how my real birth happened.

My mother could not dilate, so I had to be pushing for hours. Those words seemed to both foretell and explain my destiny, bringing to my consciousness the memory of how I deal with change.

I pushed once more, without thinking about it, like an impulse welling up from my essence. I fiercely wanted to be alive, to breathe, to free myself from that pressure. At the exact moment when I almost gave up, when I thought I was dying from lack of breath, the world suddenly widened.

When I was born, there was a moment when, after hours of waiting for my mother to dilate naturally, the doctors decided to perform a vaginal cesarean section. In a matter of seconds, the pressure turned into expansion, and I found the space to come out.

The expression of being born with a conjunction between Jupiter (expanding everything) and Saturn (constricting) could not be more literal.

Back in Bali, after all that effort, I got into a fetal position, and I cried, vulnerable, tired, and free. I cried like the baby who had just been reborn in my 38th year. I felt in every bone of my body how I embody in my being the signature of a fierce struggle with the physical world. Then I allowed myself to witness multiple scenes from my life that brought back to me that sense of frustration.

One concrete situation came to me stronger.

I was at one of the meetings that had recently taken place at my university in Thailand, where I had been working for almost ten years as a Spanish lecturer. It seemed to be just another bland and insipid meeting where everything seemed to be happening as usual. I could not have been more wrong!

I opened my e-mail inbox, and I saw reflected on the screen the materialization of one of my deepest fears. I was in a room full of people, surrounded by my colleagues from all over the world. The air conditioning and the impersonal architecture of a building that could be placed in any country in the world were draining me without my conscious awareness. Universities, like hospitals, airports, and some hotels, are missing a deep sense of soul and authenticity. They all look the same. It does not matter where they are located. They are like corpses, lifeless.

In that e-mail, I felt the fear and frustration of the creator bubbling up with these words: "Mar, you don't have what it takes to bring the children of your fantasy into the world. You have neither talent nor professionalism. Your ideas will remain eternally in your head, writhing with the pain of wanting them to be born and not succeeding. Your ideas are useless. Your ideas are madness, a formless delirium that has no end. I no longer want to accompany you in the process of giving birth to them."

While I was reading the e-mail, almost in paralysis, my colleagues kept talking about papers, about absurd details leading us nowhere as an educational center, as a department, or as humanity. Nobody cared about developing the potential of that future generation. It was all about rules, bureaucracy, and control.

A fierce, flaming, volcanic rage began to spread through each of my veins, pumping in me with the danger of exploding at the least appropriate moment. I felt like taking the laptop and throwing it out of the window. I had put so much time and energy into this project that it had become as heavy as a rock, stuck in my womb like an aborted baby.

What my Ph.D. advisor wrote to me in that e-mail was: "Mar, it would be better for you to look for another advisor. I am no longer willing to continue directing your Ph.D. thesis."

I devoted almost four intensive years of dedication and sacrifice to this project. I truly believed it was my sacred mission in the world to bring that necessary change into the educational system. The project was about the development of critical and creative thinking when studying a foreign language, which allowed the students to reflect on their own identity and the conditioning of their language and culture, opening portals to possibilities.

I believed I could revolutionize the educational system, bring a change as urgent as necessary, question the essence of what makes us human, and analyze language as a code that simultaneously both limits and liberates us.

After more than four years dedicated to this project, finding a new advisor was not exactly easy; but, in addition, the subject of my doctorate was so specific that there were not many people in the world qualified to direct it. Opting for another advisor would mean starting almost from scratch.

I felt like a war veteran, lost and without a mission. I could sense the visceral frustration of having three planets in Aries (Mars, Venus, and the Sun) opposing my Saturn and Jupiter conjunction.

I could see myself inside of the birth canal one more time: I was in the middle of the alchemy of frustration, Saturn being my dearest teacher.

My awareness returned to the shala in Bali, to that sacred space we had woven together to dive deep into our transformative process. The Shamanic Breathwork session was finished, so I began to draw my experience on a piece of white paper. Everything on the paper was on fire, except the center, where I was drawing some water with different shades of blue. We went to the small groups to process the session so we could integrate it. Everyone shared. When it was my turn, one of the girls asked me:

"Mar, do you want me to tell you what I see?"

"Sure."

"I see that you have drawn like a porthole of a submarine and you see life from there, like far away, protected, but you are not being part of all that fire."

A painful knowing in my heart when I heard her words confirmed to me that she was right.

A few days later, the Shamanic Breathwork retreat in Bali ended, so I returned to my work in Bangkok. I was still feeling lost and increasingly disconnected from an educational system that did not promote the infinite potential of the students but rather blocked it, confining it into little boxes that did not leave the room to breathe.

A year passed, and I decided to go to Mexico, to Teotihuacan, to get certified as a Shamanic Breathwork Facilitator. I felt much more confident in my purpose. Astrology was becoming more and more strong as a symbolic language to decode the potential of my soul. I was longing to bring astrology back into our cultures as the wisdom of connecting with earth and sky.

I perceived with certainty that my days working in the academic world were coming to an end. That part of me needed to die, but another part of me was strongly resisting that change.

Once again, I found myself back in that sacred space dedicated to transformation. I was lying on the mat, with the sacred pyramids of Teotihuacan anchoring us. The smell of sage and palo santo filled me with a pure intention of deepening into my essence and unveiling all the beliefs that were contracting me.

Then, in the middle of the first session, I needed to go to the bathroom, I raised my hand for one of the facilitators to accompany me, and no one approached. It hit me. I was suddenly pierced by the pain of loneliness I had been resisting for years. The voice of my inner child, one-year-old, repeated to me: "You are alone, don't trust, don't open yourself, resist."

Before me, a scene with my mother appeared with unusual force, I was one year old, and she was giving me an omelet. It was Easter in the south of Spain, in my hometown, Malaga. Below my grandmothers' house balcony, a float was passing with Mother Mary wearing a red and golden gown and a red flower on the chest. Men were carrying her on their shoulders. It was 1 a.m., and we were all awake to witness this procession. The sound of rhythmic drums and military steps hitting the floor was the background of the scene; the smell of incense impregnated the celebration of the death of Christ, a very shamanic ritual that is an integral part of the Spanish culture. My roots are interwoven with this tragic and dramatic sense of living and dying, like a flamenco song danced with a furious passion.

Many people from my family had gathered at my grandmothers' house to watch Christ and Virgin parading with the band music and the candles. The streets were overflowing with people. Suddenly, my mother turned pale, the blood drained from her body, and she handed me over to my grandmother, who was at her side. She was carried off to the hospital; my father and uncles took her away through the crowd.

I did not see her again for two weeks.

I felt abandoned and betrayed. I was an orphan. I felt like one. I did not want anyone to touch me, feed me, or wash me for the whole time my mother was in the hospital. My father, with his tender 22 years, had to run from work to the hospital to visit my mother and come home to feed me.

My mother had to have an urgent surgery between life and death. She made it out alive, but evidently, my brother did not make it into the world, so I was raised as an only child. This experience stayed with me as an imprint on the danger of giving birth and being a mother.

When my mother came home two weeks later, I looked at her, wearing a little pink gown and my curly, golden hair. I stared at her, and my eyes reflected unusual wisdom for a one-year-old little girl, then I turned my face away. My grandmother was holding me in her arms. In my whole body, I felt a visceral rejection towards that mother who had abandoned me, towards that woman who had pretended to love me only to leave me without warning.

And I told myself: "I am alone" "I do not need anybody."

That day, lost in the memory of my childhood, I stopped believing fully in love. And I placed such a solid armor on my chest that it became confused with my own skin to such an extent that I forgot it existed; so I spent my life looking for love, longing for it with a voracious hunger, while simultaneously fleeing away from the vulnerability that is essential for authentic intimacy to take place.

This is the reason why I kept falling in love with unavailable men, one after another.

On the floor of the Shamanic Breathwork session in the sacred land of Teotihuacan, with the pyramids in the background, I remembered.

A few months after that Shamanic Breathwork program in Teotihuacan, I woke up on my bed in Bangkok. It was my birthday, and I was feeling a profound hole in my heart.

I was completely alone.

I could not see anybody because COVID had started. That isolation kept growing beyond the limits of the political restrictions, and it extended for almost two years. Most of my friends left Thailand, and my house is an hour away from the city, so when the restrictions were less strict, it was still lonely because I was working with a computer day after day, living by myself. I spent weeks, even months, without seeing or touching anybody. And then I kept asking myself: How did I create this reality? And why?

The constrictions of this situation took me to decide to write that novel that I had been gestating within me for years: *The Courage of Loving you, Soledad*. Soledad in Spanish is a female name that can be translated as solitude and loneliness.

I also created two international online Summits ("I am possible" and "I am alive"), where well-known speakers of Shamanism, Astrology, and Spirituality shared their wisdom.

However, I was not fully content. I was not happy only by being recognized for my work anymore. I wanted to feel alive, vibrant, passionate, and connected.

And, finally, I have no choice but to surrender.

Writing this chapter, I am aware that the time has come to get out of that submarine which I entered when I was one year old. The loneliness I have experienced has been the pressure I needed to create and to find my voice, beyond the social conditioning that tells us what is possible and what is not.

I needed to own my Saturn.

My infinite creative power required me to move inside beyond external authorities, away from family and friends, from possible lovers, from my own culture, and my land. In these years of isolation, I dived into the deepest and darkest part of myself, that place that can never be taken away from me:

my soul.

The pressure of loneliness brought me back the memory of my birth, of the channel of my mother's body that would not open, that suffocated me, but I could do nothing but keep pushing. Sooner or later, the channel of life will open. Even when I do not have any more energy, I keep pushing from the inside out.

I am giving birth to myself!

I am a mother and a midwife at the same time - like many other women of a New Earth, of a new humanity, of a new ancient way: the way of the soul.

And the pressure, the frustration, the loneliness were (and are) the necessary contractions that activated me to keep pushing so I can give birth to life!

My sacred work is to inspire you to also give birth to your fullest potential, transforming your wounds and obstacles into medicine for yourself and our beautiful global tribe called humanity.

SHAMANIC MEDICINE OFFERING

I want to connect! I invite you to do the same.

Let's dive together to bring forward our connection with earth and sky.

You can find this ceremony at the following link:

https://www.almarguerrero.com/alchemy

I invite you to play a soulful song and start moving your body, focusing your attention on your heart and womb or the space below the belly bottom where life is created.

You can then bring your attention to the womb of the earth and dance with her with everything that you are, with every feeling, with every thought. You are Her. You are the Earth. I invite you to feel how she brings you all her wisdom, the memory of our ancestors vibrating inside of you and inviting you to drink it in and make it yours. With each movement of your body, you can perceive how the energy of the earth, the land where you stand and breathe, is spreading through your cells and your limbs. Your roots are always connected. Feel your creative power palpitating in your womb - or your inner core if you were born with a male body.

Now connect with the sky. Keep moving, feeling the music, feeling the earth, and now also inhaling the Cosmos into your being where you can embody the infinite potential that is available for you.

Now!

You are possible!

You are the Cosmos experiencing life.

Keep moving freely, paying attention to every cell, to your bones and blood, feeling how they were mountains, rivers before.

You are the Earth.

You are the Cosmos.

You can become a moving tree with the roots deeply connected with the earth and the branches growing up to embrace your full potential. Embody that potential with every step, imagine your dreams and dance them, make them yours, feel them in your cells so that you can bring them here now.

Open yourself to the magic of bringing into your presence the memories of the past, the potential of the future, and dance with them in the magic and fullness of this present moment.

You are intimately connected with multiple dimensions, and you are the infinite creative power of the Cosmos embodied as a human being.

It is your right to live!

It is your right to create!

It is your right to breathe!

Dance every emotion and make it yours.

Breathe it. Inhale it in. Exhale it out.

Let's make love with life.

And a certainty can flood into your chest, fulfilling your courageous heart.

You are Connected!

Mar Guerrero (Almakhemy) is an interpreter of the Cosmos and a catalyst of transformational and alchemical processes through Astrology, Energy work, Tarot, and Shamanic Breathwork. Mar is deeply passionate about holding ceremonial spaces where she integrates the different disciplines that she has studied for years to create an embodied experience of the Cosmos.

She is very connected with the power of words and art, becoming a bridge of cultures and symbolic languages. She has a long experience teaching Spanish internationally with her Master's Degree in Spanish Literature and Applied Linguistics. At the moment, she is writing her first novel.

Mar is the founder of Almakhemy, a school for the soul to remember, transform, and create. Her sacred work is to weave networks of connection that activate the latent memory in the soul of the people who approach her. She accompanies and encourages her tribe to remember the power of their soul, to manifest in a tangible way businesses, books, and different creative projects.

She encourages to manifest and give birth to these projects by following the natural cycles of earth and sky (like the Venus cycle).

Mar Guerrero trusts that human beings will come together as the global tribe that we are to radically embrace our vital essence and our creative power.

We are not meant to do this alone!

www.almakhemy.com

www.almarguerrero.com

Youtube: Mar Guerrero Almakhemy

(https://www.youtube.com/c/MarGuerreroALMAKHEMY)

IG: @almakhemy (https://www.instagram.com/almakhemy/)

Chapter 7

DEATH AND REBIRTH

Divorce as Shamanic Initiation

Deb Kotz, DMin, MA

What do you do when you find out
that everything you thought was true, isn't?

~Deb Kotz

MY STORY

I paused at my desk for a moment to gaze at the tiny, green leaves bursting forth from the maple trees outside the building of our family business. My body lit up with the reverberations of spring in Minnesota and the new life it promised.

My nearly packed suitcase awaited me at home, in anticipation of my trip to North Carolina in the morning. My heart soared as I envisioned being in a community once again with my soul family. My excitement grew as I thought about meeting and supporting the curious, adventuresome, powerful souls registered for the latest Shamanic Healing Initiatory Process (SHIP) at Venus Rising.

My magical second home, known as StarWalker cabin, beckoned. Nurturing heart energies pulse through this sweet little mountain retreat. The grounding Earth Temple Medicine Wheel stands below, and the ethereal Spirit Temple Blue Star Wheel perches above. They converge to create a vortex where I was called years earlier by the little people of Dove Mountain to create a sanctuary for rest and renewal.

My body startled as an insistent voice sounded in my head. *You must talk to him tonight, as soon as you are done with clients.* My shoulders tensed. Things in our marriage weren't great lately. No matter what I did to try to connect, my husband remained distant and aloof. *Oh well. After living together for 36 years, there are bound to be some rough patches. We've gotten through hard times before. We will figure it out together.*

When the last client of the day walked out the door, the voice returned with more intensity. *Go upstairs, now! It's time to talk.*

I reached the top of the stairs to see the receptionist heading out to her car. The office suite was empty and quiet. I walked into my husband's office as I'd done for over three decades and quietly asked, "Are we okay?"

Silently, he got up from his desk, stepped into the hallway, looked around, returned, shut his office door, and warily sat back down. "No," he said. "We are not okay. I've been thinking about leaving for a long time."

My body froze. *What?* My stomach dropped as my heart jumped into my throat. My mind raced. *He's been thinking of leaving. For a long time? For how long a time? He can't possibly mean that. He can't be serious. This can't be happening!*

He continued, emotionless. "I planned to leave six years ago, but then you got diagnosed with cancer, and I thought only an asshole would leave his wife when she had cancer."

My body remained completely still. My thoughts raged. *What? Why is this the first I'm hearing of this? You've wanted to leave for six years, and you never thought to mention it? That's the real asshole move!*

The next morning, he dropped me off at the airport as if nothing had happened. I went through the familiar routine of checking my suitcase, grabbing a latte, and settling into my window seat. My mountain refuge awaited as a whirlwind of chaos threatened to tear me apart.

In Charlotte, I rented a small SUV to drive to the Cove. Pure adrenalin kept me awake on the three-hour drive. The radio stations jostled between rock, country, Christian, and NPR. Entering the mountains, even those stations became spotty.

The car, hurtling down one particularly long mountain curve, suddenly lurched to the side. I vaguely wondered if I'd blown a tire, but the car recovered. Feeling numb and on the verge of panic, survival mode set it. *I can make it to Asheville and look at the tire when I stop for groceries.*

My legs shook as I stepped into the parking lot. My gut clenched as I peered at the ruptured left rear tire. *Thank you, spirit guides, for keeping me safe.*

In a daze, I purchased food for the week. A young man from AAA arrived as I loaded several full totes into the back seat. He adeptly changed the tire and told me the spare was good for about 50 miles. *My cabin is only 59 miles away. I'll be fine.*

An hour later, I parked my rental next to the Spirit Temple, gathered my suitcase and groceries, walked down my driveway, and collapsed into bed.

The next afternoon, I finally relaxed into the embrace of the community I'd grown to love and trust. A community where we knew each other's pain and joy, suffering, and strength, shadow and light. A place where it was safe to express our innermost frailties and share our authentic selves. If my life was going to fall apart, at least I had the support of my loving, heart-centered wolf pack to encourage me through another life-changing shamanic initiation.

A decade earlier, I lay in a medically induced coma while doctors tried to determine why I couldn't breathe, my body hovering between life and death. At that time, my consciousness made an inter-dimensional journey to what the beautiful blue beings there called the Blue Star Planet.

The love here is indescribable. I want to stay here forever.

"You can stay here, or you can go back. There is no judgment either way."

Yes, I want to stay. How could anyone ever want to leave this place?

Wait.

I see my children's faces. *They still need a mom. I want to go back.*

"Very well. You can go back. You will have your family for ten more years. Then, everything will change, and you will have new contracts to fulfill."

I dove back into my body with a deep love for my children and all of life on Earth.

Now ten years later, facing the end of my marriage, my 5-D higher self knew this was part of my new soul contract, but my 3-D human self was devastated. At the workshop, working as staff for a Shamanic Breathwork training, I experienced walking between the worlds in a new way. Life as I knew it was shattering. At the same time, I was tasked with supporting others through their own shamanic death and rebirth. It was a fascinating experience. I found myself going from my deep grief to being fully focused on the process group I was leading, then going back into my own process. I'd walked between the worlds before, but never when I was in a full-blown crisis. It was a mystical time and another affirmation that I'd be okay.

When I got home, he moved out. We decided to do a collaborative divorce and began the divorce process. But something still seemed off. Our interactions were civil, and we both made a point to be fair regarding the legal aspects of our dissolution of marriage. But slowly, people began telling me things that made me question the truth about my marriage. Slowly, I began to recall all the times I'd thought. . .

Hmm. That's weird. What he said didn't make any sense.

Why did that woman act so strange when she found out I was his wife?

Why are his colleagues looking at me like that? What are they not telling me?

Gradually I began to realize that the person I'd devoted 36 years of my life to, built a home with, created a family with, supported in business, and considered a partner who'd be with me no matter what was living a double life.

I'd been able to cope with everything else, but the dawning realization of the many years of infidelity and betrayal was devastating. Strangely, my body was finally able to relax as pieces of the puzzle began to come together.

I'm not crazy.

I'm not a bad person.

This is what it feels like when someone is gaslighting you.

I'm an intuitive person.

How could this happen to me?

How could he look me in the eye and lie so easily?

How could I not see what was going on?

Did he ever love me?

Was any of our marriage real?

What is true, and what is an illusion?

In retrospect, my body spent years trying to tell me something was wrong: dramatic weight gain, cancer, heart problems. My body did its best to communicate the disconnect between my holistic, healthy lifestyle and the actual state of my life.

Over the next year, I scheduled sessions with four different energy healers. Each of them was horrified when they began working with me and exclaimed their version of "I can't believe all the arrows, hate barbs, hatchets, and knives that are embedded in your field. I can't remove them all in one session. I apologize if removing them hurts. I will do as much as I can for today." No wonder my health was suffering.

While my old life continued to dissolve, I was free for the first time in decades. My children were grown. Our dogs and cats had crossed the rainbow bridge. The family home was for sale, and my only responsibility was me.

I traveled to Peru and explored Machu Picchu, allowing Pachamama to restore my body. I flew to California to visit my sister, ate delicious food, and played in nature. I drove all over the midwestern and southeastern United States, visiting friends, co-facilitating workshops, participating in sacred sexuality retreats, and going wherever spirit led.

A few weeks before Covid-19 and the response to it caused chaos in the U.S., I co-facilitated a retreat in Guatemala. Lake Atitlan was a powerful vortex. I experienced a significant soul return, retrieving soul contracts that lay dormant in one of the lake's volcanos for millennia. It was an amazing, healing time.

A few months later, our sprawling family home of 30 years finally sold, and I was able to purchase a wonderful, cozy, new home of my own. I awoke in my new bedroom, reveling in joy and freedom as my field expanded into every room of my new sanctuary. My body relaxed into deep peace.

After three years of releasing and letting go while calling in my new life, I was finally at ease. My energy field was clear, clean, light, and calm. I experienced a sense of deep gratitude for all it took to go through the immense death of my old life and miraculous rebirth into the new.

My health improved dramatically. No longer needing protection from the lies and hate barbs hurled at me during my marriage, I let go of 50 excess pounds.

I began to re-examine my work in the world and simplify my life. I saw some private clients pre-divorce but mainly focused on facilitating priestesses and women's circles, SHIP, and shamanic groups. With the divorce, I'd lost my office space and group room, and with the sale of my house, I'd lost my retreat space. With the onset of Covid, I moved my groups online.

Over time, it became clear I was being called in a new direction. As I felt less need to travel, I decided to sell StarWalker cabin to Venus Rising, where it could continue to be a place of healing for those going through deep transformation.

Back in Minnesota, I adopted a lively and loving cattle dog. I met new friends and colleagues who matched my new vibration. Old relationships that still resonated deepened. Relationships that felt dissonant drifted away. I became a grandmother. I began to embrace a life filled with ease, peace, and love.

Looking back, I'm grateful that I had skills, knowledge, friends, family, and support throughout my divorce and its aftermath. And it was still the hardest initiation of my life. Harder than chemotherapy. Harder than open-heart surgery. Harder than anything I'd ever done. Because when the bottom dropped out, I lost so many aspects of my identity. Wife. Matriarch. Family business owner. Someone who married for life.

Today, my energy runs freely. When I see friends I haven't seen in a while, they tell me how much lighter and happier I look. I'm passionate about supporting other women going through a divorce after a long-term marriage. I want them to know that after the greatest death comes the most fulfilling rebirth. Approaching divorce as a shamanic initiation catalyzes an empowered new life.

SHAMANIC MEDICINE OFFERING

I did not go through this process alone. I called on my community and worked with skilled practitioners along the way. At the same time, it was important to develop a personal practice that supported me each day, especially when I was feeling hopeless or overwhelmed.

One of the practices that evolved during my journey can be summed up in three steps:

1. Ground.
2. Connect.
3. Listen.

Grounding helps me feel supported and safe. When grounding into the earth, I often notice the roots of the trees, the stone beings, or the mycelial networks below the surface, giving me a felt sense of oneness.

Connecting to the sky feels supportive in a different way. Initially, I would pray *bring it on!* and *I'm ready for my next mission!* Eventually, I realized that I didn't need to produce in order to be loved. I began to ask for all the time I needed to heal. This was pivotal in calling back my power and sovereignty. I don't have to give myself away, to another person or to spirit, to be loved.

Listening to the messages of the deer, crows, rabbits, turkeys, or occasional hawk who appeared in the eastern portion of my yard during morning prayers filled me with hope and a promise of new beginnings.

Afterward, I would journal about my experience. Often, I would intuit the meanings of whatever showed up. When I wanted further understanding, I would look up the meaning of the animal, energy, or being who appeared during my meditation, either online or in a book of symbols.

To experience a guided version of this simple exercise, find a comfortable place to sit or stand and follow this link: https://youtu.be/HpBPqasj2no

A description of this process is as follows:

Call in sacred space by lighting a candle, burning some smudge, ringing a bell, or simply with your intention.

1. Ground.

Close your eyes. Take your attention to the base of your spine, also known as the root chakra. Imagine a grounding cord extending down from your tailbone into the earth. You may feel drawn to a specific rock, gemstone, tree root, or other underground feature. Or you may choose to send your grounding cord all the way to the center of the earth, which some describe as the slow-vibrating iron crystal core.

Once you've found your own personal sweet spot, begin to draw earth energy up through your grounding cord and into your root chakra. Allow the earth energies to move throughout your entire body, feeling the support of Mother Earth, also known as Gaia or Pachamama, reminding you that as a human being, you are of the earth. Remember to breathe.

2. Connect.

Take your attention to the top of your head, also known as the crown chakra. Send your awareness up and connect with the energies of the sky. You may imagine a ball of light about eight feet above your head, sometimes known as your soul point. Or you may choose to travel all the way to a star system that is special to you: Sirius, the Pleiades, or Arcturus, for example. You may even decide to send your intention to the galactic center, the womb of our Milky Way galaxy.

Once you've connected to this higher or faster vibrating realm, imagine it flowing down into your body. Allow the sky energies to move throughout your entire body, feeling the expansiveness of the upper realms. Just as you are of the earth, you are of the sky. Remember to breathe.

3. Listen.

Open your awareness. Notice the feelings in your body as you call in the energies of earth and sky. Relax. Breathe. Surrender. Allow whatever arises within you to surface.

As you practice this exercise, you may sense feelings of peace or love. You may become aware of deep rage or grief—no need to change anything. Just allow whatever is there to be there. Connections between your current situation and a memory from childhood or even a past life may emerge. You may think nothing is happening. Whatever occurs is perfect—no need to force anything to happen.

Take a few moments to journal about your experience.

Give thanks to the energies that came in to support you.

The end of a long-term marriage is destabilizing in so many ways. Fortunately, we can learn to create moments of stability amid the chaos.

The Shamanic Initiation of rebuilding after the end of a long-term marriage is similar to the re-creation we are all being called to go through as we move from the Piscean to the Aquarian Age. Death of the old. Questioning everything we thought was true. Visioning and manifesting a new reality.

What do you do when you find out that everything you thought was true, isn't?

1. Ground.

2. Connect.

3. Listen.

The catalyst for the most profound shamanic initiation of my life was sorting through the truth and the lies in my 36-year marriage. Much like our competing versions of world events today, I may never know the whole story. Fortunately, when I ground, connect, and listen, I know I am not alone.

Supporting women who are going through this portal is my passion and my medicine. It is an honor to midwife women as they re-create their lives.

Deb Kotz, DMin, MA, is an ordained Shamanic Minister. Integrating over 30 years of education and experience offering private transformational sessions, groups, and women's circles, she is passionate about helping women recreate their lives after the end of a long-term marriage.

Deb holds advanced degrees in Theology and Spirituality, Psychotherapy, and Shamanic Psycho-Spiritual Studies. She is a Shamanic Breathwork Master Practitioner and is certified in hypnotherapy, Reiki, and spiritual direction. She is a facilitator of the Shamanic Priestess Process and Magdalene Mysteries, the Shamanic Priest Process, and the Women's Shamanic Shakti series.

In 2010, Deb founded the first Venus Rising congregation, Shaman's Hearth Spiritual Community of Venus Rising. Through Shaman's Hearth, she led Shamanic Priestess and Wise Women circles, Shamanic Breathwork ceremonies, and the Shamanic Healing Initiatory Process (SHIP). In addition, she was part of the Venus Rising staff, assisting other Shamanic Ministers to begin their own Venus Rising congregations.

In 2021, Deb let go of her role as congregation leader and Venus Rising congregation coordinator to focus on her private online practice, where she is honored to support women during and after divorce. Her unique approach combines her vast experience in Shamanic Breathwork, hypnotherapy, psychotherapy, spiritual guidance, energy work, and women's empowerment circles to create a safe place for women to release the past and recreate a new life filled with confidence, love, and joy.

Contact Deb at:

www.debkotz.com

debkotzllc@gmail.com

Facebook: Deb Kotz

CHAPTER 8

DANCING NAKED IN A YURT

Embodying Artistic Freedom

Judy Redhawk, Ph.D., DMin

"Imagination and creativity can change the world."

~Anonymous

MY STORY

I would add to that quote: "in combination with Shamanic Breathwork."

Thinking about the invitation to write a chapter in *Shamanic Breathwork, The Nature of Change*, I began to wonder about my Shamanic Shakti Art Process and its complementary relationship with Shamanic Breathwork. What is the story which wants to be told? What is the medicine I offer? How was I going to tell the story of how Shamanic Breathwork has helped me step fully onto the spiral path of change and into being the shamanic witchy wonderful woman I already was and how it helped transform my life and create a life worth living? How my Shamanic Shakti Art Process has always been a part of me, even though that might not be what I called it from my childhood into now.

The Shamanic Shakti Art Process (SSAP) is a story—a story of embodying being human, of how our souls open mysterious doors and we step over the threshold into an inner world where we find the alchemical gold: our individual soul's language. The SSAP combines our healer within (the shaman), our life force energy, imagination (Shakti), and art processes that express our soul's messages. Art experiences are living processes. We create joyful connections within ourselves when we can share our creation stories and their meaning. We all need to be witnessed. We all need the experiences of being seen, heard, and felt by others.

My story is about creating over a lifetime and the power of play, art, imagination, and the alchemical medicine of soul return/soul retrieval.

I encourage you as you read these words to begin to use all your senses, imagination, and creativity to experience the magic, mystery, mayhem, and mean-making of your own life's story and your soul's language. . .and find your "yurt," that sacred space, in which to dance naked and to create.

Let me begin by sharing this story of finding artistic freedom or, perhaps, I need to say, how creative freedom was brought back to me in Shamanic Breathwork in a yurt. For, that experience was a soul retrieval/soul return.

The story of artistic freedom growing into the Shamanic Shakti Art Process began when my mother died in 2003. Friends are those people in our lives who have our permission to speak the unspeakable to us. They are our soul whisperers.

My friend, Lee Lipsenthal (who is now a guardian angel), was such a friend when he observed to me, "You aren't handling your mother's death very well." I confess I was confused because I didn't see or feel what Lee noticed. I thought I was approximating "normal" pretty well. We were sitting in a booth in a meeting room in a hotel in Pittsburgh, Pennsylvania, where we had a staff meeting for the Dean Ornish Program for Reversing Heart Disease. Lee was our team leader and cardiologist from California. Lee was a charming, funny, shamanic fellow. I was drawn to Lee's humor and realness from the first time meeting him. I was a group support facilitator. Lee was sincere when he continued, "I lead a healing process with my friend, Nita Gage. It is called Shamanic Breathwork. I think you'd like the process. It's a Shamanic Breathwork journey, with art, ritual, ceremony, group processing, psychodrama. I believe it would help you heal your grief. The next workshop is in a couple of weeks on the Hawaiian island of Molokai."

I wasn't aware I was feeling grief. And, I trusted Lee to observe things about me of which I wasn't aware. Lee also knew my background in drama therapy, psychodrama, theatre, and psychology. He had followed my creativity with my groups.

But Molokai? I heard my trusty voice inside say, *Go!*

When I told my husband I wanted to go to a Hawaiian island for a healing retreat, he couldn't understand why I had to go so far away; I couldn't explain that the voice inside me said *Go*, and that voice never steered me in the wrong direction.

I'd not been away from my husband and our two children by myself. As I arranged to fly to Molokai for a week-long Shamanic Breathwork experience of which I knew nothing, except what Lee had described, I felt the 'craziness' of it all.

Arriving on the island of Molokai, a group of us were met at the tiny island airport and were driven to the Hui Ho'Olana retreat center (huiho. org). It was a paradise of water, color, fresh air, yummy food, and exciting people. I was beginning to realize that the people who go to these Shamanic Breathwork workshops seemed to be 'of a kind.' By this, I mean a wild kind of energy, and a particular way of dressing. This was unfamiliar to my rather staid professional self. I didn't feel like I fit in.

Our group room for Shamanic Breathwork was in the yurt. There was a beautiful floor, an open round space, a peaceful feeling, almost like a church; it was aesthetically beautiful with a covered porch for drawing. The rain had started and could be heard making a rhythm on the roof. The wind was also starting to blow. The Shamanic Breathwork experience was intense, and we were cozy in the yurt. Nita described how during my Shamanic Breathwork, she had found a part of me, my little girl, dancing between the legs of the elders in Africa and holding a white duck. Nita brought her back to me by flying on a magic carpet. A soul retrieval/soul return. My heart felt wide open, and I felt expansive. The Shamanic Breathwork experience lead to that night's adventures.

You know that moment—the one in the middle of the night when your eyes fly open. You hear your heart pounding loudly with fear. You wonder what woke you. You lie, very still, breathing very slowly, waiting for your heart to slow its' pounding and the blood to stop rushing in your ears so you can listen.

At that moment, back in 2003, on the island of Molokai, after my first Shamanic Breathwork, I heard in the wind's voice which woke me:

Wake up, sleepyhead. Can't you hear the leaves are already dancing? They've started dancing without you. Now is the time for dancing - dancing with the wind.

Hurry.

Quick. Catch me.

The voices of the eucalyptus leaves rattling in the wind were inviting me to dance.

I heard their invitation: *leaving the ground and twirling around and stomping the ground.*

Come, join us.

The sun will change places with the moon and stars soon enough. Take yourself across the world into yourself, where you will find yourself dancing naked in the yurt with me.

The air chilled my bare arms as I reached them from under the blanket. Wrapping myself in the blanket, I stepped into the night.

The moonlight guided me through the dark to the yurt. I felt the cold on my feet with each step on the wet night grass. The cold air caught in my lungs. My feet registered the ups and downs of the path to the yurt. My heart was racing with anticipation asking the question: What would I find in the yurt?

Gather some of me, the eucalyptus leaves told me.

What do I need you for? I asked the leaves.

You'll see, the wind whispered back with a smile in its voice.

In the yurt, by candlelight, I felt my body begin to sway to the music of the leaves in rhythm with the wind.

I heard the leaves whisper, again, *Use us; dance, feel, use us as rubbings, create your pictures.*

In the yurt, I obeyed the urge to take off my clothes, to light a candle, to dance naked to the music of Sarah McLachlan. I felt daring. I was daring myself to be vulnerable. It was as if the soul retrieval/soul return of that little girl had brought me back to life. I hadn't known I was dead while alive.

I danced.

I created feeling images by rubbing colors over paper over the leaves even as I was moving to the music—pastel colors of pink, blue, red, orange, yellow, black, and green shape themselves into images of dancing, of the breath, the shadow on the paper.

For the first time in my life, I felt *free*. Free to dare me to dance naked, to create images from feelings; to follow the invitation of my soul to join the dance of life.

Looking back, the reason that experience of the yurt was so transformative was that I was creating from within, with the encouragement of my little soul retrieval self, combined with what I felt with the air on my naked body and the music in my blood. I wasn't putting on paper what I saw on the outside.

I was borrowing the eucalyptus leaves, the paper, and the pastels to show what was inside of me.

When looking at my rubbings, another may or may not feel what I was feeling, which is okay. I engaged in the alchemy of the materials and the feelings to co-create those sacred images, my soul's language.

The story of that night of wild abandon, of dancing naked and artistic freedom, grew into the Shamanic Shakti Art Process over the years. The creative freedom I felt in the yurt transformed into the sacred purpose gift I could bring to Venus Rising. If I could have that experience, perhaps others could too.

At the beginning of my story is my maternal Grandfather. He was a physician and an amateur painter. He was a profound influence on my creativity. Growing up with him until I was four, I remember the smells of linseed oil and oil paints. Images appeared as if by magic on his canvases, as though there was life in the canvas. Watching my grandfather paint, I like to believe he and I had a soul connection in the shared languages of nature and art. This soul connection made an impression on my psyche, leaving me with the desire to create magic as he did.

Before the yurt, there were the woods and summer nights catching lightning bugs and dancing in rain showers. I was always creating. Nature provided all manner of supplies: dirt and water became mud pies which were decorated with leaves, or even cupcake sprinkles; painted sticks became swords or snakes or magic wands; acorn shells became tea sets for fairies; flowers became crowns; vines on trees became swings; bushes became hidden retreats and hiding places; the snow was made into forts. Shoeboxes became dollhouses. Anything which could be painted or decorated in my bedroom was. I never had the chance to talk with my mother about how she felt about my creative expressions, and I can't ever remember being admonished for any of my creativity. Perhaps my creativity and imagination kept me occupied while she had her hands full as a single mom with five children.

My brothers, sister, and neighborhood kids were always eager to join in my creative projects. Those experiences showed me how imagination, creativity, and community are the alchemical cauldron of magic and healing. We'd enact dramatic kidnappings and rescues; hide and seek with monsters; musicals with silly songs. There was lots of laughter and shrieks and that wild abandon of pure joy and play.

While studying drama therapy in graduate school, I read that John Dewey, educator and philosopher (1859-1952), postulated that what we play as children often is taken with us into phases of our lives. I found that to be true for myself.

The story of the artistic expression, which grew into the Shamanic Shakti Art Process, began, I now know, in my childhood and continued through all my life's experiences. I took my childhood play activities with me and refined them into my soul's language.

I was led to Venus Rising through death. My mother passed suddenly in February 2003. The first Shamanic Breathwork was in March 2003. My youngest brother killed himself in August 2003. I flew to Portland or for my second Shamanic Breathwork. There I met Star Wolf and her husband, Brad. I was seriously feeling called to the Venus Rising training and was encouraged by Nita Gage. In February 2004, a friend jumped to her death from a bridge in Pittsburgh. Death again leads me to my third Shamanic Breathwork at the Dillsboro Inn in western NC.

No longer could I deny my soul's longing to be trained in Shamanic Breathwork. Using my inheritance from my mother, I signed up for SHIP. The healing I was experiencing and witnessing with Shamanic Breathwork was like nothing I had experienced so far in my role as a psychologist in an office, listening. Shamanic Breathwork helped us embody healing in a more profound way than drama therapy and psychodrama alone.

Shamanic Breathwork and SHIP training gave me the courage to reclaim my shamanic soul and Shakti Art. Venus Rising had already offered the art form of mandala making following the Shamanic Breathwork journey. I was supported in bringing more expressive art experiences for individuals and the group.

The experience of writing this chapter has given me the platform to bring forward the story of my experiences and the SSAP, to be who I am, and to publicly take my name Judy Redhawk and be the wonderful wild woman and force of nature that I am.

SHAMANIC MEDICINE OFFERING

The medicine of the SSAP is in the creating and the sharing. My role is to facilitate the creative processes, which are the learning processes. There is alchemy in creating individually and in a group. There is reclaiming the piece of a soul that went away because of comparison thinking and judgment about what is 'art.'

Experience the SSAP:

Can you find a space where you can play a piece of music that talks to your soul?

Can you gather art materials you like? Pieces of white or black paper, any size?

Can you smudge and bless your art materials and your space?

Can you play your music, close your eyes and begin to feel the music inside you?

As you feel an image, open your eyes and move to your paper.

Let your soul borrow your hands, the art materials, and put on paper what you feel.

Do this over and over until you feel complete.

See what has emerged and shown itself. Gaze at your creation with the soft eyes of love. Isn't your design beautiful? Bless it. Perhaps it has a name?

Judy Redhawk, Ph.D., DMin is the Shamanic Shakti Art process teacher and Venus University Director of Admissions. She earned her Ph.D. in psychology in 1984 from the University of Pittsburgh. In 1987, she became a registered Drama Therapist. In 2005, she became a Shamanic Breathwork Master Practitioner. She was ordained as a Shamanic Minister and awarded her DMin by VRU in 2010. Judy Redhawk has also been initiated as a Shamanic Priestess and is a shamanic/Tibetan/Usui and Brigid's Flame reiki master.

Her professional work and background have been in the fields of drama therapy, theatre, psychology, and Shamanic psycho-spiritual studies and practices. She is a core team member and teacher with Venus Rising specializing in teaching and training students to utilize the Shamanic Shakti Art Process as a tool for transformation, integration, and wholeness. She also teaches group processing skills.

Currently, Judy Redhawk is working for an online counseling business (Better-Help), building a shamanic psycho-spiritual counseling practice frees her up to take folks as a lead Shamanic Breathwork Venus Rising staff to Teotihuacan and Egypt. She facilitates workshops, private intensives, and transformative and experiential seminars nationwide.

She is building her magical house in the mystical blue mountains of NC and living full time as she embodies her shamanic self.

Judy Redhawk can be reached at:

judyredhawk@shamanicbreathwork.org

www.shamanicbreathwork.org

Judith(Judy)Merritt@betterhelp.com

CHAPTER 9

RESURRECTION
Activating the Inner Christ

Frank Mondeose

MY STORY

The first time I experienced Shamanic Breathwork, I was undergoing a great personal crisis. I was 33 years old and freshly divorced after a traumatic breakup. At the same time, my business prospects had unexpectedly turned uncertain. After investing tremendous blood, sweat, tears, and money into it, my dream of expanding my thriving erotic performance art event business into a mainstream global business was crushed. A major live events promoter company turned into my personal oppressive Roman Empire. They transformed our partnership into a pure money grab, and in the process, crushed my vision of creating an environment where love and beauty could flourish. I was suddenly confused, demotivated, and in debt. After a few years of living a self-imposed illusion, life slapped me down hard. I was now, clearly, unmistakably, at a crossroads.

But a distant part of me knew life itself was calling. I somehow knew something bigger was asking to be born. After some solid, loving advice from a dear brother, I decided to escape to Costa Rica on a personal and professional sabbatical.

My first challenge was releasing my attachment to *doing*. The shadows of my previous responsibilities were constantly nibbling at me. I resolved deeply to set it all aside and to head into the unknown instead. It took all of my spiritual muscle to focus on myself: to stop, to breathe, to release, and to recalibrate. Shadows be damned. I didn't know it at the time, but that may have been the single, most life-shifting inner decision I've ever made.

In the outer world, my original plans of beach bumming in the Gringo-infested version of Costa Rica quickly got diverted. Spirit had other plans for me, and I was drawn to a mysterious community in the jungles of Guanacaste. After a few days, I told myself: *I think I've just experienced a taste of true love for the very first time.*

Life in the jungle was magical. The interdependence of nature poured into communal living. Cacao treats in marble temples, simple casitas embedded in flourishing wildlife. It was a full system reset for me. Amidst the sweaty symphony, everything somehow just worked. Life became simpler. Somatically, I felt my body relax and open.

I invested my time learning about a new form of health: focusing on the body, getting regular massages, juice cleansing, yoga, and silence. What happened next I can only describe as the cracking of my heart armor. I released emotional weight and parasites I was carrying for way too long. I cried, laughed, opened, and softened. I invited life to take over.

I was fully immersed in what I imagined was a utopian world. It felt like my heart rebooted, and I experienced joy and happiness in the simplest of things—mostly being in nature.

Returning to Canada was a rude awakening, living in a city, moving from one mouse cage to another. It was a moment out of the 1988 cult classic *They Live*: I too felt like a drifter who discovers through special sunglasses that the ruling classes were aliens concealing their appearance to manipulate people into mindless consumption and breeding. It suddenly all became very visible to me.

In my early 20s, I started as a hotshot corporate marketing professional before stepping out on my own as a "playboy" event producer. In one instant, it all came together, and I began to see how marketing was slowly brainwashing humanity into very small, predictable, and limited lives. Even though I was living quite an extraordinary life expression, I was still a slave to the idea of success, driven by self-promotion and achievement. This all limited my ability to connect with my soul.

As enjoyable as it was, my time in Costa Rica led to my first existential crisis. I decided I would reflect and refocus my energy on my newly defined personal mission related to my core values and unique gifts. It was clear I was put on this Earth to do much more than entertain. I wanted to create a truly human impact. I wanted to inspire! I wanted to express the fire in my heart.

I remember realizing that the work they were doing in that eco-community was "healing work." I had never really considered anything other than western medicine as healing.

Maybe I'm a healer too, my gut exclaimed. That led me to the next question: *What kind of healer would I be? Reiki, Massage, Yogic?*

I laughed and joked to myself, *it'll probably be something to do with sex, a 'Sexual Healer.'* I followed those thoughts with research and discovered Tantra and Sexual Shamanism.

It was late April 2012, and I was days from returning to Costa Rica until a series of random and mysterious synchronistic sequences played out. After some guided alignment, I found myself on the International School of Temple Arts website, and I landed on the one-month apprenticeship program with the school founder starting May 1st. This spoke to me tremendously. But, I had my doubts, and it was way over my budget.

I found myself on the edge of a cliff. *Do I return home and do what is easy and comfortable? Or, do I leap in the unknown, trusting divine guidance, support, and my soul call?*

Of course, I jumped.

When I arrived at the School of Temple Arts a week later, one of the first experiences was participating in their annual conference on Sexuality and Consciousness, and it was there where I met Crystal Dawn Morris (also a co-author of this book). She looked so familiar to me. I felt that somehow I knew this woman, whether it be through finding her on a website almost half a decade prior or from another lifetime, it was clear to me. We had work to do together.

Her first offering at the conference was a guided Shamanic Breathwork session. "Yes." I said, "That is exactly why I came here!"

It was my first experience of the like. I had done plant medicine like Ayahuasca and Peyote, but nothing could prepare me for the profundity of the experience I was about to have.

Shamans always tell you, "You don't know what you will get, but usually, it is exactly what you need."

That first experience with Shamanic Breathwork was breathtaking. I got a clear vision of the most beautiful woman emerging from sacred waters. I could remember her long blue flowing dress draped over the water she walked on. She seemed to be floating in front of me but moving away from me, into the empty abyss. I remember feeling intrigued, reaching out to her, longing for her. I remember warm celestial light from the heavens and cool flowing waters beneath me.

Who is she?

She was the first glimpse into my inner feminine. Of course, I didn't know it at the time. All I knew was that she inspired me; she lit my heart ablaze. I got butterflies in my stomach and chills up my back. She had something for me.

That first Shamanic Breathwork experience turned out to be a pivotal moment for me. It was the moment when I truly saw my potential to blossom as an agent of love. She was the mirror. The Magdalene to my Yeshua. I was all in. I was ready to do anything to learn the Path of Love.

And, as it is said, "When the student is ready, the master appears." My teacher was Crystal Dawn Morris. From that moment on, we have been inseparable in spirit. For years, Crystal Dawn taught me the ways of Tantra, Sexual Shamanism, and Shamanic Breathwork. Through her loving guidance and support, I was led back to my inner beloved, and I continue to integrate her within me.

A large part of my development journey has been choosing, courting, understanding, and honoring my inner feminine.

I learned later in the Shamanic Healing Initiatory Path offered by Venus Rising Association for Transformation that the Inner Beloved is the fourth right of passage of shamanic healing and coming to wholeness.

There is absolutely no way I could be the confident, grounded, bold, strong, centered, loving, and compassionate man I have become without this inner marriage. For too long in the past, I was busy leaking energy and giving my power away to people and things outside of myself in the hopes of receiving the reflection of love from another: "If I am not loved by another, am I worthy?"

At first breath, Shamanic Breathwork led me right back to my inner beloved. Exactly what I needed to harness my will, focus, and love. In that breathwork, I began to activate my inner Christ. I took a giant step closer to my path of clear service and devotion. Yesterday didn't matter. At that moment, life pivoted.

Based on my experience, I have come to think that Shamanic Breathwork is the single most powerful and accessible tool we can use to come to know ourselves. A constant circular breath to oxygenate the body brings on states of non-ordinary reality where we can access our divination senses and direct ourselves into our inner worlds to clear, heal, or expand. It can help jump timelines and switch realities.

The most remarkable thing is that these extraordinary realities are embedded in our physical bodies. The method is very simple, completely free, and can be done almost anywhere, anytime. It also has none of the side effects or after-effects that often come with ingesting substances to get into similar states.

I had the luxury of meeting Star and Niko Wolf in Iceland in 2018. We had a wonderful heart connection, and we immediately saw the gifts in each other. Since then, I have become fully immersed in the Shamanic Breathwork Initiatory Process philosophy as well as the impact of the SBW practice. The Shamanic Healing Initiatory Process (SHIP) has completely changed how I deliver my work body.

Since my initial breathwork with Crystal Dawn Morris, my life has completely changed. I transitioned from producer/entertainer to humble student, apprentice, facilitator, and now Lead Facilitator of the International School of Temple Arts (ISTA).

ISTA has its gifts. It is a seven-day immersive spiritual, sexual, and shamanic experience to clear the body of shame, fear, and guilt and reprogram it with love, power, and freedom to live a life of ease and purpose. Crystal Dawn Morris and I add Shamanic Breathwork to all our ISTA programs.

Since incorporating the SHIP principles, I fundamentally have changed how I design, frame, and deliver content to my participants. The Shamanic Healing Initiatory Process, created by Star Wolf and her late husband Brad Collins, is the clearest and most comprehensive map of personal development and shamanism I have ever come across. They hold the key codes and rites of passage for personal expansion and integrity, and the process never ends because we work with the spiral path and not a linear one.

This supports the seeker to return and continue to peel back the onion to unveil another deeper layer of our psyche, trauma, and addictions. It is a process of constant alchemy, spiritual hygiene, and emotional clearing!

The five rites of passage of the SHIP are:

The Spiral Path

Family of Origin

Shadow Work

Inner Beloved

Sacred Purpose

SHAMANIC MEDICINE OFFERING

Jesus was an activist. He had values, abilities, and influence. This is particularly why he *chose* to go to the cross.

Christ is a metaphor for waking up to the light of one's true self and the choice to live with clarity, courage, and conviction.

Jesus was a man. Christ is an idea.

Christ translates to the Hebrew term Messiah, meaning the "anointed one." This title indicates that Jesus' followers believed him to be the anointed son of King David, whom some Jews expected to restore the fortunes of Israel.

Scripture hints at the second coming of Christ. We often interpret it as a man who will return to influence our life and times. The second coming is a journey of personal revelation. It's the awakening that no one is coming to save us. What happens in this life and time directly correlates with how we choose to show up in the world. This dimension acts as a holographic mirror, and what we radiate, we magnetize.

We are the first and last line of inspiration. How we think, what we say and what we do matters and has personal and collective implications. It truly is that real and serious.

Receive that you have been anointed by the Divine, in this incarnation, to wake up and claim your existence as the light and spirit of Source and to live an inspired life, *in Spiritu*, with Spirit. In French, "inspire" means to breathe in. In living an inspired life, we are *breathing in Spirit.*

First, wake up from the illusion and delusions of psychological, emotional, and social programming. Purposefully and diligently burn away the limited beliefs inherited from traumatized generations. By courageously going through the five rites of passage, we burn away all that does not serve and is *not true.* We do this not only for ourselves but for our ancestors and the next seven generations.

Crossing the threshold of each rite of passage is what creates the space for the most authentic self to emerge. This is the journey of resurrection.

When we have burned it all away and watched our staged personalities die a thousand deaths, it is from there we can rise.

Resurrection is the awakened incarnated soul, free from self-imposed shackles, clearly comprehending free will. Each outcome is an act of conscious or unconscious consent.

"Do we let ourselves be seduced by the victim archetype? Or do you choose to meet life as the conscious creator?"

When we recognize that we are the conscious creator of each moment, we must seize opportunities towards personal expansion and the pursuit of happiness. We do this by choosing ourselves foremost and moving with integrity, clarity, and honesty. We do this first to ensure we are well resourced as an illuminated channel and to strengthen our relationship with Source. Re-*Source*.

When we live in alignment with our values, fueled by integrity, we can live a value-driven life. When we align these values with love and service to the collective, we step into Christ Consciousness.

The Activated Inner Christ does not self-sacrifice, suffer or martyr as the story would have you believe. They inspire through their brilliance, love, and embodiment.

The following activation code contains deep succinct wisdom. A suggestion is to create a daily meditation and journal practice using one point per day.

1. Decide that you want a happier life, one that excites you. Be willing to jump into the unknown guided by deep intuitive calling.

2. Get clear with your values. Allow them to guide your decisions. Be willing to refine and upgrade them.

3. Investigate your interests and fan the flames of curiosity.

4. Choose the direction of your journey. Set off, open, for growth and expansion. Focus solely on the next steps, and do not get lost in the future. The past is a reference point for dissatisfaction. Keep it there.

5. Trust, when you are committed to living in Christ Consciousness, you will be taken care of and live the exaltation of your choices.

6. Commit to living with integrity as a guiding principle.

7. Develop a loving relationship with yourself. Stalk your self-talk. Be encouraging. Limit emotional self-flagellation, paralyzing worry, and self-doubt.

8. Let go of stories and habits that commit you to grasp and/or aversion in times of doubt. This is your immature inner child screaming for attention. This will only lead to suffering. Love your little one and surrender.

9. Face your fears, and choose love. When we choose love, it always comes right back around, often from unexpected sources. Receive graciously.

10. Recognize that you always have a choice. Choosing the easy way, because it seems the only way, is still a choice. The path of the Activated Inner Christ will always make decisions based on their intentional core values and discover the options that exist to live within said values. The path of the righteous is rarely easy. It comes with work and challenges. This is the path of the initiate.

11. *Everything* is love. Integrate that.

12. Challenges are also an expression of love. They exist to bring you greater awareness or forge the steel of integrity. They also serve in alchemizing new ways of being and support you to level up. Choose grace when dealing with challenges.

13. Bring love into every moment. When you forget, wait until you remember and then bring love into every moment.

14. Love is generous. It is an act of service and devotion to the well-being of others. Do good, wish well for others. Bless people with your presence by being fully you, with care and consideration.

15. Create intentional prayerful space for pleasure and ecstasy.

The Activated Inner Christ chooses to create from love in every moment. They do it in service to the highest good for all. When aligned with that intent, love moves through you. The Activated Inner Christ empowers people and shares this gift to others, so others can also be in love, and with that, a fellowship of lovers.

Through the journey and challenges, we are pressured and alchemized into diamonds that can reflect the light of consciousness in countless directions and colors. We are limitless.

We become the beacon, first to light our path, and soon to help light the path of others.

You are the conscious creator. Choose to live life from a place of love, joy, and ecstasy. Feel it, embrace it, make conscious choices, face every moment, and experience it fully.

What does your illuminated life look like? Set out on the journey to Activate your Inner Christ.

Inspire love and awaken joy-filled hearts.

Visit Loveanderos.com for more.

A contemporary voice on Love, Eros & Relating, **Frank Mondeose** embodies both pray and play, which is reflected on his YouTube web series "The Spiritual Playboy."

Lead Faculty with ISTA, the International School of Temple Arts, co-founder of ReMENber Brotherhood Journey, Shamanic Minister for Venus Rising Association for Transformation, curator and educator at LoveandEros.com, and creator of the lifestyle brand Monde Osé.

Frank has touched the hearts and minds of many, whether it be through tantalizing their imaginations at his multi-sensorial events to inspirational interactions that have navigated people to accessing their personal power.

Frank holds an unapologetic, no-nonsense container. It is a space to step out of one's comfort zone and meet their edges in a compassionately ruthless manner. His containers are solidly held in a protected and safe environment where all emotions and expressions are welcome and celebrated.

Frank has taught Sexual Shamanism in over ten countries, including Canada, the United States, Mexico, Costa Rica, Iceland, England, Italy, Netherlands, Spain, and Turkey.

You can experience Frank online in one-on-one sessions, a passionate lecture, five hours intensive workshop, and/or week-long immersive training.

Frank specializes in:

- Helping singles and couples live more ecstatic lifestyles
- Bridging the gap between traditional relationships and modern sexuality
- Rediscovering Love
- Supporting couples to up-level the way they relate to each other
- Understanding the spiritual elements of sexuality

- Discovering the New Awakening Masculine
- Honoring the Resurrecting Feminine

Visit FrankMondeose.com for more.

CHAPTER 10

MAKE A NOISE

Sounding, Toning, and Emoting to Release Fear, Grief, and Rage

Kathy Guidi

MY STORY

My childhood family life was filled with silence. Born to deaf and hard of hearing parents and the sole child until I was ten years old, my home world was a place of quiet: no radio, no record player, no loud discussions around the dinner table. That is until negative emotions arose, which had no soothing voice to be understood. In our family, negative emotions were not processed or discussed. Either they burst forth with yells and screams like the loud clanging of discordant cymbals, or they were driven down inside, shushed, ignored, and tucked away.

This early childhood imprinting carried forth into my early adult years. I held a lot of anger and frustration, and when triggered, my acerbic tongue was quick to lash out.

As the adage goes, "You can run, but you can't hide," and decades later, the anger caught up with me until I'd hit a breaking point. Spirit guided me to breathwork, and a long multi-year healing journey ensued. The breathwork process changed the course and trajectory of my life, connecting me to my long-suppressed intuition.

September 2017:

Lying on the floor with 20 others, we do the circular breathing technique they taught us. Five minutes: *What am I doing here? Why did I come? I don't know anyone here. This kind of stuff never works for me.* Ten minutes: Tingling sensations surge through my hands and feet. *Whoa. This is strange. Just trust and breathe.* 15 Minutes: Energy, like plasma, pulsates through my hands. *Wow, this is cool! I think I'm getting the hang of this.* 20 Minutes: Sobs erupt, and tears stream down my face. I am touching the void, tuning into the oneness of all things. I know I am part of the greater universe. I am love. My heart is open. *How is this happening? How could I experience all of this from breathing?* 25 Minutes: The soothing voice of the facilitator brings us back to regular breathing and back into our bodies. *What the hell was that?*

At 53 years young, I was at a low point in my life. My quick temper and anger issues were making a fierce showing during my menopausal years and were impacting my marriage and other relationships. "Nothing is going right," I was often heard saying. "You know, you might benefit from some breathwork, and I know of an upcoming Rebirthing seminar you might like to go to," my friend said to me. With nothing to lose, I enrolled and found myself breathing in a room with total strangers and learning about the benefits of conscious connected breathing. I was hooked!

In the ensuing months, I signed up for individual breathwork counseling and had ten sessions with my practitioner. I began revisiting and unraveling several of my early adult romantic relationships that had ended badly and in which I carried residual anger. I started sensing where the stuck pain was held in my body, and through the breathing process, these tensions slowly released. I got further in those ten sessions, both physically and emotionally, than I'd done with years of talk therapy.

"I am so angry at all those people. They aren't listening to me. They're pissing me off," I'd say. "Perhaps," my practitioner said, "the truth is that you're not listening to yourself. Perhaps the anger is a signal from your inner child telling you something about your boundaries. Perhaps you have disconnected from your inner knowing." Catching me off guard, I mused on her words and began the slow journey of reconnecting to my higher self. 'Self-parenting' became my new buzzword.

Thirsty for more understanding of the conscious connected breathing modality, I searched for local training programs. Not much was on offer. A Google search returned links to Rebirthing, Holotropic, and other similar breathwork modalities. Then, in reading an article on shamanism, I noticed one of the author's credentials: Shamanic Breathwork Facilitator. *Oooh, I like the sound of this.*

Piqued, I landed on the "Venus Rising Association for Transformation" website and read about Linda Star Wolf. *This feels right. I'm getting a strong yes.* I ordered her seminal book and devoured it within days of arrival. I immediately felt connected to this breathwork process.

July / August 2018

Tossing off my people-pleasing and self-sacrificing hats, I embarked on a two-month sabbatical to Bali to rediscover and rebirth my 'authentic self.' I intended to learn to operate from a place of compassion and love (for myself) rather than out of duty curtailing towards resentment (for others).

Before my trip, I discovered Levi Banner, a teacher offering Shamanic Breathwork in Ubud. *Exciting!* Days after my arrival, I join one of his classes. In a room of 60 intrepid souls, we are led on a journey into an altered state of consciousness.

Purple, white, and pink Balinese flowers adorn the altar at the front of the room. Incense wafts in the warm tropical breeze. Drums, rattles, and a didgeridoo are strewn on the floor. After a short introduction, Levi bangs his medicine drum and welcomes in the directions. I feel the sacredness of what is about to happen. We lie on our backs, pull the sleep mask over our eyes, and begin to breathe. In through the nose, out through the mouth. The music is loud and thumping. After a while, my body tingles and activates—energy courses throughout.

Someone comes over and gently massages my abdomen. *Whoa.* My body contracts as the tension builds in my neck and throat. The helper continues to press on my abdomen and taps near my collarbone. Suddenly, as if a floodgate were opened, my tears release, and a well of sadness surges through my body. I roll over on my side, curl up with a blanket, and hug my Little Me.

In the ensuing weeks, a spate of earthquakes rocked the island. Though I had been enjoying Bali, these shakes stirred up some post-traumatic stress. Feeling frightened and needing to release some of this energy, I enrolled in a full-day Shamanic Breathwork workshop where we would have time for the complete mandala art process and integration sharing circle.

On the day, 40 are gathered, and introductions are made. The group is split in half, with each person partnering with another; we have the breathers and the co-journeyers.

I'm a bit of a mess and very activated. We decide I will breathe first. "I'm really nervous," I tell my partner. The music starts, the eye masks go on. Within minutes a tightness and constriction arise in my chest and lungs, and I begin to cough, gasping for air. *I can't breathe. I'm drowning. Am I going to choke myself to death?* Multiple pairs of hands are on my back while I'm sitting up, coughing and spitting.

"Turn over and get on your hands and knees," I'm told. Someone pushes on and simultaneously rubs my back. "AAHHHHHH." A deep, loud wail releases from my throat, and I let out a little roar. With snot running down my nose, I collapse to the floor. Pain and sadness exist deep in the pockets of my heart about aspects of my marriage. *We're never going to make it.* More sobbing.

As the music moves us into the higher realms of the upper chakras, a feeling of unconditional love for my husband washes through me, along with an understanding that our energies have gotten too entangled, and it was time to separate. I am experiencing an energetic marriage death, and whether this transpires into the physical, time will tell. But it's now time to say goodbye to the old ways of our relationship.

We pull oracle cards, and I receive a clear message from Nut and Geb, Egyptian deities of the sky and earth. "If you've pulled this card, you've completed a great round of transformation in your life and are ready to step out into the world with sacred purpose and a strong sense of your wholeness." *I love everything about Shamanic Breathwork. I want to become a facilitator and bring this into my community.*

Before leaving Bali, I commit to coming back in five months to begin my Level 1 training and immerse myself in SHIP, the Shamanic Healing Initiatory Process.

January 2019

Back in Bali for the two-week SHIP immersion course, I'm ready to dive deeper into my healing journey. I still have some big questions to answer about my life and marriage, and I'm prepared to experience another shamanic death and rebirth cycle. We will have five breathwork sessions interspersed with alternating teaching days.

Again, I lay back on my mat after speaking to my co-journeyer and setting up our agreements for touch and assistance. Eye masks on, we are taken on a guided visualization, and then the music blares through the speakers.

My neck tightens, and my jaw begins to open and close. My hands pull imaginary strands of stuck energy from my throat. I writhe on the yoga mat. *Something needs to come out, but I am afraid.* One of the facilitators places a hand on my sternum. The rattling sounds are all around me.

"Make a noise Kathy, open your mouth and make a noise," he whispers to me. Deep in my process, I unclench my jaw and let out an "ahhhhhh." "Do it again, more." "AAAAAHHHHHHHHHH," shoots from my lips, a piercing howl and scream that travels up from my root and power chakras and out of my mouth. Tears flow down my cheeks. "Sit up," he says as he taps my back.

I feel someone tugging at me, and soon I flop onto my belly. The conscious part of my brain knows this is the beginning of a rebirthing experience. The unconscious part only knows that this is a life or death situation. I have to fight against the unseen thing opposing me. Pushing through, I feel myself going down the birth canal. Someone holds my leg back, and another pulls my arm forward. *I can't do this. I don't have enough strength. I want to die.* Pause. Breathe. *No, I want to live. I want to make it through the other side.* Pause. Breathe.

I push through until I am released, dripping in sweat, dripping in tears, collapsed on the floor. I am in the muck of my despair. As the music plays, I slowly regain my strength and stand up. Though my eye mask is still on, I pull my long hair over my face because I don't want anyone to see me. *I will prevail.* My Shakti energy entwines my spine as I dance to the pulsating music, and I connect to the deep universal life force within and around me. I am the phoenix rising. I am a medicine woman.

2020:

Our world radically changed in the early months of 2020 with the onset of the Sars-CoV-2 virus slithering like a snake throughout the globe. Online trainings replace in-person trainings as we adapt to the rapidly evolving environment. From the comforts of my home, I finish my training and certify as a Shamanic Breathwork Facilitator.

I've come far since my first breathwork session and learned much about my inner guidance system. I've delved deeply within myself and claimed my right to feel the full spectrum of human emotions. And just like positive emotions such as laughter have an associated sound, so too do the negative ones of fear, grief, pain, or anger. In societies where it's not the norm to express the range of negative emotions, or only cursorily perhaps with tears, most people don't have the support or opportunity to safely release these powerful sensations when they course through the body. In my offerings, I support people in tapping into their own deep emotions that have been hidden away. I love to help them "make a noise."

SHAMANIC MEDICINE OFFERING

Allow me to help you "make a noise."

The following toning practices are used in my breathwork sessions to help people relax and open their throats. These exercises prime the vocal cords and allow for the exploration of mouth shapes and corresponding sounds. This permits people to make sounds and noises during the subsequent Shamanic Breathwork journey.

Please have a journal and pen ready to record your experience.

Grounding

Sit or lie in a comfortable area where you will feel safe to make some sounds. I like to do this process in conjunction with an immersion with the elements: sitting in front of a fire or under a big tree; relaxing in the bath or other body of water; perched atop a hill or mountain.

Place one hand on your belly and one hand on your heart, and close your eyes. Begin taking long slow inhalations and exhalations. Feel the belly rise on the inhale, taking the breath into the upper chest and lungs, and then let out a long slow, easy exhalation, allowing the breath to wash over your shoulders and back down like a wave. In and up, the wave crests, and then down and out, the tide recedes. Do this five to ten times to ground and center yourself.

Sensing, Discerning, Perceiving

For this exercise, we're going to tone the vowel sounds "Ooo, Ohh, Ahh, Ehh, Eee" (U, O, A, I, E) which are linked to the chakra energy centers of the body. The order starts from a low "Ooo" sound (base chakra) up the scale to a higher-pitched "Eee" sound (crown chakra).

For each vowel, make the sound on the exhalation and hold the sound for as long as you can. Tone each vowel five to seven times.

Put your hands below your belly button onto your root/sacral chakra. Taking a few inhalations and exhalations, tone the sound "Ooo." This chakra area pertains to your needs for safety and security, comfort in the world, and your inner and outer home. What do you perceive? What qualities of your home and home life do you love? What needs to be changed? Feel the vibration of the "Ooo" sound clearing any obstacles to create the home of your desires.

Next, place your hands above your naval onto the solar plexus chakra and tone the sound "Ohh." This is your power center, the seat of fire that inspires your creative actions in the world. Tuning in, notice what you feel. Are you inspired with your life? Do you feel you are living your sacred purpose? Or do you feel stagnant and powerless? Feel the vibration of the sound digesting and eating any blocks and obscurations that prevent you from tapping into your full potential and creativity.

Moving up, shift your hands on your heart chakra. Tone the sound "Ahh" with each exhalation. This is the seat of your higher self. Allow the sounding to help you connect deeper and deeper. Love, compassion, joy, and equanimity exist here. What do you sense in your heart? What is your higher self telling you? Feel the vibration and imagine connecting your beautiful heart into the grid of infinite love and compassion.

The hands next go to the throat chakra. Tone the sound "Ehh." This is the place for self-expression, communication, and self-actualization. What do you sense? Do you feel any tightness or contractions? Do you have a hard time saying what you mean? Or does your communication flow effortlessly with authenticity and integrity? Feel the vibration relaxing the throat muscles and the sound "Ehh" flowing like crystal clear water gently down a stream.

Now, place the palms of your hands above your brow, the third eye chakra, and relax your fingers onto the top of the head, the crown chakra. Tone "Eee." This is your connection to Source and the place of self-transcendence. What do you perceive? How is your mind? Is it always busy, or can you relax easily into a state of peace? Do you have a connection to something greater than you? Feel the vibration of this sound dissipating any negative chatter. Feel any busyness melting away into the vastness of a clear blue sky. You are not alone. You are part of the great big web of universal infinite intelligence.

Noticing tensions and blocks in any of the chakra toning areas indicates where energy is stuck and where emphasis or focus may be placed during a breathwork session.

Feeling

Place one hand on your belly and your other hand at the base of your throat. Inhale, the belly inflates. On the exhale, make the sound "Ahhhhhh" in a way that is comfortable to you. Feel the vibration in your throat. It may just be a soft "Ah" with your lips slightly parted. Do this three to five times.

On the next go, try opening your mouth a little wider, feeling the back of your throat opening. And as you sound "Ah," see if you can push the sound from your deflating belly, up and out your throat and mouth, and feel the vibration moving throughout. Do this three to five times. Notice what you feel. Are you confident in making a longer, louder sound, or is this a new experience? Is the sound even and strong or a bit shaky and croaky? What emotions, if any, are surfacing?

Lastly, try this again. Take in a fuller inhalation and open the mouth even wider into a big 'O-shape,' and sound "Ahhhhhh" as loudly as you can. Feel the energy coming from your belly. Notice what you feel. Any physical sensations? Body tensions or pains? Can you tap into any emotions? Sadness? Anger? Grief? Do any tears want to come?

This is a great purification exercise to do when activated or triggered. By the last "Ah," you may release some tears, have a sob, or even a scream. Remember, it's okay to feel these emotions; the important part is to let them pass through you.

Check out my resource page for an audio version of the above practices: https://birdsongretreat.nz/Shamanic-Breathwork/

Kathy Guidi is co-creator and kaitiaki (steward) of Birdsong Retreat & Sanctuary, a place for wellness and spiritual healing. She is a certified Shamanic Breathwork Facilitator and ordained Shamanic Minister through Venus Rising Association for Transformation, a Reiki master, a retreat facilitator, caterer of plant-based nourishing kai (food), earth-honoring ritualist and apprentice in the Pachakuti Mesa Tradition of Peru, and a spiritual mentor. She holds bachelor's and master's degrees in business and finance.

She is an all-around WOW-girl (ways of wellness) seeking to optimize body, mind, and spirit. She left a well-paying corporate and urban lifestyle in San Francisco for greener pastures in rural New Zealand, where she has been living with her husband on a ten-acre slice of paradise since 2006. In the early days, the retreat and sanctuary were for their own healing, then slowly became a place for friends and travelers to find respite. Since building their Temple of Venus, they have been hosting and facilitating small boutique transformational wellness events with a focus on shamanism and shamanic practices.

She is passionate about earth stewardship, sacred relationship/ayni with all things and beings, and helping people with their journeys towards wholeness. In this second phase of life, her passion centers around personal development, understanding the psyche, healing our internal wounds, and becoming conscious, heart-centered humans.

You can find her dispensing wisdom to friends and guests from the garden, from the kitchen, or from the comforts of their cozy couches. She offers group Shamanic Breathwork sessions and co-facilitates women's retreats: www.birdsongretreat.nz She is currently working on her doctorate in psycho-spiritual studies with Venus Rising University and is soon to launch her personal website www.kathyguidi.com.

CHAPTER 11

SPIRITUAL TORMENT

FACING NEGATIVE ENTITIES
THROUGH SHAMANISM

Heidi Steffens

MY STORY

Racing out of my room in the middle of the night was better than staying in bed. I leaned into my sleeping mom's ear, whispering, "M..m..mom? Mom? Can you come? There are people in my room again. Please help me? Will you chase them away?"

"Huh…what?" Cracking one eye at the clock, well past midnight. "Go back to bed. There's no one there, and *don't* wake me up again." My feet are bolted to the floor as tears stream down my eight-year-old face. Mom's breathing went back to sleep mode as I waited for help that wouldn't come. This ritual went on for years.

Eventually, sleepiness overrides my fear. With my eyes scrunched closed as much as possible, I ran to my room and dove back into bed, hiding under the perceived safety of the covers.

I saw spirits and unknown entities night after night in the room I shared with my younger sister. She never saw them, was never affected. I became the protector to keep her safe should any spirits decide to go for her. I slept closest to the door to block anyone from getting her. If they were going to get anyone, I would rather it be me.

It was harder to see these beings during the day when there was light everywhere, but they were clearer at night. Some looked like they wanted something from me, and some seemed only to want attention. Some tried to trick me or made themselves look scary. I blocked all of it as best as I could.

Nobody ever believed me when I told them what I saw. "It's your imagination." "Wow, maybe something is wrong with you." "Are you crazy?" Sharing what I experienced led to ridicule and speculation of my mental state. I could feel this was all real but started keeping it to myself.

Through my teens and early twenties, I did what I could to avoid translucent beings. I kept myself so busy I would drop from exhaustion when it was time for bed. If I relaxed at all, spirits were one step away. I didn't know how to stop it.

There was one spirit who didn't scare me. He would appear for only a few minutes and talk about what I was experiencing, but it was hard to understand everything he told me. His delicate appearance, honest demeanor, and consistent care for my well-being were enough to help me trust him over the years.

"What do you think is the worst thing these beings you see could do to you?" He asked me one day. "They could kill me." I really thought this was true.

"That hasn't happened yet. Don't you think if they wanted to hurt you, they could have done that by now?" His transparent arm reaches toward me with affection.

"I suppose."

"Then it won't happen going forward either. Try and look at this part of your life through logic instead of emotion. You have come into this life with a unique gift, and we need assistance from humans like you to maintain a balance between the worlds. It's time for you to help us."

Is he serious? Why me? But how could I say no? If I could help people, then it would be worth it. "I do want to help others who fear spirits or need help understanding them. Please show me how to do this." I took a deep breath, and my studies began.

More Spirit Guides showed up to share wisdom and training, explaining I was already walking the path of the shaman, but now I would learn how to do with intention. They showed me how to travel to other realms for healing energy, guidance, and wisdom. I learned how to perform negative entity extractions and spirit attachments from people, places, and things. I completed soul retrievals, channeled energy to heal past life traumas and initiate cellular healing, and so much more. It was a profound journey of learning.

They led me to books, classes, and therapies to help me heal my own past traumas and clean up my life energetically and physically. I began opening to people in my life and started sharing my authentic self, which was scary, but the lifted weight was miraculous. Friends asked me to help them with guidance and healing, and I realized I *could* help them. I felt empowered and centered for the first time in my life.

"As you continue your work, you will encounter so much good and healing which will always fill you with wonder." Said one guide. "But on the other side of the coin, you will be faced with challenges and darkness that will be unimaginable. You decide where and when you want to stop." It never occurs to me to stop. The overriding need to help others keeps me going. My Spirit Guides always connect with me through the power of unconditional love and Divine Source.

Back in 2008, I was inspired by the paranormal investigating shows I saw on TV and thought this would be an excellent way to find out more about the spirit world and why spirits are stuck or, in essence, haunting a location or people. Paranormal investigations soon became the other bookend to the work I was already doing in the healing world. So many people feared spirits and were being hurt or traumatized in ways that they couldn't tell most people. I knew how much they suffered. The more I investigated, the nastier the cases became, and my instinct to protect grew even stronger. I had zero tolerance for people and animals who couldn't help themselves and were getting picked on by spirits and entities.

I discovered that I could see troublesome and nasty beings better than others by journeying between planes and dimensions. My spirit guides communicated during investigations, just like in healing sessions. It was like receiving insider information on how to best go after an entity and remove it from our dimension. My strength grew, and I knew this work would help many people. I found two halves that made a whole between the spiritual healing and the paranormal torment sides. I had found my true calling and walked the path of my inner shaman.

SHAMANIC MEDICINE OFFERING

I am fortunate to work in the spiritual and paranormal realms as my full-time work, and I love being a safe container for others on both sides. What I have found is both sides need to address protection and healing. Anyone who knows me knows that I'm all about protections, and a person can do a ton of healing when there is a safe space available. Being able to walk the path of the shaman, I create a safe space to dive deep with those looking at a healing journey and connect them to wisdom and opportunities for healing.

Not everyone is aware of or affected by spirits or entities. When I say spirits, I'm referring to a soul that has been human and is now without a body. An entity is a being that has never been human. There are good and evil spirits and entities; just like anything else in this universe, there is balance in everything.

Commonly, I receive an email where someone is experiencing paranormal activity in their home, making them feel uncomfortable or scared. It's better to teach people how to keep themselves safe and set proper protections, as that is a valuable skill to have for a lifetime.

I don't believe in bargaining with spirits or entities. For instance, people say to me that a spirit is in their house and can stay if they behave, or they assume the spirit is a recently departed loved one, so they want them to stay. I'm afraid I have to disagree. Spirits had their time here, and there is so much more for them in the next leg of their journey! It's better if they keep moving. Entities also have other places and dimensions other than hanging out in someone's home. When I tell people this, they get worried and state, "What if it's Grandma coming to visit? Or my recently departed friend? I want them to stay at my house."

Here's what you do if you find you have a spirit or entity present, even if you think you know who it is. You remind them of the golden rule. You say out loud or in your head, with clarity and certainty, "If you aren't here for my highest good, you must leave."

That's the golden rule. This phrase draws a line in the sand and reminds spirits and entities that there is a balance between beings with physical forms and beings without. If you aren't here to help, then you must move on. This means your spirit guides, angels, helpers, and *helpful* loved ones get to stay. This phrase works for about 90% of the activity in people's homes. Like speeding, there are consequences for interfering and getting caught. You remind those who shouldn't be here that there are consequences if they continue by saying the golden rule.

If you have more than just an eerie feeling or hearing bumps in the night, you might want to do the second step in creating a safe space for you and others in your home. This is called a clearing. Did you know the most significant item in your house is the space between all things, and it's what gets neglected most often? We paint, change furniture, scrub windows, vacuum, but most people rarely clear the energy of their space. You might not think about it until bumps in the night turn into doors opening on their own, or you hear people talking when no one is there. If there is activity in your home that shouldn't be happening, a home clearing is an excellent next step.

When you do a home clearing, the number one piece of advice is to trust it will work. If you doubt it will be effective, you are leaving holes in the process and likely won't be effective. If you are too scared to do a home clearing yourself, find someone who isn't afraid to do it. The keys are confidence and certainty. Aggression or taunting during the clearing is also not effective. You are challenging whatever is there and could make the situation worse instead of making it better.

Here are some basic steps for a home clearing:

1. Start earlier in the day if possible. You'll feel more comfortable doing the clearing when it's daytime, plus you'll have a reasonable amount of time after you're done to ease back into 'normal' before going to bed.

2. Before you begin, call in your personal protections. Whether you call in God, Buddha, Archangel Michael, or whoever you believe in, do this before you start and even say a prayer to keep you safe and thank Divine source for helping clear the space.

3. Use a tool that helps focus your intention while clearing the space. For some, this means carrying a smoldering stick of dried sage, or for others, it means using a chime. Whatever your tool, you will be taking this throughout the space to remind yourself and other beings that this space is being cleared.

4. Pick a place in the house to start, like the basement if you have one, or start at the farthest end if you have an apartment. With your sage stick smoldering, or while tinging your chime, say the golden rule as you go into each room and each area of your home. You'll want to open closet doors and go into all the nooks and crannies. You mean business, and you want to make sure you clear the whole space.

5. Work your way through the house and finish in the attic or highest point. If you are in an apartment, work your way through the entire unit from one end to the other. When you are complete, thank those you called on to help you.

6. I don't believe you need to open doors and windows to the outside while doing a clearing. Beings didn't use doors to get in; they certainly don't need them to get out. Plus, if you live in Minnesota as I do, you don't want to leave the windows open while you're doing a clearing during winter.

7. Limit any distractions and the number of people, pets, kids, etc., in the home while the clearing is being done. That means turning off the TV and having the family go out for ice cream while you are doing the clearing. Make sure your family brings ice cream back for you since you did the work.

This type of clearing is a perfect all-purpose clearing. If you would like more details on this type of clearing, please visit my clearing video at https://www.myspiritexperience.com/clearings

When I say all-purpose clearing, it should help in most situations with a spirit causing problems. Paranormal investigation TV shows have you believing that a demon is behind all paranormal activity, which isn't true. I have worked with thousands of people, and actual demonic activity is rare. It doesn't make the haunting less scary, though. If you find these techniques are not working, you will need to contact someone well trained to deal with a more advanced haunting situation.

After protections and ensuring people are safe, we focus on healing emotional, mental, physical, or spiritual trauma. For years, I have channeled Divine healing energy through Shamanic Reiki sessions. In these sessions, I can journey to the healing and wisdom places to connect a client with the Divine energy needed at that time. I also work with my Spirit Guides to remove blocks and perform soul retrievals. Shamanic Breathwork is another tool that offers clients to connect directly with their higher self or their loving Spirit Guides for healing and wisdom. We hold the Shamanic Breathwork in the studio to hold a safe space allowing many to journey at once.

In some cases, when working with a client, there is a negative being responsible for, or attracted to, the trauma they have received. This negative being (spirit or entity) must be removed for someone to have the opportunity for complete healing. This process takes years of training to be done safely and effectively. Most often, inexperienced practitioners do the equivalent of pulling a weed by breaking it off where it enters the ground. If you don't find and remove the whole root, the issue is not solved, and the situation will resume.

People who have been harmed or tormented by spirit often develop a fear of all spirits, and in most cases, in a healing journey, I can teach people how to connect with their Spirit Guides and higher self safely. *I am first and foremost centered on protecting*, and sometimes it is in the best interests of the client I am seeing if they don't embark on this journey. Now or ever. A person needs to be emotionally stable and in the right frame of mind before embarking on a quest to communicate with one's Spirit Guides through journeying. If a person has a ton of trauma they are currently processing (or denying there is any to process), then it isn't an ideal time to go on a deep dive to enhance one's intuitive connection with their Guides. I would recommend someone does their healing work first to clear this energy out. It might take some time, but your Spirit Guides will wait. If you would like to learn more about how to safely connect to your spirit guides, please visit my site at https://www.myspiritexperience.com/develop-your-intuition

Every day I am learning something new from my Spirit Guides. After working with thousands of people for years, you think you've seen it all, but how can you know everything when dealing with an unlimited source? Over the years, cases have gotten more dangerous and more extreme. At times, I have stumbled upon negative entity traps that are incredibly harmful or deadly to humans. I am grateful to be married to the person with whom I do this difficult work. We have dismantled enough traps that we are on a watch list by negative beings. They are biding their time and have promised they will find a way to stop us. We keep our faith strong and take care of ourselves to ensure we are strong enough to continue helping others.

Heidi Steffens is the owner of the spiritual center My Spirit Experience in Minnesota. She is an intuitive and psychic, Master Reiki Instructor, Ordained Shamanic Minister, and a Shamanic Breathwork Facilitator. Heidi works full-time doing in-person and remote individual sessions, teaching classes, and hosting events with people in Minnesota, throughout the United States, and overseas. She has investigated hundreds of haunted locations and worked paranormal cases all over the United States, Central America, and Great Britain. She has been the organizer of MPRS – Minnesota Paranormal Research Society (minnesotaparanormal.com) since 2008 and co-hosts The Gathering, a weekly paranormal radio show on the ParaX Radio Network. Heidi creates My Spirit Experience Podcast available on all podcast networks, and one of her spiritual torment cases has been featured on Paranormal Survivor, Season 1 Episode 5.

She holds a Bachelor of Elemental Studies and Master of Shamanic Intuitional Practices through Venus Rising University. She has spent decades focused on helping people navigate their healing and soul-purpose paths in this world, as well as working with lost or unwelcome spirits as the lines between planes and dimensions become more and more intertwined.

You can connect with Heidi through her website at www.myspiritexperience.com

CHAPTER 12

DARE TO BE YOU
WHAT LOVING YOURSELF REALLY LOOKS LIKE

Zeina Yazbek

MY STORY

"The truth is, I am in love with someone else," I told the man I was seeing at the time, right after he had an unexpected heart surgery. He was in his late twenties.

I held on for so long, fearing his health would take a turn for the worse if I told the truth.

For years before meeting him, I was immersed with lies, the kind of fabrications my old self thought only existed in movies with unfortunate endings. I was manufacturing them daily and living a parallel life of secrecy.

Wherever I felt safe to show a side of me, I did. When I felt threatened, I hid and lied. Some were conscious. Others weren't.

Rewind to just three years before that night, and I would have said, "What? Me? I would never!"

Honor, honesty, and doing the *right thing* were the air I breathed. I solely thrived on not being that kind of person.

I was surrounded by narcissists, takers, and liars—ones who fed off of my misery and constant giving because it was convenient. I started looking at myself as a joke—someone who was unworthy of living.

These words aren't just uttered letters.

I hated myself. It was dark and self-destructive. I was mysteriously sick for two years with a constant body pain that doctors couldn't figure out. I was also hurting loved ones around me. They could see I was not well. *I am okay. I can handle anything* was my recurring inner dialogue. I even received death threats at work and was still playing strong and *keeping it together.* I was a workaholic insomniac business consultant who mostly lived at the office. I had teams to run and clients *to save.* I thought I would be condemned to a life of suffering had I admitted to my pain.

Little did I know that I already sentenced myself to that.

"You're a wh—" he said to me in a split second as his beautiful, loving eyes turned from sparkly honey brown to raging despise. I was already destroyed physically, emotionally, and psychologically. Confessing was my asking for absolution. I was ready to throw in the towel.

I left the table and stormed out as fast as I could, endless tears blurring my sight as I ran towards the parking area on the rainy narrow streets of Beirut. I didn't care if a car hit me. Although what he said shattered me, I was already living in fragments. He also didn't say anything I hadn't been telling myself.

I wanted to be exposed and end everything right there and then.

That night sent me on a deeper spiral of self-loathing. I smoked more packs of cigarettes, ate less than one meal a day, and over-caffeinated my body. I didn't want to see anyone. I saw myself as a fake, unworthy of being loved or happy. I constantly saw myself as a threat that needed to be annihilated.

My self-conversation of unworthiness was running the show which became my life. It orchestrated a silent symphony that creepily choked the real me to death. This wasn't seen by my conscious mind. My mind would have told you a different story.

As I take short breaths between the words I'm typing, I keep trying to locate when this self-hate started. I was a highly dissociative child. Going down memory lane isn't the easiest. I often catch myself envying people who can tell past stories and share memories with such ease. I have always been forgetful as far as I can remember. I'm unsure whether it started with the Lebanon civil war I was born into, childhood sexual abuse, being bullied, or the fact that I always felt that I didn't belong here.

These memories would have never made ink had I not met Shamanic Breathwork. Everything I'm sharing in this space started being readily available after I started breathing cyclically.

And so, it began.

I had fabricated stories to myself and others from the age of five. I wanted to be someone I was not.

How could they love me if they knew who I am? I had a deeply embedded belief that I wasn't loveable. Letting anyone get to know me was the ultimate fear. Hiding my real self became my biggest talent.

I am still picking up pieces of that to this day.

My story didn't look like this at all to the outside world.

Growing up, I was seen as the poster child of success. I was the one who excelled at everything effortlessly, from sports, singing, and dancing to competitions and school. It was of my nature. I never had to scheme, plan, or compete to prove myself. I just did.

I was also intuitive. I would see something, and then it would happen. Not knowing it was intuition nor expecting it would take place, it just did. I never told anyone.

Just as Lebanon was coming out of war, I was eight years old. I will never forget the moment I looked at the television screen in my parent's room and saw teenage kids dancing. Something within me said *this is where I am going to be.* Not even months later, in a stroke of luck, I met the executive producer at a gymnastics competition I had won. She asked me to join the team of that same TV show I saw. I did that for the next ten years of my life. Around that same age, I used to endlessly watch MTV music television with a feeling I would somehow live in New York City and work at that network. At the age of 21, this also happened unexpectedly.

"You have a very strong personality," people often told me. Some even suggested that it was "too strong." What they didn't know is that behind the scenes, I was struggling with being in the spotlight. I began playing small so that I didn't win, pass a test with flying colors, or be noticed at all. I chose to take the backseat of my life because it felt safest.

I wanted to be accepted so badly by the ones who used to bully me. So, I tricked them into liking me by creating an accessory of myself. I became the listener, the one who understands, the shoulder to cry on, and the giver. To the child me, there was no tricking at all. I had no idea what was going on. I just did anything to avoid the pain of rejection. At times I even posed as a bully, class clown, or a mean person. All of this role-playing was in the name of mission "love me."

Being the overachiever meant being called nerd, good girl, know-it-all, teachers' favorite, and a bunch of other names I felt I was the farthest from. At home was another stage. I had to show my parents I was indeed the overachiever because average would mean punishment.

I was living a parallel life already.

Fast forward to that night of confession at a bar in Beirut; I slipped away furthest from my body. I kept replaying the way he looked at me over and over in my head. I was in disbelief at the amount of hate that could come out from someone's eyes.

A few months later, a doctor prescribed me yet another unnecessary pill that I was allergic to. My swollen body was on the threshold. I decided there and then that I would no longer seek medical counsel. On the same day, a twist of fate put a guide in my way in the form of a person who told me about a place called Bali. Believe it or not, I had never heard of it.

Without questioning or researching it at all, I booked a flight to the island under the pretext that I would be taking my first long vacation in six years where I would enjoy my time, learn surfing, and of course, work.

During this trip, the heavens conspired with my living hell.

On the fourth day of my workcation, a bottle of lotion spilled, ruining my laptop. Something beyond me forced me to stop. I could no longer distract myself from the pain I had become. I was able to see that the end of me was near if I didn't change something. I no longer wanted my life to end. Something shifted.

To this day, I cannot make sense of what got into me. What happened wasn't logical. It still isn't. I quit me. I left the business of control and pretend. I cannot say if it was fear, courage, or surrender. Today, I'd tell you that they're one and the same.

I dropped everything, including clients, cigarettes, and caffeine, in one week.

A deep inner knowing started surfacing, letting me know I could heal myself.

My old self would have made fun of this statement.

I took on yoga, meditation and shut off my phone.

On my second week in Bali, I discovered Shamanic Breathwork. I will never forget the afternoon when I walked into my first journey in Ubud. I was the farthest from the world of holistic healing, let alone the idea of trust. Deep into the session, and just when I was saying *this is not for me*, a facilitator placed a hand on my heart. I cried so deeply without sound. Showing emotion wasn't in my code after all, although screams and loud music were governing the room.

For the first time, I felt a conscious connection to my heart. This breathwork journey opened a way for so much mystery and unraveling expansion and transformation to come. I breathed, discovered, and opened my eyes to hidden memories and lies I hadn't seen. The breath activated my soul power and saved my relationship with my body. It still does. Every shamanic journey opens space for memories, feelings, and visions. It rips open rigidly locked-in self-beliefs and exposes them to the light.

From that day onward, the girl who hated herself started remembering love by daring to be herself. This is how the biggest romance of my life to date began—painful, heart-wrenching, joyful, and expansive all at the same time. Day in and day out, I am remembering to be my own unconditional lover by being me.

It turns out that there isn't one way to love me. There are infinite ways.

No, my personal process is neither perfect nor squeaky clean. I still feel like a child learning to walk all over again on a daily basis. I aim for the road, stumble in potholes, and take shade to rest. I then get up and walk again. Getting out of bed can be hard for me on many days. Sometimes, my mind repeats a certain thought like a broken record of why I shouldn't be seen, heard, or loved. The difference between then and now is that today I choose myself with love, compassion, and patience through it all. I no longer tend to hide or mute myself. I'm not scared of uncovering my lies and seeing my tendencies in wanting to fabricate more again. I hold the flashlight and ask to see. I then surrender to my inner wisdom with trust. I see myself in my rawness, messiness, and humanness.

I embrace my unique self and celebrate with others. Life inspires me again, and I can feel it beat through it all. There is magic in daring to be me.

Today, I am a spiritual mentor residing in Bali. My core teachings are around self-love and activating the individual's original essence of the real you.

SHAMANIC MEDICINE OFFERING

The you that took the first breath in this body before being told rights, wrongs, goods, and the bad; its nature is unconditional in love. When the baby starts developing and being exposed to society, culture, and family dynamics, they start stepping away from the real self. The mind is then slowly trained to attach itself to conditional love: "be this way, so I like you, love you, accept you and/or reward you."

The journey of daring to be you is the path of loving you, no matter what.

Remembering the self is to allow the real self to be. It is not a journey for the faint-hearted. The path of self-love is one and the same. It is a very unique and individual journey. It has its beauty, initiations, medicine, and contribution. There is no one-size-fits-all when it comes to the form of you or loving you. You are not like me. I am not like you.

You are creation itself and the universe in motion.

When you feel that you have strayed afar from yourself at times, questions and statements such as "How do I do it? What would happen if I actually allow? What would family, friends, children, society, or lover say, or will they accept me? I will lose so much." Or scripts such as "It's too late" or "It's impossible, I have always been like this." This process is called resistance. What are we resisting? The real self. This happens because we have been conditioned, on a deeply subconscious level, to *fear* the self.

Why? Because it is endless layers of constant change and mystery. She is unknown to the mind. Our mind is conditioned to fear that which it doesn't know.

Here are ten ways to help support you on the journey of remembering your real self in love:

1. Meeting and loving yourself can only happen with your permission, choice, and non-attachment to the outcome.

2. Your secrets, darkness, most inner deep demons are the way. They are here in the depths of your being and in your body, waiting for you to catch up and let love.

3. Love your body, for it is the vessel of your soul. Nothing happens outside of it. Not one dream, desire, achievement happens without it. Honor it as the tree honors the sun rays as they kiss its leaves. Speak to your body with gratitude. Ask it what it needs.

4. Boundaries are freedom. Have an honest conversation with yourself about what you are letting in and out. Speaking yes and no to you first is speaking the truth to yourself. This is equal to saying to you, I have got you.

5. Trust you. No matter how hard, impossible things may be or if the entire world seems to be against you, choose you. You are the journey unfolding.

6. You are unique, sovereign, and whole onto yourself. There is no one like you, nor there will ever be. You are the visionary of your own life.

7. Honor the seasons of your being and remember that change is the only constant. The moment you believe that you have met you, it changes. You are an infinite journey of mystery, depth, and magic. Gift yourself curiosity to keep meeting you.

8. Every inch of you, of it, is just as scrumptiously lovable as the love that you are. Even on the days when it's hard to love, send yourself love anyway. The depths that you are willing to go through to love yourself then get mirrored outside of you with partners, work relationships, friendships, and the universe.

9. Patience and compassion with your process, whatever it may be, could be the catalysts. They are your secret tools for stepping into creator-ship.

10. That which we call a dark night of the soul, where one feels the darkest at times, *is* the light of the self-shining through. Stuckness, confusion, depression, split are just headlines that have been conditioned to be looked at as bad. In truth, these processes are the self speaking to you. This is not to say that the process is easy. It is often not. However, what is the hardship in the face of not living my own truth?

So, touch the tears as they fall down on your face, kiss that thought that is telling you that you are not good enough, and love that cake you ate because the path of least resistance is the path of love. It all starts in the journey of least resistance to you at the moment.

There is magic in meeting you, for you are the magic and the magician.

However long, rocky, crazy, or steep the path may seem to be, love it because it is the road of you. It is the road to you.

Join me for a live guided journey to awaken the inner beloved. Allow yourself the chance to start exploring how ravishing every part of you can start to look. Open the way for love, for you are it.

You can find Meeting the Inner Beloved on my YouTube channel https://www.youtube.com/channel/UCNIMoyjr1TRG4qoHjFiQ3Gw

Originally from Lebanon, **Zeina** was a television host in the Middle East since the age of nine. After moving to New York City, Zeina's professional journey shifted to television production, talent management, and business consultancy. After over a decade of "a successful career," her path had other plans for her. She had then found her calling through a physical illness that forced her to stop and reconnect to her life's calling and wildest desires yet. Zeina is dedicated to the forever journey of transformation. It is her mission to activate change-makers into their original power through meeting love within. She currently resides in Bali and holds transformation space through her retreats and online creations. Her most recent works include visionary and practical programs such as Dare to be you: An Online Deep Dive into the Power of You. She is a spiritual mentor, internationally published co-author, soul guide, Shamanic Breathwork Facilitator, shamanic astrology counselor, meditation teacher, and dream journeyer.

You can further connect with Zeina by contacting her on IG @zeinayazbek or via e-mail at rebirth@dreamanewworld.com

Chapter 13

FROM PARTY GIRL TO SHAMANIC PRIESTESS

How I Learnt to Get High Off my Own Supply

Patricia Silverwolf

MY STORY

Since I can remember, I have always been surrounded by mysticism. There has always been a guiding force holding me behind every move and decision I make.

I was born on the last day of Samhain when the doors to the Otherworld were close. During this auspicious time of the year, the barriers between the physical and spiritual world break down, allowing more interaction between the living and the dead. I believe that being born on such a powerful portal allowed me to have a deeper connection with my ancestors—my guardian spirits—who have held and carried me throughout my life.

When I was born, my mother could not care for me—she had no emotional or financial means. Her sister offered help, and I was placed in the care of my aunt and uncle. My father was not in the picture. I learned later in life that he proposed to my mother after my birth but caught her with another man a couple of days before their wedding. Carrying anger and humiliation in his body, he left for good.

My auntie was a woman of heart, however, a fundamentalist Catholic. I was raised in a system that always felt constricting for me. I felt like I didn't belong. Growing up was not easy. She developed Alzheimer's quite early and was addicted to benzodiazepines.

Furthermore, she was growing extremely jealous of my relationship with her husband, who turned out to be my rock, my everything. Our bond was from another world; it's no wonder I ended up in his care. In between my aunt and mother, I went through a lot of abuse, neglect, and grief, which is something I carried for many lifetimes. I now understand that this was just history repeating itself, Spirit offering me an opportunity to change the behavioral and karmic loops through forgiveness, acceptance, and selfless love.

I wandered through this earthly walk for a long time with a deep sense of disconnection. When I descended from the stars, the ties with the world of Spirit remained strong, and the pain of separation was still dwelling in my heart. I doubted my beauty, ancient wisdom, and power throughout my life. I knew I was a bit different. I always felt protected by something greater than I could ever explain. I had gifts but shut them down because otherwise, I could not be loved in my home. I had this feeling I could heal people and animals with my touch. My hands would sometimes burn hot, and I knew they held something beyond my understanding.

At the age of twelve, my life went upside down. I left the church and got into Wiccan studies, consecrating myself as a solitary white witch. I was sexually harassed by my best friend's father and blamed for it. I was slut-shamed at school by all my peers. I shaved my head and got into the punk culture, and I started to smoke marijuana and drink alcohol. I developed depression and anxiety and was placed on medication, which wasn't a good combo with alcohol. I was a little hot mess.

At home, things were getting worse. My auntie was persecuting me more than ever, leading to colossal fights. She would burn my books and call in a Catholic priest every six months to exorcise my bedroom, accusing me of being a witch. History repeating itself. Karmic loop. A light version of inquisition. At age 15, I was raped and lost my virginity. All these experiences led me into years of self-abuse. I went completely wild and rebellious, known to be a hurricane of emotions, and ostracized from my peers at school. I got into cocaine and binged on alcohol weekly.

At age 18, I got into University to study for a Bachelor of Nursing. The partying life was getting out of control. My addictions to drugs, alcohol, and sex got worse. At age 19, I was admitted to rehab. It didn't work. My issues were purely emotional and not addictions, per se. The problem was the crack in my soul I was trying to fill in. Drugs were just the numbing agent I found to replace the pain of abuse, trauma, neglect, and the core wounding of abandonment suffocating my heart. Not being acknowledged and desired by your parents can screw you up. Unconsciously, the message I received was that there was something wrong with me. I spent half my life feeling like I was unworthy of love. That's the limiting belief I held deep in my subconscious mind, which led me to get into so much trouble. I had to manifest lessons that would remind me of that until I could turn the game around.

I graduated from University and started working with newborns in intensive care— that made me even more depressed. I was in an abusive relationship suffering bad domestic violence. Soon after, my uncle sent me out of the country. Thank God; otherwise, I would have been dead by now.

I moved to Australia and decided to change my life. I started studying hospitality and was free from illicit drugs. However, alcohol was easy to reach. And so along came the bad crew and back on weed I was. In 2008, I decided to go back to nursing and did a major in Mental Health. I was smoking a lot of pot to help me cope with loneliness and pressure. It kept me numb enough. I got married and was hired as a mental health nurse. I was still battling with my addictions to sex. My marriage ended in 2011 because I couldn't be faithful.

It was then that my life changed. I was 29—Saturn's return. I felt like I could not keep on going like this anymore. I broke so many hearts throughout my life—a typical defense mechanism of an abandoned soul. I was tired of hurting and abusing myself and significant others in my life. I prayed fervently for divine intervention. Soon after, while going for a walk,

I saw a banner of a spiritual gathering called "Being Woman." I decided to Google it, and in the description of the workshop, it was all I was praying for. It was time to grow up and deal with my shit!

I attended the festival and had my first deep shamanic experience, finding my power animal: a massive grey wolf—my faithful partner who has been by my side since. I also met a medicine woman who took me as her apprentice. Just after I completed my studies, I fell pregnant with my boy. I barely knew his dad. It was a one-night thing. Even though I was afraid, it felt right. One must be careful with what is asked for. I prayed for the gods to turn me into a woman, for I could not mess around with men's hearts anymore, so I was given the biggest initiation into womanhood—a child! It was a powerful year of intense inner work. That was just the beginning.

In 2012 my son was born, and I had a massive quickening in my path. I deepened in shamanic practices, and my shadow came to make herself known like never before. In 2013, I received a vision from a dark goddess, half woman, half crow. She guided me into the lower world and helped me craft a dance to meet with my shadows and to learn lessons from them. I was in awe. I could not believe I had created that. My friends encouraged me to bring this out to the world, but I was not confident enough because I had no facilitation skills. One day, Spirit sent me a nudge. Once again, I saw a banner, this time for Kundalini Dance—a guided tantric shamanic practice that has the power to rejuvenate the body, clear old stagnant emotional energy, bring insight and clarity into limiting beliefs, and support the awakening and integration of higher consciousness. It's the art of emotional alchemy and a dance that teaches you how to embody Earth and Heaven and how to become one with your divine parents. It was a seven-week alchemical dance with the chakras that blew my mind—weeks of purging the emotional dross, fears, limiting beliefs, and behavioral and karmic loops from all layers of my body.

After this journey, I joined a retreat with the creatrix of this modality. At the end of the experience, I had my first kundalini awakening; a huge cobra entered my root chakra and left my body through my crown. I was thrown on the floor crying and shaking for 30 minutes. It was the wildest embodied experience I ever had. I was told I had been initiated and offered the opportunity to expand in my studies to become a Kundalini Dance Priestess. I completed the mystery school in 2014, and since then, I have been serving humanity in their process of awakening. However, as I serve humanity, I'm humbly reminded I have to keep deepening in my evolutionary process.

Since then, life has been a massive dance of death and rebirth. Every cycle of Kundalini Dance I held helped me shed another layer of my soul. And so I keep deepening in my evolutionary process of awakening, digging deep, and flying high, shedding ancestral layers, karmic ties, behavioral and patterned loops that have been keeping me in isolation and separation, and retrieving all the lost parts of my soul. I am traveling within and without, searching for wisdom, expanding and contracting, receiving initiations from my inner guides and Spirit, many of which were quite painful to experience, but were very necessary for the woman I'm becoming. It's a wild, messy, ecstatic unfolding journey. I believe that the more ancient your Spirit is, the more shit you have to clean up.

In 2016 I was in another abusive relationship with my greatest soul mate. This container provided me with the most sacred mirror I ever had. Through the eyes of this man, I uncovered rage, my old friend. She was killing me silently, numbed by ganja and alcohol for the last 20 years. However, she had already consumed my stomach. I developed an ulcer by age 15 and suffered from gastritis until Kundalini Dance entered my life. But rage was now allocating somewhere else, eating up my bones and joints. I had a nasty hip injury that forced me to be still for an entire year. All the suppressed anger was becoming apparent. My ex's rage permitted me to bring my rage to the light of my consciousness. As I write this, I cry in gratitude because he set my shadow free. From then on, there was no more hiding. Rage was out of the cage, wild and rebellious, fueling my creative projects. But her flaming fire was burning all the bridges and important relationships in my life. I have come to understand that rage is my greatest shadow, suppressed anger due to all the abuse and neglect. However, I've learned to have a deep appreciation for rage, for she served her purpose. She kept me safe from further hurt, protected me from abuse, and gave me fuel to keep moving forward every time I wanted to give up. She gifted me with grit and fire. She awakened my wild woman and taught me how to hold the warrior's torch. Despite her gifts, it was getting too tiring. It was time to remove my shields and lay my sword down.

Again I prayed eagerly. One should never underestimate the power of prayer! I was smoking a lot of weed, and my soul knew I couldn't go ahead like this anymore. I asked for guidance, for a sign, for a savior, a master Yoda to show up in my life.

And so the gods replied. I was Googling something shamanic one day, and Star Wolf's book, Shamanic Breathwork, came up. I didn't think twice; I bought the book and devoured it in one week. The book awakened a sparkle within my heart. I resonated a lot with her history and prayed to my guides to help me cross paths with her. I knew she had something for me. My soul was craving a rebirth. At this stage, I was just daydreaming about our encounter.

In 2017 I decided to stop smoking marijuana. A big effort, but I managed, and I offered this sobriety for my evolutionary process and beseeched to be guided towards the right teachers who would guide me towards my next step. My power animals were communicating to me via dreamtime, guiding me towards the East. Once again, I decided to google Star Wolf and found out she was holding an event during the solar eclipse. This was so divinely orchestrated. I already had a ticket to fly to the U.S. for Eclipse Festival in Oregon. On the same day, I broke up with my ex. I changed my route, my flights and got hold of the last bed at Venus Rising. You just can't make this shit up! It was time.

I arrived at Venus Rising and had the most beautiful experience. The blue mountains, the cove, the animals were all talking to me. The community held me tightly. I felt at home. I got what I wanted. In my first ever breathwork, I received a rebirth from Star Wolf. It was huge. I had to leave back home in three days. I could not even walk properly; my legs and knees were weak. My foundation was being reestablished. Once again, life turned upside down, and I decided to come back for more as the edge walker that I am. I knew there was something big in there for me.

I came back to Isis Cove to receive more healing. Rage was still consuming my life and destroying my relationship with my child. I signed up for SHIP with no attachment to become a facilitator, but once I started to walk that floor—WOW! It was like all the guides would possess my vessel and use me for the work. The timing of my connection with the breathers, the ecstasy running through my veins, the crying and screaming coming out from my body, feeling every pain and emotion from each soul that I would touch, the dance between our souls—it was recharging, uplifting, and ecstatic. I felt worthy. I felt like I had a purpose. I remember thinking *I was made for this work, for this work uses me.*

It is truly humbling to be able to serve humanity this way. Through breath! So simple yet so powerful! It amazes me to see the potential of life and humanity. Unfortunately, we are not taught about it. We are much more than what we have learned in this western culture. Inner work, I believe, is one way to restore this remembrance. To be able to travel between time and space, to retrieve fragmented pieces of our soul that have been scattered through trauma, to come back to sovereignty, to heal, to reunite with one reality only through a simple process of circular breathing is pretty amazing! I have all respect for medicinal plants, but after finding out this modality and coupling it with movement and sound, I never needed anything else.

I have learned how to get high on my supply. Do you want to know how?

SHAMANIC MEDICINE OFFERING

Kundalini Dance is an alchemical ecstatic dance that complements Shamanic Breathwork. We use movement, sound, and breathwork to enter an altered state of consciousness for greater healing and transformation. Through this practice, you will be able to retrieve soul parts, reclaim your sovereignty and embody inner union, and through that, rejoice in ecstatic rapture.

For the entire process of how to work with the kundalini energy, check this link:
https://www.youtube.com/channel/UC__z8WTuCsPvcQb_j_DJMNg

- Relax your body. Engage your senses
- Place your attention and intention on connecting to the core of the Earth
- Invite the divine feminine energies of the Earth to support you on your ecstatic dance journey.
- On the exhale, relax your perineum and feel your feet connected to the Earth. On the inhale, draw earth energy up through your feet, through your legs into your perineum, and collect the energy in your lower belly. Do it a couple of times.

- Stomp your feet, call in earth energy, Shakti fire, pray to awaken your kundalini energy.
- Once you feel warmth in your lower belly, let your body intelligence move you.
- Dance to feel. Dance to heal.
- Shake, sound, breathe. Exhale all fear-based emotions from your field.
- Dance from the witness. Dance with your shadow. Dance to empty yourself.
- Once again, connect with the core of the Earth.
- Raise earth energy to your heart chakra - the center of transformation.
- Take some sipping breaths through your central channel and out through the four auric layers of your heart chakra, sounding out: Ahhhhh.
- Let the intelligence of your heart guide you. Focus on forgiveness, self-love, compassion, acceptance, unconditional love, and loving awareness, and breathe this energy into your field.
- Keep sipping until you feel your energy rising.
- Continue to breathe energy up from Mother Earth, into your central channel, and up into your heart. Expand the energy from the heart out through all the four layers of your energy field and through the spirit body layer to Source. Connect up from your root through your crown to Source—Divine Father Sky.
- Find an organic flow in your dance, feel the stream, and play with the currents. Dance into the one. Hang out in the golden light of ecstatic union.
- Next, inhale the golden light of Source. Allow the downflow of Divine Masculine current to fill the back of the chakras all the way down into the Earth.
- Feel the connection of the solar current and the Earth current as they meet in every cell in your body.
- Open to receive the integrative balancing power of this tantric union of feminine and masculine polarities.

Patricia Silverwolf brings a fresh edge to ecstatic awakening, guiding you with her experiential gifts. As a Ceremonialist, Kundalini dance priestess, Munay-ki teacher, Shamanic Breathwork Facilitator, Womb Awakener, and a former Mental Health Nurse, she shares the magic of bridging heaven and earth authentically, thus encouraging you to channel your souls truth. As an agent of transformation, she opens a transcendental portal for you to journey through your inner mysteries and clear knowing, assisting you in reawakening, expressing, and transmuting patterns of being. Her journeys are for anyone curious to explore, open to change, or willing to immerse on a path of transformation—pure alchemy.

Patricia loves to support others to initiate their inner healer. If one is willing, they will be guided with the tools of deep ethno, tribal, and trance beats, sacred breath techniques, heartful sound infusions, and Patricia's strong and soothing voice. Honorable invocations of ancestry illuminate the path of realization and rising in consciousness. Senses may be heightened as one can access altered states of being naturally through the techniques that Patricia shares.

Patricia shares an understanding that there is no great separation between darkness and light. Union is discovered and explored as one adventure through the chakras with intentional dance, breathwork, and sound. This wolf woman shares medicinal ceremonies that support you in deepening connections to Mother Earth and Father Sky. She will inspire connecting with your power animals and spirit carers, therefore, empowering the journey further. All ceremonies she holds are a celebratory experience to realign your life and your sacred purpose. Designed to assist you in awakening your shakti energy and raising your Kundalini, the serpent energy that lays dormant, once arisen, will burst through your paradigm, and a new world will flow.

You can also connect with Patricia through her website: www.patriciasilverwolf.com, and on Instagram: patricia_silverwolf

CHAPTER 14

A JOURNEY INTO THE GREAT MYSTERY

LEAPING THROUGH THE PORTAL OF DEATH

Freyiia Milléh, ID Life Coach, Spiritual Mentor, Shamanic Shadow Facilitator

"The only constant in life is change.

~Heraclitus

MY STORY

The drum sends me off into the journey, and I only manage to take a few deep breaths before I feel an intense inner cold cut through my bones. The temperature in the room around me drops to zero. I become briefly uncomfortable lying alone on the floor in the middle of the night in this online breathwork journey. But at the same time, I'm aware my father simply confirms his presence with this sense of cold. I just called him and my grandmother from the other side to guide me. "Thank you, I understand you're here, Dad," I said out loud. "But will you please regulate the temperature so I can relax?" Immediately, my inner cold sensation disappears, and I feel his presence on my right. He wants to show me something important!

Then, I'm running in a panic across a vast field. The darkness is dense, and all I can hear is the fire from the crashed car burning behind me. *An adult will stop me in a minute*, a voice in my head says. I remember for a split second when, shortly before my father's death two years ago, he told me about a car accident he experienced as a four-year-old. He remembered nothing, other than he somehow must have managed to get out of the car and run in a panic across a field, and that an unknown person appeared and brought him back to the car and to his foster mother, who had driven it. He told me he wondered throughout his life who the person was because it was utterly deserted on the road that night.

I'm now witnessing the scene of the accident from above. I see my father as a little boy running in a panic across the field away from the burning car. I expect to see who stops him, but no one's coming. He runs and runs, but doesn't get anywhere. I suddenly notice his little body is almost transparent, and I'm shocked realizing it's his soul trying to escape. I then see the tiny lifeless body lying in the backseat of the car. It's quiet on the empty road in the dark. No one else has arrived at the scene, and the car burns quietly. His foster mother is unconscious. His soul has left his body, and he has a near-death experience where an unknown being brings him back to his body.

I'm trying to understand what's going on right now with this authentic inner experience. My deceased father shows me he died as a little boy in this accident. My mind is running fast, and I hear my voice: *If he weren't brought back to life, I wouldn't exist.* Then, I'm back in the experience and find myself in the backseat of the burning car in the tiny lifeless body. I feel how I physically slip or almost get sucked back out through the back of the little body. It's the point of no return, and the strong pull from death is taking me through the portal!

I'm now standing in the driveway of my parents' idyllic blue wooden house. They built it after my brother and I moved out. My father loved it and died here. *But if my father died as a child, this house doesn't exist either.* With a flick, the house disappears, and there is only the green lawn. Then

I see every other home in the area disappearing, and only the green grass stretch as far as the eye can see. *Time goes backward,* I think to myself, and next thing I see, old horse-drawn carriages bumping across the ground. It all happens in seconds, like a movie playing backward. I still feel the shock and sorrow in my heart that I, in this lifetime, don't exist—a profound feeling that everything I've ever known is gone. My parents' first meeting. My creation. My upbringing. Our home. My story. My body. My son. I didn't even have to go through the well-known resistance of letting go because there was nothing to release. It's never been there. Suddenly, the images began rolling for my inner eye again, and I saw the modern world as we know it disappear from the face of the earth, like a clock ticking the wrong way and the creation of everything going backward.

Suddenly time stops again, and I find myself in a warm, damp jungle. I can feel a heavy snake sliding silently over me. I can see its one yellow eye with an oblong black pupil flashing, focused on me. I'm a large flat rock. I'm lying heavily on the wet forest floor. I don't have the physical ability to move or interact with the snake, but I sense it and feel its energy. I'm conscious, like any other natural existence in our world. *No matter what physical form I take in life, I will always have the gift of life itself with me. Consciousness.* I'm reminded that I also called in the long-deceased spiritual teacher, Martinus, to guide this journey. At this moment, he gave me an experience of consciousness in its purest form. The experience of being a rock, with no physical or emotional responsiveness, but as conscious as any other life that springs from nature's creation. My mind wandered to my beloved trees in my garden, which I always greet and touch lovingly and respectfully. At this moment, I experience how nature senses and feels me when I interact with it.

Time again runs backward and takes my attention with it. In the glimpse of an eye, the whole planet disappears as if it never existed. I'm now getting used to these shocks and staying calm, witnessing it as a movie. *It must be the time just before existence began,* I think, but then a new thought replaces it. *No, because time is an earthly illusion and does not exist in this dimension.* I feel my human mind and logic come to an end here. For a moment, I'm losing my mind and can no longer comprehend what I'm witnessing. Then a deep sensation of just being present replaces the feeling of trying to understand. I feel the pure consciousness as a dark emptiness. There's nothing there. I'm nothing. I'm everything. I'm just conscious. I am. It briefly triggers an awareness of myself, and I feel my body back on the floor. I shortly have double-directional attention to the certainty that I'm just in breathwork and I will come back again. I manage to let go of the fear and go even deeper into the experience.

I'm back in the witness position to the burning car on the deserted highway. I see the lifeless little body in the backseat of the vehicle dressed in a little red sweater and dark blue pants. One foot is hanging over the edge of the back seat. I see the tiny body in a white transparent version on the field, followed back to the car by another transparent being. A deep understanding strikes me like lightning from a clear sky. *I created all this myself. From a higher place, I created him myself as the perfect father to my story. I wrote the story myself.* My mind wandered to new horizons. *What was it I came here to experience in this life? My purpose? Oh yes, I came here to explore the mystery of equal conscious relationships! The purest form of love between people.*

Right at that moment, I understood it all. I could see the big picture of my life, as clear as the sky on a sunny day. We learn through the nature of polarity. So, I created the upbringing that could awaken this desire within my human awareness from a higher place. All the emotional hardship my father has experienced in his upbringing shaped him into the perfect father role in my dysfunctional story, which has facilitated my awakening, like a perfect little piece in a vast puzzle game. Our human desires are born out of polarity, and I accepted at that moment, that all people in my world are precisely as they should be! That there is divine order in every chaos working towards transformation and human evolution. Everything is in the most beautiful divine order at all times!

I forgave my father deeply in my heart for everything I've ever blamed on him. I felt a tremendous love expanding my heart and a new degree of confidence in life itself. I was back on the floor with my headphones on. I heard the drum bring me back from the journey. I decided in that second that I don't have to experience any more codependency in relationships. I'm now ready to appreciate and love myself. I will embrace the polarity of anima and animus within me and be my own equal lover and best friend. As within, so without!

In retrospect, I understood that my father needed to share with me that he came back to life at four years old so he could bring me to life one day. He lived a life in difficult emotional conditions and died of cancer at just

68 years of age. He was sick the last six years of his life, and I sat by his side for the final six months. In that time, I got to know my father deeply. I was supporting him in a deep emotional release before he finally left his body. This breathwork journey happened two-and-half years after his death. I found the most profound forgiveness and love for both him and myself.

SHAMANIC MEDICINE OFFERING

"Only when you embrace death, life can begin.
Everything else is called survival."

~Freyiia.

"You can let go now, Dad," I said to him several times in the last weeks of his life. His body was dying, and life slowly ebbed out of him. I witnessed his strong body shrink into skin and bones. I told him again, "You can let go now," and he answered me with a question one day: "How do I do that?"

His question hit me like lightning. How do we do that? What mechanism inside ourselves do we use to detach on such a deep level that we move through all resistance and let go of everything? I gave him healing and told him to relax completely into the pain and let himself float off. He couldn't, no matter how much he wanted to end his suffering. I could not help him with that one thing.

The question lit a spark deep within me. Death has always drawn me to try and understand it, and in my younger days, I read all books about near-death experiences. My personal and professional path with clients has always worked around a present theme: letting go of control. Learning the art of detaching and indulging into the reality of the present moment completely. Life has forced me to that edge between control and surrender often. But I could not help my father to let go at his edge. He didn't pass over until the day his body couldn't maintain enough strength to breathe anymore. His body 'turned off' from starvation before he managed to let go of his resistance and leave his body voluntarily.

My dark night of the soul started in the last six months of his life. After his death, I felt torn into atoms with no job to return to. As always, a light appears in the dark when we hit the edge. A powerful light called me to travel to Levi Banner's Shamanic Yoga Teacher Training in Bali. I went. I had no idea how much the combination of yoga and the medicine of Shamanic Breathwork would help me heal, recover, and rebirth myself in the following five-week program.

WE MUST LEARN TO DIE BEFORE WE DIE!

My father's question, "How do I do that?" has guided my life's journey since his death. Often since that day, I've experienced leaping through the portal between worlds. I now know how to move through my natural fear and resistance without fighting it and getting stuck.

Shamanic Breathwork taught me to go through the portal of death while I continue to breathe! Each time I go through the 'inner death' and am reborn, my reality has forever changed! My consciousness expands, and I can feel the energy shift in my entire body. It's a move to the next level in the spiral path of life, in huge jumps!

Birth and death are the doors in and out of your present reality. You can say that birth and death are the same, seen from each side of the same door. When you approach the door from the dying perspective, it feels like you're being pushed and squeezed to a point where there's no escape. If you fight it, you'll just prolong the process. You will have to surrender at some point because the cycle of life is more vital than you are. When you slip through the portal, you'll forever be gone from that place you just left, in energy. But when you see it from the other side of the door, you're birthing yourself into a unique new experience of reality.

Step 1 – Recognize when death is calling you

First, you have to learn to recognize when death is calling you. I call it the downward spiral, which is pulling the energy in and down. Like trees pulling the waters back from the leaves, so they wither and let go. You are also following inner energetic cycles. Nothing in life is consistent. It can be a job, relationship, emotional phase, or a limited belief coming to an end.

A version of you is called to let go and die, so you can birth yourself into the next level of being you.

Write down in which areas of your life you feel the energy is pulling back, inwards, and downwards. Often it will feel like a struggle, fight, and chaos because you have tried for some time to uphold something meant to die.

Step 2 – Identify your inner resistance

Next, you have to identify any inner resistance to the pull. You may be very aware of it, or maybe you're attached by subconscious programming. This creates struggle, a feeling of powerlessness, or stagnation. Imagine you can split all of your inner personalities and talk to each of them. You might have an inner fire of independence, very ready to let go. But then you also have your inner youngster, afraid to stand alone. And then you might have an inner child, that doesn't want to give up this dream you've always striven for to make your father proud.

Write them all down on separate pieces of paper, and place them on the floor with a distance. Now, step upon the paper with the personality that empowers you the most to let go and move on. Close your eyes and feel this energy as the only one within your whole body. Ask yourself where this impulse to let go is coming from, and whatever questions arise intuitively. Now move around the floor on each paper, feeling and talking to each personality within you. Embrace them all. Identify any resistance and ask for the root cause of any fear. What are you holding on to that does not serve you any longer – and why?

Step 3 – Bring all parts of yourself in alignment

You now have to integrate those younger parts of you in resistance. Create a little ritual where you honor each one of them and give them your thanks. At some point they helped you deal with your life. All parts of your inner split personality have to join forces and become one focused energy before you can move through the rite of passage. If you don't do this inner work, life will eventually force you, when you can't hold up resistance any longer.

Sit in silence and connect to your heart. Allow every feeling from the younger parts of you to move through. Feel the doubt and fear. Be aware that the feelings have arisen from younger parts of you and they no longer shall be in charge. Take them all home into your heart and confirm that you are the adult now taking over from here.

Step 4 – Surrender to that which is bigger than you

Complete steps 1-3 as many times as you need until you feel all parts of you are in alignment. You have to reach an inner knowing, that there is only one way to go from here. You will feel no more doubt, but maybe still some anxiety. It's okay to feel alive when we surrender to the unknown. If you don't have all parts of your inner self unified, the energy cannot flow in only one direction, which IS the key to the portal of the deepest possible state of surrender.

Finally, do some bodywork, to move all of your awareness into your body. It can be a ceremony of any kind, Shamanic Breathwork, plant medicine, yoga, body therapy, EFT, Matrix re-imprinting, etc.

Surrender yourself completely to the power of the universe, to complete detachment, the unknown, the great mystery, and to God. Say a prayer with your deepest heartfelt intentions, trusting the divine power of love will always guide you home! And then let life take you on a ride to your next level. Whenever you close a door, you make room for a new one to open.

On my webpage, you will find a YouTube video, where I guide you into visualization on an inner journey to complete surrender: https://indresandhed.dk/sbwbook.html

Freyiia has, since her rebirth in Bali in 2019, become a light in the dark for many in Denmark with her free intuitive astrological updates and guided meditations. Brought up in a family with chronic illness and dysfunctional patterns, she's been walking the Shamanic path on the edge of light and deep darkness ever since her birth.

Her awakening journey started when she divorced at 25, with her baby son on her arm. Alongside many codependent relationship wounds, she got one after another certifications in spiritual healing, personal development, shadow work, and trauma release. She started her business, "Inner Truth," and struggled to crack the code of flow and abundance from a place of inner scarcity.

In her late 30s after many years of struggle, life took her into her spiritual rite of passage through the dark night of her soul, and she broke into a thousand pieces. After her father's death, she received her spirit name, Freyiia, from above, which she deeply recognized. She decided to move through her resistance and rebirth herself into a new identity in this lifetime. She turned 40 in Bali, where she was reborn in a Shamanic Breathwork ceremony on a profound level. Her voice and clear sight have cracked open since that shift. After only doing one-on-one sessions for many years, she is now speaking in public, on YouTube, facilitating ceremonies, and deep-dive transformational retreats. She's an ordained Shamanic Minister and in service as an open channel, bringing spirit into matter and shadow into the light for thousands in Denmark.

You can read Freyiia's personal story and articles on her webpage called Inner Truth. Her videos are in Danish, but maybe this book project is her first step to go international with her spiritual service.

Get in touch with Freyiia Milléh:
Website: https://indresandhed.dk
Instagram: Freyiia_indresandhed
Facebook: Freyiia Milleh, and the page: Indre Sandhed
Email: freyiia@indresandhed.dk

CHAPTER 15

BREATHE TO HEAL

How Breathwork Can Heal Physical and Emotional Pain

Walid Ablounaga

"You were born with wings. Why prefer to crawl through life?"

~Rumi

MY STORY

As I lay on my back staring at the ceiling of the tightly cramped insides of the MRI machine, I couldn't help but think, *how did I get to this point? Why am I, a healthy athletic young man who's always taken good care of his body, now finding myself laying helplessly inside this intimidating, claustrophobic machine so that doctors can try and figure out what's wrong with me?!* Time seemed to stand still, with many thoughts, memories, and decisions vividly flooding back.

The life our parents envision for us when we are young is imprinted on our subconscious. Our culture and society also play a role in creating the image of our future from our early years. Were you a doctor or nurse on career day at school? A lawyer, dancer, or a vet? Maybe some of you knew your destiny from the beginning, but I didn't. This is a short chapter of a bigger story; the rest of my story unfolds with each treasured breath of my being. Each word a fluid, ever-moving, and evolving expression of life. At the age of 39, in so many ways, was when I started breathing for the first time.

I sat with the top neurosurgeon at the American Hospital in Dubai as he explained to me the scanned images of my brain. "One of the treatments available is to undergo a surgical procedure which involves opening your skull. We would then freeze some nerves to relieve the pressure placed by blood vessels that are touching the nerve to cure your problem."

I stopped breathing for a few moments, which felt like hours, then took a deep breath as I tried to grasp what he was saying to me in total disbelief. "You're going to open up my brain?" I was diagnosed with Trigeminal Neuralgia, a chronic pain that affected the Trigeminal nerve. The veins on my head would thrust and pop out of the side of my eyebrows, mainly at nighttime. I couldn't put my head down on the pillow because the pain was excruciating; pain killers were my only path to reach sleep.

My thoughts threw me into many scenarios, none of which were positive, and I felt shivers down my spine. The doctor was very calm and continued to talk about medication and previous experiences from those who've healed. However, I was no longer listening to his words, just thinking only of the size of the hole to be made in my skull. *What if they freeze the wrong nerve? What if I have permanent damage? What if, what if.* Nothing but negative thoughts.

For some time, I could only struggle through my day and keep my sanity with the support of powerful painkillers. The constant pain and electric shocks I felt in my jaw and teeth were so severe I even woke up my dentist one morning at three a.m., begging him to pull out all my bottom teeth. He reassured me I was fine, but the painkillers stopped working. I was given a shot in my gums with a stronger version. Leaving the clinic, I was overcome with anxiety as I asked myself, *what would happen tomorrow night? And the next?* After doing some research online, I read that what I was experiencing was the number one disease that causes people to commit suicide. Reading this, I felt a sense of panic rushing through my body, only amplified as my mind showed me a worst-case scenario.

I refused the idea of surgery and having to open up my skull and started contemplating my options. I decided to go on a journey of self-healing. I thought to myself, *I'm too young for this. This shouldn't happen to me or anyone else.* I let stress get to me. The constant negative inner dialogue resulted in an emotional downward spiral, but I refused to be defeated. Even with the turmoil this situation brought, with the physical and mental battle raging inside me, a sense of knowing emerged. It was a knowing that this was the first step of many leading me to health and to a life purpose that would empower others with the courage to take their own steps. My life's healing adventure began.

Throughout middle school, my Judo teammates nicknamed me *Abu–Nafas*, which translates from Arabic to *Father of the Breath*. Abu (Father) Nafas (Breath). They would say that "Walid never runs out of breath!" I didn't know then that 30 years later, breath would be my destiny. *Nafas* derives from the word *Nafs*, which translates to (Spirit/Self), and breath and Spirit are the same word in many languages. I started to see my emotional state's profound effect on my health. Once my mindset changed, I realized I was not simply breathing in air or oxygen, but a sacred life force; Spirit. In Sanskrit, the Hindus call it Prana (the universal energy), the traditional Chinese call it Chi (balancing the negative and the positive), the Latins call it Spiritus, and Arabs call it Nafas. You are breathing in Spirit with every breath.

Growing up, sports was my main calling. I played every sport I could find and excelled later on in Judo. Martial arts have been an integral part of my character formation. I also ran track and field, focusing on the mid-distance races, the 400m (the man-killer) and the 800m. I knew then how important the breath was to run faster and to recover quicker but didn't fully comprehend the sheer power it had until later in life.

After graduating from business school, I worked in many corporate jobs with large-scale companies that try to mold and frame you to become who they want you to be—dress the part, talk their way, and live their culture. There's nothing wrong with that, but it wasn't my nature, nor did it resonate with me. By accident and sheer coincidence, my partner and

I co-founded our marketing company. We grew our vision from a one-person show to a 100-strong team by the second year, eventually leading over 1,400 employees within the first few years. Handling clients in 14 different countries across the Middle East and North Africa wasn't easy, and I was lucky to have an amazing team.

As we continued to grow, the pressure and stress grew as well. Deadlines, targets, demanding clients, and the continuous stress of cash flow all slowly affected my health. The 2008 financial crash and the 2011 Arab spring also led to more obstacles and further pressures, which took their toll on my well-being without my realizing it. I was anxious about what the future may hold, and negativity was ever-present and filtered from work into family life. After fifteen years in the marketing and business world, things changed: the clients, their attitude, the profits, and most of all, the fun. I no longer felt fulfilled at work; there was an emptiness to everything—even my successes and achievements. The ever-present questions included: *Is this all life has to offer? Is this my soul's calling and life's purpose?* I look back and say, the wake-up call at the hospital that afternoon was one of the greatest things that happened to me.

My shamanic journey started as a result of wanting to heal naturally. At first, I looked into stress and anger management courses. I began focusing on my physical healing in parallel to working on the mind and soul. I started detoxification programs which included juice fasts, water fasts, coffee enemas; you name it, I did it. I attended a silent retreat (Vipassana), searching for answers and understanding buried deep in my subconscious. This eventually led me to experience different plant medicines such as Ayahuasca, Wachuma, and Peyote. I tried various animal medicines as well. The journey continued into meditation, yoga, breathwork, sound healing, energy work, and many types of healing modalities I'd never heard of at the time. I met incredible practitioners along the way: crystal healers, pranic healers, and bio magnetic therapists. I connected with Reiki masters and countless healers sharing their gifts and light with the world.

If you had told me back then that I would be burning my skin and placing frog poison to heal and purify my body, or talking about Spirit animals and lower worlds, I would have laughed. But having experienced these amazing healing methods first hand and journeying to places I once thought didn't exist, I'm here today sharing this gift with the world.

I succeeded in healing myself with the grace of God, the support of my wife and family, and the assistance of the many healers and wonderful souls I encountered on my journey. I no longer needed surgery, my life drastically changed its course, and for all of it, I'm grateful. I learned we are all shamans (healers), and we can truly heal physically and emotionally.

Today I invite all those who join our Shamanic Breathwork sessions or Soulventure Journeys to meet their inner shaman, their inner healer. I always say, had I known then what I know now, I would have handled so many situations with my clients, suppliers, partners, family, and others so differently. This is my journey, though, and I'm forever grateful about where it has led me.

Having experienced the wonderful healing effects of different types of plant medicines, particularly Ayahuasca, I found answers to why certain situations happened to me in life, learning from the pain about the keys to healing and awakening. The local shamans facilitated journeys I could never imagine I would be on. Unlocking a part of your inner mind and opening up your subconscious to explain the entire universe and everything in it is something you have to experience for yourself. I had all the answers all along within me.

In such a short time, the grandmother plant explained so much about the planet, the plants, the galaxies, and everything in between. A few months after my first encounter in Peru with the psychoactive brew, I experienced my first deep breathwork. This was hosted on the last day of a festival held in Mexico, and my friend Gregorio Avanzini facilitated what would be one of the most powerful sessions I've had. I could not believe the incredible insights I received, the downloads of messages and learning, as well as the healing that took place all from just one session of breathwork. Similar to my Ayahuasca experience in the jungles of Peru, it was as if all the pieces of the puzzle of my life came together, and everything was clear. I knew what I clearly wanted, and what I no longer wanted. This blew my mind.

The benefits were evident in my mind, body, and soul. My breathwork journey truly began then and there. From that day forth, I've been on a ceaseless quest for learning everything I can about the breath, its benefits, healing powers, and non-ordinary states of consciousness to which it leads. My mission has since transformed to focus on helping other entrepreneurs and high-powered executives like myself deal with the stress and pressures of everyday life and put them on their personal paths to self-discovery. I thought this feeling and connection could only happen with the use of chemicals, psychedelics, or plant medicine, not knowing that the answer was in the breath all along.

My training began, and I was fortunate enough to have traveled to learn from the greatest masters in all corners of the world, including Peru, Mexico, the US, Europe, and Bali, to name a few. During this time, I decided to close my company which was causing me the most agony and stress, and almost instantly, I felt lighter in my thoughts and spirit than ever before. I still love setting up, launching, and investing in businesses, but only those with purpose and meaning. My wife, three daughters, and I all decided to move from Dubai, where we called home for fifteen years, and relocate to Bali to start our new adventure as a family.

I studied many different breathwork techniques trying to learn the similarities and differences between them and dove deep into the various available methods. Having studied Stanislav Grof's Holotropic Breathwork at the start, one of the most famous and first methods known to many, I attended several of their training modules and found it quite interesting, technical, very powerful, and full of knowledge. Yet something was missing. My first Shamanic Breathwork experience was with Levi Banner in Bali. It was something special and new, inviting in spirits and connecting with different worlds. I always believed in the spirit world but never had a fully immersed experience. After reading Linda Star Wolf's book, *Shamanic Breathwork – Beyond the Limits of the Self*, I was immediately drawn to learn more about the shamanic practices offered by Venus Rising. Studying with her and the team in North Carolina and in Teotihuacan, Mexico, I learned more about shadow work, different worlds and realms we can travel within, energy, psychospiritual practices, bodywork, and more. It was a deep and powerful learning experience for me on many levels as the training landed at the right time, just when I needed it. After becoming certified as a Shamanic Breathwork Facilitator and ordained a Shamanic Minister, I was fully ready to share this knowledge and healing with the world.

SHAMANIC MEDICINE OFFERING

Nafas Journeys was set up to provide Spiritual Adventures we call *Soulventures*, an adventure for the Soul. The vision, logo, offerings, and many of the elements of the company all came to me during breathwork. I remember finishing one of my early-on breathwork sessions in tears, having seen the logo so vividly. I drew it on tissue paper and asked my brother Sharif who is a creative artist, to design a logo following the shape I scribbled. He shared what we have today, which to me is something extraordinary. I future-traveled during that session and was able to envision the first journey I would later host, feel the feelings from the hearts and souls of all those who've attended and sense their deep gratitude for the adventure of healing and fun. I had the biggest smile on my face. A vision, a dream, then shortly after, a reality.

Many of our members join the breathwork or Nafas Journeys to heal, stating that they are stressed, anxious, or have panic attacks. A few are seeing therapists for help, while many are taking antidepressants, and the rest are either consuming alcohol or drugs as a means to escape. Going through a difficult time, whether it be a physical or emotional injury, loss of a loved one, death, losing a job, business or investments, is not an easy situation in which to be. Whatever state you may be feeling, I invite you to come back to the breath. Allow the breath to be your guide, measuring how you feel. Taking slow deep breaths while you are calm and relaxed, consciously aware of the inhale and the exhale, will help you be relaxed and focused in times of stress or any tense moment.

In my personal life, having given so much focus to finance, marketing, and sales, the most important parts of life are often forgotten, such as breathing and having fun. Here are five simple tips that have helped me on my journey to use for yours.

1. **Breathe:** Be conscious of your breath, for it controls your state. Take several deep and full breaths throughout the day and be aware that you are not only breathing air but taking in energy, Spirit. Fuel up and hyper-oxygenate your body and mind.

2. **Meditate:** Time with yourself is crucial and important. Starting with five minutes a day and slowly increasing the time when you are ready. With endless benefits, there is no better way to begin your morning.

3. **Manifest:** Be crystal clear of what you want, visualize it, feel it, and even breathe it. And more importantly, believe it. Have trust in a higher power and keep your vibrations high. Sometimes things take time, be patient.

4. **Healthy Lifestyle:** "Let food be thy medicine and medicine be thy food." It all starts with the diet, so make sure your day is full of nourishing foods, lots of water, and daily exercise.

5. **Have fun:** Life is one beautiful journey; enjoy the ride. Don't let yourself be taken by the little things; always keep a positive state of mind. And remember: just breathe!

A transformation doesn't happen overnight, and it doesn't happen on a week-long retreat. It's a lifelong journey. Whether practicing yoga, playing a musical instrument, or learning a new language, three key points will make the experiences fulfilling and richer, allowing you to thrive: focus, commitment, and consistency.

My intention is to set the stage for you to have a glimpse into a higher realm of knowledge, to experience something you've probably never felt before, to awaken parts of you that you never knew existed. Making a positive change in yourself will only inspire you to help change the world. We help others tap into their inner soul, the fire within, to transcend their minds and bodies, become at peace, and live the life for which they are destined. I continue to grow and learn every day, and I believe everyone else should as well.

Walid Aboulnaga co-founded, managed, and ran multiple successful businesses in the Middle East and North Africa with a team of over 1,400 members from 14 different countries. After witnessing and experiencing first-hand the destructive effects of stress, he sensed a need for a deeper connection with our true potential and awareness of our mind, body, and Spirit. As a result, *Nafas Journeys* was launched in 2018, a Transformational Travel Experience helping those embarking on their lifelong journey and quest for self-discovery by bridging adventure with spirituality.

He has trained with some of the most knowledgeable and experienced breath masters, including Shamanic Breathwork under Venus Rising, Stanislov Grof's Holotropic Breathwork, the Wim Hof Method, Breath Mastery with Dan Brule, and many more. Walid is a Certified Shamanic Breathwork Facilitator and Ordained a Shamanic Minister. He is also a member of the Entrepreneur's Organization (EO) for the last nine years and current board member.

Bringing in his experience from the multiple different breathwork techniques, he has led thousands of people across different countries between his Breathwork Workshops & Transformational Retreats. He is an adventurer committed to helping others see their true potential and experience profound transformation by bringing breath awareness and conscious breathing into everyday practices.

He currently lives in Bali with his wife Katrina and three daughters Luna, Skye, and Theia.

~ The key is not to complicate life; live free and simple.

Walid Aboulnaga, Founder NAFAS Journeys

Let's connect and one day breathe together: walid@nafas.life

For videos on Breathwork, Shamanism, our Journeys around the world and more please visit: www.nafas.life/blog

@nafasjourneys

CHAPTER 16

BABY YOU WERE BORN TO BREATHE

Being Initiated by the Greatest Secret in the Universe

Mariko Heart Wolf

MY STORY

Was it a longing from the distant past being answered by destiny?
Or the sacred wound of a lifetime of a broken heart and unworthiness,
acting as a forgiving crack allowing the light to finally shine through?
Was it fragments of a dream being woven together as a tapestry of medicine?
Or the readiness for a breakthrough to the other side to shape shift my world?

Perhaps all of the above. I found myself amidst the majestic Sedona red rocks, with heart-pounding, nestled in a blanket, anticipating the dive into uncharted waters of my first Shamanic Breathwork journey guided by Linda Star Wolf and Brad Collins.

Smiling on the outside, yet somehow that moment, feeling like my six-year-old pigeon-toed self, awkward, without a voice, and feeling like I didn't belong. But sharing the space with Star Wolf and Brad was like being with a kindred soul family, gathering around a warm hearth prepared with love, intention, and meaning. My shoulders and stomach melted and relaxed as I received a deep breath.

DIVINE APPOINTMENT

Star Wolf's words resounded like the heartbeat of the great mother drum, with the voice of truth resonating to every cord in my being. I recognized some of these notes to have come through dreams in years past. "Be with what grows corn," Star Wolf shared, referencing the words of her Seneca Wolf Clan Grandmother Twylah Nitsch. These very words, "Be with what grows corn," were offered in a dream I had 20 years prior by a native elder while we watched a sunrise together atop a mesa. This was the spark that ignited the fire of leaving behind the life I knew in Santa Barbara to venture onward to Sedona. Was I crazy leaving the "ideal job" at the ABC-TV affiliate I aspired a lifetime to achieve as well as uprooting from friends and my energy practice from the home of mountains and sea I so loved? It was a quantum leap of faith into unknown territory. I followed the call in trust that my new life would *grow corn*. The words being delivered by Star Wolf were not only familiar but were connected to the original *voice* that echoed in my dream in a faraway land, yet still reverberating deep within me.

And, during the week leading up to the Shamanic Breathwork weekend, I awoke three mornings in a row with the words *blue star* etched in my mind and heart. Like a new mantra, I repeated the words *blue star* aloud while trying to make sense of its meaning. While living in Sedona, I had come to know the Hopi families living on Second Mesa and related the words *blue star* to the Hopi Blue Star Kachina, the spirit which signifies the coming of the new world by appearing in the form of a blue star. This satisfied my curiosity at the time as it felt like a time of new beginnings. Then my eyes widened while my jaw dropped as soon as Star Wolf mentioned she was to pass on the blue star mystery teachings that were given to her by her Grandmother Twylah. My heart leaped with a wolf howl of elation, knowing that the rivers of our connection ran deep and that something so much greater was being orchestrated—being in this room was by Divine appointment.

I had found *home*.

Star Wolf and Brad shared the breathwork instructions and then opened with an invocation of welcoming the Spirit Keepers of the Four Directions, the Great Above, Sacred Mother Earth, and the Great Within. As Star Wolf drummed and guided us into the journey, "Breathe. . .see you on the other side and back again," she surely meant it. Within the safety of the ceremonial container and Star Wolf's and Brad's loving presences, I free fell into the breath in a way that I had never breathed before, all effort had dissolved, and the breath was breathing me. The evocative tribal music elicited immediate immersion into an extraordinary landscape of direct soul guidance beyond the mind's constructs, logic, conformity, and ego control.

initiation

At that moment, I discovered the breath as the initiation into a deeper reality, as if the greatest of mysteries was now in charge and I was flowing within its direction. Without a thought, my body spontaneously shook, as if being given permission to feel into all the places where I had ever stopped breathing or walled off my heart, and layers of tension were peeling off and being shed from a lifetime of silence. Wild, untamed sounds vibrating through my throat opened pathways I didn't even know existed. This was a far cry from my "quiet, reserved" Japanese upbringing. Within my next breath, I unexpectedly found myself transported to the island of Japan. Unlike watching a movie, I was upfront and center, with the cries of men, women, and children buried amongst the rubble. The atomic bomb had just exploded near Hiroshima, at the foot of my grandma's family home. In disbelief and horror, my head uncontrollably shook from side to side; *Nooo! How could this be? How is it possible for such devastation to be cast upon life?* My heart was like a sinking ship.

The veneer of my frozen tears broke loose, and there was no damning up of the raging river pouring down my cheeks. This decimation was never talked about in our household. And only whispers were caught of my mom and dad, grandparents, aunties, and uncles as Japanese Americans to lose and leave their homes with only one suitcase to live in internment camps from 1942 to 1945. On the surface, I did not feel any emotional repercussion from family members who had undergone this experience. Their conversations were about the community and their friends.

It seemed like a point in history after which life went on in its somehow resilient nature, but perhaps the scars of its impact and aftermath were calling for a miracle release.

And now, this release was happening through every cell, muscle, and fiber of my being. Looking fate straight in the eye sent tidal waves of despair. The oceans of tears flooded through this collective wound. I turned in the direction of my ancestors and dropped to my knees to honor their spirits. I felt their story, their bravery, and their loss. At that moment, time stopped, and I felt the soul of the world at its core—the dark, the light, strength, fragility, vulnerability, fear, and the purity of love that reaches beyond understanding. I wept until becoming a puddle on the ground, being held safely in the arms of Star Wolf and Brad. Instead of pushing the waves of feelings away, feeling into the deep pool was the opener of the way and the tide turned a corner, as did fate. Particles of radiation, thousands of them which appeared as tiny lights, were being extracted and lifted out from my body, leaving my head, neck, shoulders, arms, back, and legs. The places and spaces within—which held generations past—were now being hollowed open to breathe and welcome new forms of life, including waves of forgiveness and unconditioned love. These waves began to cleanse and soften my heart, and I opened my arms to not only return to but receive my humanity.

I was becoming lighter and lighter, and I found myself rocking back and forth in a fetal position. Brad and Star Wolf shape shifted their bodies into a birthing canal, a cosmic portal where I was being *birthed* right then and there on the breathwork floor. A birthing experience is a highly experiential and palpable process that often naturally occurs during breathwork, where one physically and energetically experiences a rebirth. My timeless spirit was propelled forward through time and space, being welcomed like a newborn into this world.

HEART WIDE OPEN

How would it have ever been possible to spread one's wings fully in the light while overcast with such shadow? It's no wonder that leading up to this release, no matter how many years and layers I had consciously worked through in the personal loss of my father with his gambling and disappearance and my mother's sorrow and despair, unresolved grief engulfed my heart. This grief became the medicine that would break my heart wide open to feel into the full spectrum of the dark and the light, including how deeply I loved and cared. I didn't want to care. I wanted to shut down. But the truth was, I did care and wished for all of life to thrive in the fullness of freedom. And now, how could life ever be the same? Following the breathwork, without these denser energies carried in my bones, I grew two inches, walked taller, felt 50 pounds lighter, and the heavy rains which clouded my existence began to lift for the first time. Having delved into the healing arts most of my life, this revelation and soul return was unlike any other.

My sacred calling was illuminated, and all that I had ever collected and embraced in my medicine bag was to be part of this expansive living field of service through Shamanic Breathwork.

The floodgates of heaven had opened new pathways within my soul. My spirit soared with new hope when feeling into the potential of humanity, receiving the opportunity to breathe in this way. *What extraordinary shift is possible for the evolution of love, consciousness, and wisdom upon our planet? What if all of life were to breathe fully? What then?* I immediately hopped on a plane to the Blue Mountains in North Carolina to train, apprentice, master-apprentice with Star Wolf, and the wolf tribe at Venus Rising to offer this sacred work in the world. As Star Wolf teaches, "Our healing is the training."

In childhood, in contrast to the world where much emphasis was on logic and the physical, dreams and intuition were places of refuge where knowing truth was accessible. Dreams brought angels and ancestors who delivered messages along with vivid scenes of the past, present, and future. There was a way of direct revelation that went beyond the structures of this time-space continuum. I often contemplated the possibility of creating conditions to access higher wisdom, truth, extraordinary states of consciousness, and meeting guides and angels. And if so, how could this be shared? Spirit delivered the grace and vehicle to do so through Shamanic Breathwork.

AWAKEṄING THE SHAṀAṄ WİTHİṄ

What I love about Shamanic Breathwork is its nature in being a vehicle for direct experience and that no one is playing the role of healer for another. The healer and shaman are within each of us, and we have access to all resources and medicine within and throughout our universe. However, with conditions such as a safe, sacred space, the presence of the heart, working consciously with the breath and music—the soul is supported in awakening the shaman within. All is possible. *Be ready for miracles.*

Every journey is unique. The soul's medicine is as infinite as the multi-dimensionality we are, and will be delivered in the way, shape, and form, according to where we are in our journey, what is up for us, and what we are ready for. This can include receiving through our senses and feelings, insights, emotional release, transforming core family of origin and collective unconscious patterns, embracing our shadow, communing with our inner beloved, aligning with our sacred purpose, co-creating with the cosmic universe, activating our imaginal cells and destiny, and beyond.

Love is love and is expressed in its infinite wisdom and beauty. There is also something extraordinary and magical that happens in the field of a group! It's as if Divine Intelligence of the *field* takes over and orchestrates the perfect medicine within this super alchemical bubble of transformation for each of the journeyers. Though each soul is on a unique sovereign journey, we are all connected. And one person's release, awareness and connection serves the release, awareness, and connection in each one of us and the entire field.

SHAMANIC MEDICINE OFFERING

Through the privilege of being a journeyer and co-journeyer, I have come to appreciate beyond measure the mystical and magical relationship we share with one of the greatest secrets in the universe, which lives right under our noses!

B-R-E-A-T-H-E

Each of us has inherited this Divine gift, and it is our birthright to realize its treasures.

This medium lives outside of time and space. Yet, its medicine has been known and practiced throughout the ages to initiate soul connection, shine the light of awareness, activate life-altering change, shift, and transformation. This secret is so sacred that we have been initiated into life by its power and mystery. And in our last precious moment, we will be initiated by it into the next phase of our soul's journey. And within every one of our inhales and exhales, we are being initiated through the cycles of change of life, death, and rebirth.

This secret of all secrets is Spirit, the great initiator, alive in our breath.

It's up to us to be conscious of its power and use this wisely.

We may be surrounded by those who love and care about us, but no one else can breathe for us. As a Hopi elder once spoke, "We are the ones we have been waiting for." Perhaps this includes, *"We are the ones we have been breathing for!"*

I have joyously facilitated hundreds of Shamanic Breathwork journeys with thousands of amazing souls. What I have come to learn is this:

If you are here, you are a brave soul! You have chosen to come to this dimensional reality from Infinite Source to have a unique experience, to grow, and to love.

It takes courage to be here and to breathe,
no matter how rough, you are good enough,
to feel, to heal, to be real,
to relieve, conceive, believe,
to release trauma, stories, and life as drama,
to free yourself from a conditioned life of survival,
to see with the eyes of Infinity, a truth revival,
to learn, to teach,
to turn things around when all is a breach,
no longer needing to pretend,
to forgive and to mend,
to embrace the whole, rock 'n roll, return to Soul. . .
you are made of earth and star,
a student of life, an Avatar. . .

here to walk with the dark and the light,
the brightness of day and the soul of night,
and when all is said and done,
you are never alone; you are the Breath of One.

Close your eyes. Make contact with your breath as if saying "hello" to your best friend ever! This friend is a sacred ally, master teacher, healer, guide, and portal to the universal field of all potential and possibility.

Often in life, there are things we must wait for to attend to in the future, like meeting a friend, preparing a meal, turning in an assignment, but we can always tend to our breath in the moment we have now. This is the best day ever to be in the ceremony.

Breathe as you've never breathed before—breathe your trust, breathe the risk of being different, breathe your prayer, breathe what you love, breathe what has meaning, breathe your dreams, breathe your true nature, breathe your sacred purpose, breathe what sustains you, breathe your destiny.

WAKE UP CALL

An old Chinese proverb states, "The way it begins is the way it ends."

How do you spend the very first moment as you awaken in the morning?

Is it reaching for your cell phone?

Perhaps change it up a bit and reach for the breath of all breaths. Recommit.

What do you most value? Our greatest currency of exchange is not money.

Some of our most precious blessings are our attention and our breath.

Where we give our attention and what we breathe life into matters and creates our world.

Whatever is most important to you, breathe it.

For instance, say what is most important to you is "connection with Spirit."

Pause. Close your eyes. Receive a breath.

B-r-e-a-t-h-e your connection with Spirit.

The other morning, it dawned on me that the first four letters "b-r-e-a" in the word "breathe" is in b-real! This can be a reminder that within our breath is our great calling to *be real* and return home to who we are. This includes being real with what is dying, being real with what is living, being real with what is birthing.

YOUR PRECIOUS HEART

Your heart is the first and last frontier. You were born with wings on your heart—the wings of awareness, the wings of feelings, the wings to know and speak your truth, the wings to set your spirit free and soar.

There is nothing within you unworthy of love, mercy, compassion, respect. Offer a breath of love, mercy, compassion, respect for yourself for being here. Offer a breath of love, mercy, compassion, respect for your loved ones for being here. Offer a breath of love, mercy, compassion, respect for your global family, which includes the animals, trees, rivers, mountains, all of Mother Earth, the stars, and the cosmos for being here.

THE SACRED NOW

This is it! This moment. You got this. The New Earth is not somewhere in the future. It is here now, in your very breath.

You were born to dance your Soul song.

Raise your eyes to the skies,

Outstretch your arms to the heavens and earth,

With your heart wide open, give and receive the full love of who you are.

In the beginning, was breath, and the breath was God.

Baby, you were born to breathe.

Mariko Heart Wolf, Certified Shamanic Breathwork Master Practitioner, Ordained Shamanic Minister, Certified Soul Coach, Certified Matrix Energetics Practitioner. She is deeply grateful for the privilege of training and mentoring with Linda Star Wolf, visionary teacher, and originator of Shamanic Breathwork, and to wolf brother Nikolaus Wolf and the Venus Rising family. Since her late teens, she has studied with native teachers and healers from around the world.

Mariko shares a deep respect for personal and global awakening in cultivating love, wisdom, beauty and compassion, and the liberation of heart and soul. She is passionate about transformation and magic, where one has direct access to their own eternal medicine, truth, and shaman within.

She has facilitated hundreds of Shamanic Breathwork journeys with thousands of brave souls in highly experiential deep soul dive initiatory journeys. She is a gifted intuitive, angel guide, and soul midwife with over 40 years of experience in the Holistic Health, Shamanic, and Consciousness fields. Mariko has joyously devoted the past ten years to facilitating Shamanic Breathwork journeys with individuals, families, women's circles, communities, and holistic health centers, including the Sanctuary at Sedona Integrative Mental Health Facility where she offers weekly Shamanic Breathwork journeys as an integral part of holistic recovery.

While relaxing, you will find her hiking on the sunlit red rocks receiving a refreshing breath of life-renewing winds, laughing with her loved ones, enjoying a quantum consciousness book with her two amusing basenji wolf dogs puppy piled on top of her, dancing wildly to native hip hop music, preparing a batch of raw cacao treats, enjoying a great movie, playing with the magic of oracle cards and taking a deep-sea dive into the ocean of Shamanic Breathwork for herself or beloved soul tribe in person and online.

Mariko Heart Wolf is writing a book of consciousness-altering quantum questions to shapeshift your life. Mariko Heart Wolf can be contacted at:

babyyouwereborntobreathe@gmail.com

www.sacredheartmagic.com

CHAPTER 17

NON-ORDINARY RECOVERY

A Shamanic Initiation of Trauma and Healing

Rev. Gail Foss MA, RN, LADC

MY STORY

Every person has moments when they realize they have a choice to make. This moment of clarity marks when their journey begins. They exchange the "I was" for a new "I Am." Their skin splits, and the new bursts forth. This is a shamanic initiation.

My first was at 20 months old. My two sisters and I were taken to St. Michaels, a foster care/orphanage for Catholic girls. Mama and my sisters were silent and frightened. I was alert and curious. I remember the blue spruce in front of the mansion, the smell of baking bread in the hall, and the warmth as we came in from the cold. I screamed and resisted when the stranger pulled me from my mother. Mama collapsed, sobbing, fragile after many shock treatments. Dad was cold and staunch. They took us to a bedroom with large windows, wide sills, and three beds. My sister, Mary Lynn, tried to comfort me and stood me on a windowsill and pointed up. In the dark, clear winter sky was the milky way. I asked, "What is it?" She whispered, "Stars." Wonder replaced pain as I stood with her arms around me and absorbed the beauty. I trusted my sister, and I slept.

My broken heart awakened my spirit. I didn't know it was a safe place or that the routine, stability, and continuity for three years would establish a foundation to survive the chaos of the coming years.

I moved many times after St. Michaels, between parents, states, and neighborhoods. Resilience is the byproduct of love, recognition, and support, given and received, from beyond the circle of suffering. It's in the presence of angels, saints, and next-door neighbors who see and dare to care.

I've come to know that the narrative of suffering, though shocking, is common. More interesting is what wakes us up and causes us to step out, leaving behind the familiar to immerse ourselves into the difficult and extraordinary. I have heard my story of alcoholism, emotional, physical, mental, sexual, and spiritual abuse, tragedy and triumph, abandonment, and deprivation, told in fragments in a thousand recovery rooms, accompanied by a story of gratitude and the golden thread of love that runs through every triumph.

Some extraordinary women have guided my path to healing. Everything that happened was training for my life adventure and my work. I've faced and tamed my monsters, befriended Baba Yaga, delineated mother, maiden, crone, the beauty, and the hag. I carry within me the gold of my quests and powers acquired. I'm a shapeshifter. I've learned to love despite and because of pain. What a trip!

In the middle of my second divorce to a raging alcoholic, I sought ways to heal my children and myself. Churches helped little. I finally collapsed into the arms of Al-Anon. I fell apart so I could separate, authenticate, and integrate the story. I healed, matured, and built a village of strong women to support me. My Al-Anon sponsor said, "You can't undo the past, but you can stop picking the old scabs. Let them heal. Glean the gold in your stories but be more than the story. You're not powerless over your choices now.

Change the trajectory of your life for a different outcome." Here was good news. This initiation left behind a life consumed with battling the snarling beasts and aroused my curiosity to seek a world of healthy possibilities.

I worked hard for three years, and life was better. But I had a secret shadow whispering. I told myself I was okay now; I could drink safely now. Within three months, with a box of wine in the fridge and a restocked liquor cabinet, I was in trouble. I continued Al-Anon, masked. Al-Anon saved me.

Friends and I went to a meeting. It was locked, so we slipped into AA next door. The woman in front of me told her story. A bolt of lightning coursed through me. I fidgeted; my head screamed, *shut up!* Unmasked! I wanted a drink and felt the tension as I tried to compose myself.

Once home, I offered my therapist friend a cup of coffee. I needed to sort this out. I hoped he'd say I wasn't alcoholic. He said, "Look, I'm not saying whether or not you're an alcoholic. I'll just say your story is mighty familiar." He paused. "Let's go to a meeting tomorrow, and see if it resonates." We went into a smokey basement with chairs and a big coffee pot. My palms were sweaty, my voice shaky; I said, "My name is Gail. I'm an Alcoholic." Raw and exposed, I trusted. Pouring the alcohol together felt like ceremony—another initiation. I slept deeply and peacefully.

There was a new alcohol counselor on staff. I chose to trust this coincidence, and Rachel became my first great teacher.

She told me to write, but I didn't know how to put the snarled mess of my inner experience into words. I had vivid dreams and visions between wake and sleep. I used a childhood breathing practice to sleep. She used guided breathwork exercises and verbal questioning to untangle my circuitous thought patterns. I gradually wrote my dreams and visions and shared them with her because I was afraid of madness. She said, "You're not mad. These are metaphors for the traumas you've experienced. Ask them to be clearer." It worked. "Your dreams seem truthful. This is the gift of prophecy, a gift of the Holy Spirit. Your drugs and alcohol suppressed your gifts." She urged me to go to the Caron Foundation for the treatment of childhood trauma and encouraged me to do the training and advanced training. My body, mind, and spirit were strengthening, and my brain was untangling. Rachel was a Certified Spiritual Director and knew I was hungry and thirsty for spiritual knowledge outside the mainstream. She encouraged me to use what worked for me and recommended a breath/prayer exercise.

I went into my closet and breathed as directed, with no expectations. In minutes, the walls disappeared, and everything was light. I was light, held by a being of light filled with love, without shadow. I saw that matter was the illusion, and light was everything. I came out of my closet, changed—another initiation.

When I shared with Rachel, she looked at me, then off into space for a minute, turned back, and said, "I've signed you up for next year's retreat." I asked, "Do I need to give you a deposit?" Her voice softened, and she said, "No. You'll be facilitating." She saw my fear; she looked softly at me and said, "You know recovery, and now you know God. You're an instrument."

At the Spiritual Recovery Retreat, I couldn't imagine someone like me being an instrument. I felt a new current flow through me when I spoke, which emerged as information I'd never known, and hearts opened. From 1989 to 2016, I facilitated one or two 11th-step recovery retreats every year throughout Maine and New England and in the Virgin Islands.

"I'm afraid to go deeper," I said. Rachel looked squarely at me. "I trust your spirit consciousness more than the fears of old religions. Your curiosity is like a divine carrot dangled before you. Follow where it leads."

It led me to attend the four-day Maine Healing Arts Festival for several years and, I did the first of many sweat lodges and fire walks. I attended dozens of trainings and workshops. But meeting Jeannine was the best. She is a traditional healer from northern Maine, a member of the Mi'gmaq people, a substance abuse counselor, and my teacher and friend. I spent many weekends driving the three hours up and back to northern Maine for gatherings, sacred fasts, sweat lodges, and just hanging out.

From 1990 to 2015, I pursued shamanic and mystic studies. My husband Harley and I bought land, built a house, and began to build a retreat center in central Maine. I studied transpersonal psychology, Gestalt expression, psychodrama, expressive therapies, movement, and art therapy. We planned together how we would build this joint business. He'd manage the property and marketing, and I'd be the director of services. I developed a unique shamanic-experiential trauma healing practice. We dreamed a big vision.

In September 1997, he woke with a grand mal seizure, and on March 18 of 1998, he died in my arms at home of Glioblastoma multiforme. It was an excruciating sacred journey and passage. Life as I knew it was over. For the first time in my life, I was alone. Another sacred fucking initiation.

The retreat center became apartments. I managed Harley's business to solvency then sold it. I finished my bachelor's degree, closed my agency for private practice, then hunkered down. Whew!

In 2006 Rachel died of cancer. Grief became the name of the road I trudged. Acceptance with love was the lesson.

I did small ten-woman retreats on my land, including sweat lodges, sacred fasts, shamanic drumming, and journeying. In one retreat, we developed a stone labyrinth. Every time I needed something, a solution came whispered in the night. "Is the snow too deep for a sweat lodge? Do a sacred sauna with rounds. Are oil prices too high? Buy a wood stove." I learned to stretch, evolve, and listen for answers. Harley often came between dream time and waking. A tree fell across my woodland path. "Call Bob."

Bob came with chainsaw and humor. I started laughing. At 58, I fell in love. The wheel of time turned. I made my last mortgage payment and realized I had arrived somewhere. Something was coming. I had a past life memory in ancient Briton as head woman of a learning temple for girls and young women, destroyed by Roman troops. I was spared. The head of our order and the main temple was my sister. I refused consolation and blamed her. Emerging from the regression, I felt deep grief for those lost and for my sister.

I attended a Matri Breath session and felt stirred. It was time to find my village of kindred spirits.

In the spring of 2016, I heard "Gail!" I picked up my phone; the time was 3:33 am. I googled "shaman, breath, recovery." *Venus Rising* popped up. I went into the web page. I saw her face, Linda Star Wolf. A chill spread. *Was this my landing place?* I ordered her book and read it.

I bookmarked the web page. For months I re-examined the material, like reading a newspaper from home. I signed up for notices of events. One day I received a phone call from North Carolina. It had an urgent ring. I said, "Hello?" The voice said, "This is Ruby from Venus Rising. You sent inquiries, and you visited our page. Are you ready to come to S.H.I.P.?"

Was I ready? "Ruby, I need to check my money situation. Can I come in the fall?" "The fall? No, you can't come in the fall. We're not doing it in the fall. If you're meant to come, the money will appear. Not a problem. Call me when you know. We're filling up fast." I went out onto my land to talk to my grandmother trees. Earth spirits whispered excitedly. Grasses caught the breeze and late afternoon light shimmered. *We're going home!* My heart whispered. I wanted to talk to Bob. By the time he arrived, I was clear. "I'm going to a training in North Carolina in two weeks. I have my flight." It was my old friend the carrot calling. The next morning, I called. "I'm coming!" Ruby replied, "Oh good, I saved you a spot. Check your email. I've sent the instructions. Send your itinerary."

From Bangor to Asheville was complicated with big winds. Still, I arrived barely on time in a non-ordinary fashion. Where the trickster blocked me, strangers stepped up and showed me another way. I kept my eye on the carrot and stepped out in faith,

The people there were mostly under fifty. The energy of her space both calmed and excited me. The mountain was spectacular. After being blessed with sage and directed into the temple, I heard a strong, soprano, earthy laugh as Linda and her assistants came in and greeted us. She did a beautiful seven-direction prayer to establish the container. She told her story. I was amazed at how it paralleled mine. Here was a kindred. Her knowledge was greater and more integrated than mine and when she passed the talking stick, the stories told by the healers, therapists, and energy workers humbled me, and I was grateful.

I can tell a good teacher when they lean in wide-eyed and say, "Then what happened?" When I tell my worst behaviors, they say, "Oh, I've done that!" And then laugh and say, "I didn't like the outcome much; it was an awful mess to clean up, but what the hell, it's how I learned." The ordinary never held satisfying answers for me. This is how Linda teaches—humble, real, and not apologetic about the side travels and mistakes she made to learn her lessons. Because it was the exact journey she needed to do what she does.

Next, she spoke of the spiral path and re-experiencing and expanding knowledge at deeper levels. The similarities in our visions and downloads were comforting. Her experiences were more extensive than mine, yet they were cut from the same cloth. This was the school and teacher I was seeking.

The first breathwork session I was furious and trapped in a deep cave, pushing the stone away. My body was not strong enough. I heard Ruby's voice coaxing me, and suddenly the way was clear, I pushed through, wept, and someone comforted me. It was rebirth. A weight fell from me, and I drifted into peace.

When I rode on the back of a dragon in an Icelandic setting, Star Wolf told me that she, too, had ridden the dragon. I took notes in the lectures, but the journeys made me realize how very ancient we all are and who I am. When I shared with her my Briton past life experience and my belief, she was my older sister then, she said there was something in it that felt familiar. It took several more trips to the mountain for me to make full amends for that lifetime.

Some journeys seemed random, others very connected to the information in the lectures that related to my life. In one journey, I was in a giant spaceship headed for earth, another filled with geometric symbols and crystals. There were animal helpers and angelic beings. I even went into a deep place like a void but later had vivid dreams all night. The music was epic and suited to the theme of the day. The mandalas were non-verbal descriptors, and the process-feedback groups integrated the experience through tactile, kinesthetic sensory expression. Witnessing and being witnessed helped give language to the experience while fresh. I returned for four-week facilitator training and shamanic skills development, and shamanic ordination. I attended a four-day writing retreat and completed two yearlong mentorship groups and a yearlong Shakti Rising women empowerment group.

I recently received my master's degree through Venus Rising University, a non-traditional degree accredited through North Carolina State University. I treasure it above any degree I could have. I have sent my advanced clients to her program. I have begun to offer deep shamanic immersion retreats here in Maine. I am designing a new recovery curriculum that brings the science and the mystery together and incorporates Shamanic Breathwork and other practices for a deeper spiritual recovery experience. I'm scheduled to attend an Avalon British Spirituality Retreat with Star Wolf and other shamans.

I am a seasoned professional. Her shamanic teachings and the breathwork as she teaches it are the most complete and comprehensive I've experienced. It is thorough. In many of her teachings of ancient practices, she cites recent scientific validation. She teaches the value of intentional journeying and yet allows each a learning curve and freedom. She believes each person's guidance will get them where they need to go. The music tracks are designed to move through all chakras and have an overlay intended for a specific chakra. Her curriculum is easy to follow and has nuances that carry the learner to increasingly larger circles of wisdom and influence depending on their level of knowledge and practice. Repetition brings newer insights; practice strengthens the gifts and allows the personal nuances. Like a melody played in different genres, still true, but the rhythm changes the dance, and the musician's ability and experience enlarges the hearer's response.

She is the Maestro supreme, and all who learn from her will improve their gifts. I do not imagine I will ever grow tired of learning at her feet.

SHAMANIC MEDICINE OFFERING

What are you afraid of? That is what you must face.

What we can name, we can heal.

Identify the false head chatter that keeps you in a shame bind.

This starts you on the journey of championing your inner wounded child.

This simple exercise breaks down the false narrative.

Take a piece of paper and divide it into three columns marked
LIE, TRUTH, AFFIRMATION

In the first column, write the false names and negative head chatter
until it repeats.

(There will be an end.)

In the second column, marked Truth, write two proofs.

In the third column write an Affirmation about it.

E.g., LIE: "I'm stupid." TRUTH: I graduated college, head of my
department. AFFIRMATION: I am competent, teachable, and capable.

Do this till you have challenged all the lies on the paper.

Then sitting before a mirror as if talking to your inner child, say:

"They said you're stupid, but the truth is you were head of your department and graduated college. You're competent, capable, and teachable."

Go through each one aloud, making eye contact with yourself.

Then make affirmations (I am statements) and put them around your home to remind you of your true magnificence.

I teach four important sacred ceremonies to support the work:

Gratitude and Remorse Ceremonies

Protection

Calling in Abundance

Calling Forth Teachers and a Village

These are free on my YouTube channel (Gail Foss) as well as on my website: elderberryrecovery.com

For further information or upcoming programs, check my website or gail@elderberryrecovery.com

Rev Gail Foss MA, RN, LADC, Reiki Master, Trauma Specialist, Psychodrama Specialist, Certified Shamanic Breathwork Facilitator.

Gail began work in the healing arts in 1970 as an LPN. She used breath as a therapeutic tool in Lamaze breathing and with therapeutic touch in the ICU. In 1979 she completed RN school and continued in Hospice Care with breath and guided meditation to ease peaceful passage. As Nursing Director of the Chemical Dependency Unit, she used it as a technique to quiet the anxiety going with post-acute withdrawal, Drop-In meetings and in Insight Groups. As clinical director of a free-standing treatment program, she introduced daily breath and morning and evening meditations to ease healing. In 1990 after experiencing a workshop in Shamanic techniques, including trance dance and Holotropic Breathwork Gail began to incorporate breathwork and trance dance in her private practice with ACOA groups and at recovery retreats. Gail sought more study of shamanic techniques, which she incorporated in her recovery practice, including shamanic drumming and journeying, Native American indigenous practices, sweat lodges and sacred fasts as well as Akashic record retrieval. She is a Usui Reiki Master. She began training with Venus Rising in 2016 and continues her ongoing association with them. She has a private practice in Bangor, Maine, and at Elderberry Sanctuary in Winterport, Maine, where she also conducts shamanic and recovery retreats and shamanic ceremonies. You can reach Gail at gail@elderberryrecovery.com or her website elderberryrecovery.com.

CHAPTER 18

GRIEF TSUNAMI
LEARNING TO BREATHE UNDERWATER

Edmundo and Kimberlee Lopez,
Shamanic Breathwork Facilitators and Shamanic Ministers

OUR STORY

Kimberlee's Story: With the words, *it is over*, my world dramatically shifted. In the twinkling of an eye, I was in a surreal daze. I felt like I was punched in the gut and that my heart was ripped open. I could not believe this was happening. I lost my breath and felt like I was drowning. I kept saying to myself, *this can't be happening. No!* The life and dreams I'd built with this person were gone.

When I got into my car, I was shaking. I started to cry. *No*, I thought to myself, *I need to hold it together until I can make it home.* I stopped and took a long breath in. I drove home with tears streaming down. I felt like I had shifted into the twilight zone, where time stopped. I was frozen in limbo. My mind couldn't comprehend anything beyond what just happened. Making it into the house, I lay in bed and cried to let out the pain. My body was shaking. I could not stay afloat in the grief. I called a friend. She came over. Although her presence was a comfort, everything she said was just background noise.

Eventually, out of pure exhaustion, I fell to sleep. I welcomed the relief from the pain of my new reality. This loss was the end of a significant relationship in my life. Edmundo and I had integrated our lives, except living together. We met in the dance community, where we both served on the Board of Directors of the Alamo City Swing Revival. We were in a Bible study and went to church together. We did holidays together. Our families and children formed a bond. We were planning on being married. I had been a single mom for nine years, taking care of three kids. Edmundo was my first relationship since my divorce. I was ready to find a life partner, and Edmundo was it. That day Edmundo decided he didn't believe in God anymore, doubted the Christian way of life, and did not see our relationship as a positive one. He was a loner and thought relationships were too complicated. This was not on the radar before! I could see we were going in two different spiritual directions. The relationship was no longer sustainable. Edmundo called it; *it is over.*

The next morning, I woke up. The pain from the day before came flooding back. It was like a nightmare became real. Ugh! Grief so stinks! It felt heavy on my soul and took the breath out of me for days and weeks. It was hard doing day-to-day life because everywhere I turned, Edmundo was not there anymore. Our normal rituals of connection were abruptly gone. Then I had to explain to others what had happened. That was another wound in itself; disclosure of our new status, broken up. This was especially hard for my youngest son, who formed a bond with Edmundo. My emotions were all over the place. I felt like I was drowning in a tsunami of painful grief.

The Holy Spirit began showing me how to breathe underwater in this grief. I just started Shamanic Breathwork in my community. I attended their monthly sessions. I knew I needed help. I was afraid I was going to drown in the heaviness. But God was so faithful. He placed this spiritual tool of Shamanic Breathwork at my feet. I took a leap of faith and jumped into this practice. Little did I know where it would take me and what powerful medicine it would offer me. I was desperate to get better and heal.

Breathwork became another form of prayer for me. It was a way to slow down the mind chatter of all my fears and day-to-day worries. My breath lifted me up into the realm of the spirit. Here, my emotions could be released and given to the God who cared about me. In exchange, the Holy Spirit would pour hope, guidance, and rest into my soul.

In one of my Shamanic Breathwork sessions, God showed me to pray for Edmundo. This was a commitment of three months. The Holy Spirit told me it would help heal my broken heart. It would also keep my heart from becoming hardened, bitter, and full of self-pity. There was no promise of an outcome. Just pray. In my mind, the relationship was over anyway. I was to pray the Bible scripture Ezekiel 36:25-27, which said, *I will sprinkle clean water on you, and you will be clean; I will cleanse you from all our impurities and from all your idols. I will give you a new heart and put a new spirit in you; I will remove from you your heart of stone and give you a heart of flesh. And I will put my Holy Spirit in you and move you to follow my decrees and be careful to keep my ways.*

In another breathwork session, God overwhelmed me with love. He showed me that I was seen and known by Him. He was at my side all the time. Every tear was precious to Him. He collected them in a bottle. That experience inspired me to keep a gratitude journal. Daily, I would write down where I saw God's activity and the things I was grateful for. I began to see God's miracles every day. I began to be more in the present and less in the past or future.

In a different breathwork session, God showed me I needed to breathe often. I did a 30-day challenge for myself. Thirty minutes of breath work daily for 30 days. In this spiritual realm, I was called to release my emotions to the healing presence of God. It was here that He would begin to bring spiritual healing to my broken heart. With each breath, I was breathing in the healing power of the Holy Spirit's love. God showed me specifically how my breath is an umbilical cord to the Holy Spirit. I could see how I was literally breathing in the nourishing breath of God. That was mind-blowing! What a tender loving God.

I continued to attend my Alanon 12-step support group. This fellowship is for family members and friends who have been affected by Alcoholism. The family disease of addiction affected me in my first marriage. I used my group and sponsor to support me through this life change. I worked with my therapist on triggers of loss that came up. I eventually got back to my love of partner dancing in my dance community. I was getting stronger. I was healing and creating a new life with God and without Edmundo. I was going to make it.

After 3 months, I was released from my spiritual commitment to pray for Edmundo. I felt sadness, but not the tsunami size. I was not drowning in grief anymore. I felt peaceful.

Oddly, the very next day, Edmundo rode his bicycle to my neighborhood. I saw him and stopped. "Is there a chance of getting back together?" he said. I told him, "No." God had brought me to a stable place. I was not ready to jump back into an unstable relationship, only to have it abruptly end again. I was setting boundaries for myself. This was growth for me! I encouraged him to seek God to find the answers he was looking for. I was open to meeting up in a few months and reevaluating. He was open to that too.

Later, Edmundo found stability with himself and God. He surrendered his life to Christ as his Lord and Savior. He got into a 12-step Alanon support group. We got back together with a new spiritual foundation. We married. Shortly following our wedding, Edmundo and I spent the entire year of 2019 growing together in our faith by participating in the Shamanic Healing Initiatory Process (SHIP) offered by Linda Star Wolf of Venus Rising. It was magical and birthed our ministry of sharing Shamanic Breathwork with others in our community.

Edmundo's story: For decades, I was raised in a world with little to no spiritual health. I was handed down a protocol of worship rather than a relationship with a God. I worshipped not because I believed, but only because the routine of going to church was expected of me. It was my family's tradition.

When my relationship with Kimberlee ended, I started a list of character traits I sought in myself and my partner. As I wrote out my items, I slowly realized that the traits I coveted in a partner were exactly what Kimberlee offered me. The traits I wrote down for myself brought me out of my comfort zone. I was overwhelmed. I had work to do. *Where do I start? Oh my God. What was I going to do about Kim? Can I get her back?* I went running. I prayed. I breathed to calm down. *Worst case, Kimberlee will not meet with me. But I have to try anyway.* I was drowning in a grief tsunami; the loss of Kim, the loss of who I thought I was, and the loss of not being who I wanted to be. I got on my bicycle and rode to her house. She wasn't home. *This wasn't meant to be.* I rode back to my apartment. On the way out of Kim's neighborhood, I ran into her. *Maybe it was meant to be.* I asked if she would reconsider making another go at our relationship. She said no. *Maybe it wasn't meant to be after all.* She said we could talk about this after the new year. Kimberlee asked, "What will be different this time in this new relationship? How have you changed?"

I threw out several reasons. She responded, "I need action, not words." *Fair enough,* I thought.

I sought out the support of strong spiritual men to mentor me. I got into an Alanon 12-step support group to examine how the disease of addiction had affected me. I saw a Licensed Professional Counselor (LPC) to help me see through the veils covering my past. I attended the Shamanic Healing Initiatory Process that included six Shamanic Breathwork initiations. I began the first initiation in pursuit of Kimberlee. I came back to session numbers two, three, four, five, and six in pursuit of myself. Shadow work had the most powerful impact on me. Shadow work was acceptance of my strengths, needs, past abuse, fears, and behaviors that did not serve me well. I was human. Once I accepted all aspects of myself rather than pretend they were not there, I began to find peace within.

I began to make sense of my past dreams. My life long recurring dreams were about a vigilante's life where I was making wrongs of the world right. In these dreams, I was anonymously changing history, bringing justice, and preventing wrongs. I did this because in the real world, I felt I was utterly afraid, weak, and useless. I was afraid to hear my voice out loud. I was fearful of being judged. My shadow brought me face to face with those characteristics of myself I considered failures.

I should point out that in all of these breath sessions I had a co-journeyer looking over me and holding protective space during the entire time. I also created a safe haven to retreat into should the journey prove more than I could handle at that moment.

It was in a Shamanic Breathwork session when the vision came to me. If I truly loved Kim, I wanted the best for her. God would take care of her and me. For the first time, I let go of Kim and started working strictly on myself. I began working on that list of character traits I wanted to manifest in myself. My conversations became different with God, myself, Kim, and others in my life. Peace was a bigger part of my life. I was handling my financial problems head-on. I was able to see a bright light in my life. I was living a life of gratitude. Meditation, Shamanic Breathwork, and the Holy Spirit were helping me clean up a previously hectic and chaotic life. But this new way of life is not a one-and-done deal. I have to keep breathing, praying, and opening myself up to God daily. By God's grace, Kimberlee and I are beginning to give back what we have been given. We are offering powerful Shamanic Breathwork sessions in our community. We offer this service at Breath of Hope Professional Counseling.

SHAMANIC MEDICINE OFFERING

Here is the medicine that worked for us:

1. Breathe for a minimum of 30 minutes (max 60 min) a day for 30 days. Find a comfortable place for lying down. Set an intention prior to breathwork. If you have chakra attuned music, use that during your breath session. If not, you can use instrumental new-age music. Begin your breathwork by breathing quickly in through the nose and out through the mouth in a cyclic fashion. Do this quickly for about five minutes. Then breath normally. When finished with the session, write an affirmation and draw a picture of a significant piece of the journey. Share your experience with a trusted person.

2. Keep a daily journal. Write things you are grateful for. List where you have seen God or your Higher Power's activity in your day.

3. Get involved in a Shamanic Breathwork community and breathe with them regularly.

4. Attend a SHIP through Venus Rising or another congregation in your community.

5. If you have been affected by the family disease of addiction, get involved in a 12-step fellowship, like Alanon or AA. Find a sponsor and work the 12 steps. Attend at least six meetings before deciding if this community is for you or not.

6. Get a wise mentor or a sponsor to support you in your healing journey.

7. Find a professional therapist that specializes in working with trauma and loss.

Edmundo and **Kimberlee Lopez** live in San Antonio, TX. Kimberlee Daughtry-Lopez founded Breath of Hope Professional Counseling in 2012. Her private practice was voted best private practice in San Antonio for 2018, 2019, 2020 by the San Antonio Awards program. She thoroughly enjoys working with couples and individuals. Her specialties include couple work, using the Gottman Method. Kimberlee has a BS in Elementary Education and a Masters Degree in Counseling. Kimberlee is a Licensed Professional Counselor Supervisor (LPC-S). She is certified in EMDR and is a Registered Play Therapist (RPT), concentrating in sand tray therapy. Edmundo Lopez has a BS in Electrical Engineering. He is currently a technical sales consultant with AT&T. Edmundo and Kimberlee are trained as Reiki practitioners, Shamanic Ministers, and Shamanic Breathwork Facilitators. They offer their services at Breath of Hope Professional Counseling in San Antonio, TX. Visit https://breathofhopecounseling.com to learn more about the services offered.

Edmundo and Kimberlee love partner dancing, hanging out with family and friends, watching a good mini-series, cooking and eating delicious foods, reading, studying the Bible, and working on home projects.

CHAPTER 19

JUMPING INTO FIRE

ELEMENTAL ALCHEMY

Lisa Asvestas

MY STORY

The autumn waxing moon illuminates the live oak and juniper trees that make up the Texas hill country while shining light on the white stones that shape the awe-inspiring labyrinth we women have centered ourselves in. The heartbeat of the buffalo drum and our voices fill the air.

"May this labyrinth bring healing to me, my family, and my community," the intention and prayer for my sister's creation flow in words from our hearts.

We pray with song, "Mother, I feel you under my feet, Mother I hear your heartbeat."

We pray with gratitude, "Thank you, ancestors ... thank you life-giving waters."

We pray for ourselves, our families, our communities, and we pray for the children, "May our bodies be healthy, and our minds and hearts be in peace and joy."

The cleansing scent of copal and a sense of calmness fill the air. *There is no hurry* feels like a collective sentiment. In rhythm, we share and listen to one another.

"How long have you been on your spiritual path?" One of my sisters asks.

"When did this become your life?" I am surprised when I hear myself say almost as a question, "Hmm, six years ago?"

I recognize I'm now present in this moment of bliss because the last six years of my journey taught me the shamanic language of elemental alchemy. I'm grateful to be here; I silently thank myself for saying yes to this divine invitation.

Through the lens of elemental alchemy, we see that as the natural world around us, we too are beings made of water, earth, fire, spirit, and air. Just as nature is in cycles of transformation, so are we. Transformation can be messy, chaotic, and terrifying. It can also be regenerative, powerful, and joyful. We are made for change. It is written in the spiral of our DNA. Understanding the language of the elements allows us to identify where in the cycle of transformation we are, helping us move through our lives with greater awareness.

My story of elemental alchemy began six years ago on an early summer morning. In my sunny, spacious bedroom, painted the perfect shade of blue, I lay in my bed, eyes closed, listening to the morning routine sounds of my husband of over two decades. I am in love with the wrought iron forged into vines that make up my bed. I love all the colors, art, furniture, and tapestries I have chosen. I have poured my love and attention into my beautiful home on top of the hill. As my husband leaves for work, the front door slams with such force, the whole house shakes. My body comes alive with tension. A sinking feeling enters my stomach, and my con-grams (the programs we inherit from family, lineage, culture, religion, mythologies, ethics, decisions. . .those that do not serve our highest good) take off running, down their well-trodden tracks. My mind teeters and totters in co-dependency. *I can fix this! What am I doing wrong? I can't do this anymore!*

Looking back on this time, I recognize that elementally I am overly attached to the water cycle in my relationship with my husband. I have been running this racket for a long time without any way of knowing. At the time, I did not have the language. In shamanism, water can be a beautiful element to immerse in. The cycle of water has the attributes of trust, dreaming, nurturing, and resting. We all enter this world through the waters of our mother's womb, ideally a safe space in the dark where all our needs are met. Water in excess can be dissociation, confusion, numbing, and depression. I learned how to dissociate early in life. When I entered this world, my parents were teenagers, and they suffered ancestral lineage trauma of physical and emotional abuse, addiction, co-dependency, and depression. All this I inherited. As a child, I did not feel safe. At age 11, I discovered alcohol, a highly effective way to dissociate. I put on my perfect shade of co-dependency, and I tap danced and performed my way into adulthood; this did not allow for healthy boundaries. The need to be seen as good to feel love dictated my life. I cultivated an efficient way of checking out, all while smiling.

In aspects of my marriage, I oscillated between the elements of water and earth. At times I felt squeezed, uncomfortable, stuck. These are attributes of the earth cycle showing up in my life. Experiencing the earth cycle is necessary for alchemy. Focus, groundedness, planning, stability are attributes of how the earth cycle can show up. How we do the earth cycle determines the quality of the foundation of our creations. The negative characteristics of the earth cycle - anxiety, indecision, co-dependency, stagnation, crises, deterioration happen when we stay in the earth cycle too long.

When the door slams that early summer morning, my waters break, and my body floods with emotion and pain. I sob and heave, all while wallowing in my stories. To relieve my suffering, I mindlessly scroll on social media (an alarmingly captivating way of dissociation). A friend's post on the beach catches my eye. *I want to be in the ocean right now.* The ocean has always gifted me with a sense of peace. *I want to be away from all this pain.* With surprising certainty, I check flights and my calendar. I become increasingly frantic as I look at the following week and realize that it will not work; two weeks seems too far away. I have a novel idea - *what about today? What about now?* I search, and to my astonishment, I find a flight that leaves in two hours. I book it! With excitement and fear, I pack my backpack and am out the door. The same door that started it all this morning.

Before sunset, I am in Tulum, Mexico, a sacred space on the magical Caribbean sea. I rush into the warm waters, my salty tears mixing with the ocean feels like a homecoming. The waters cleanse me, and for the first time in a long while, a sense of calm floods my body. As the sun sets, Grandmother Moon greets me in her fullness. Sitting on my knees in the sand, I fill my belly with deep, rhythmic breaths. I listen to the sound of the ocean. With clear awareness, I witness my mind begin to retrieve my con-grams. In this moment of clarity, through the roar of the waves, I hear a voice, *Stop, no more! What does staying in your marriage look and feel like?* I can see! I see my future life in front of me. It feels familiar, predictable and by western linear standards, it looks successful. My mind says, *don't be selfish. It's enough.* I hear, *You have a choice, go back to your marriage, and make a vow never to be stuck in these stories again.* The familiar sinking feeling enters my stomach. *Or.* I suck in my breath and peer into a parallel version of my future. All I see is black! "I don't know what's out there," I gasp. "I am so scared!" To this, Grandmother Moon says in the most soothing voice, "And it is okay." As I exhale, I feel a deep sadness for what is coming to an end, and at the same time, a curiosity, a new sensation stirs in my heart. A whisper of longing. With this, I jump into the fire! Death is finally here.

The dissolving of my marriage is brutal, and the effects ripple through me, my family, and my community. When the divorce is final, I think, *all is good. I made it through!* I continue with my career as a restauranteur, business as usual. *This is what you have always done; keep it up, do more of it. Show everyone how good you are.* Creative energy in action, passion, momentum, and proper use of will are all aspects of fire. The negative aspects of the fire cycle are addiction to drama and adrenaline, burnout, impulsivity, and workaholism. I am unaware that my creative energy is in the confines of linear thinking and driven by my con-grams.

Until one day, out of the south, I receive an invitation to the Pyramids of Teotihuacan, Mexico, for a week-long shamanic retreat. I say yes! I am curious about shamanism, and time away from my self prescribed busy life seems perfect. In Teotihuacan, standing on the Pyramid of Quetzalcoatl, breathing deep, staring into the eyes of the feathered serpent, a prayer emerges from my heart, *Guide me feathered serpent, take me into the darkness, take me within myself, wherever I must go to heal and to be free.* That evening, I experience my first Shamanic Breathwork. I hear a crystal clear voice, *you are frayed, you are tattered, you don't know who you are.* It is a surreal moment, and I feel the truth of it in my bones. I surrender. This is the element of spirit on the shamanic elemental path. I feel spirit/love as surrender, forgiveness, humility, and grace. My heart opens, and I am curious as a wolf pup about shamanism, Shamanic Breathwork, ceremony, ritual, initiation, and most delightful, I am curious about myself. *Who am I, and why am I here?*

The next few years are a spiral of quickened transformation by elemental alchemy. First, I find my community in the Blue Ridge Mountains of North Carolina, home of Venus Rising. I soak in the shamanic language and teachings. It is here that I experience feeling seen, heard, and cared for in a community. Then, I follow my heart to Egypt with Star Wolf, Nikolaus, and many of the writers in this book. I am initiated in the Temples of Isis and Sekhmet. I experience a shamanic journey through Peru's Sacred Valley. In ritual and ceremony, I connect to the wisdom and power of the indigenous healers and the Andean Mountains. Soon after, I find myself on a small boat, heading deep into the Amazon jungle. It is here that I receive the powerful medicine of Ayahuasca and the Shipibo healers.

On the last day of 2018, in Ubud Bali, I step into the next higher version of myself. I am ordained as a Shamanic Minister and Shamanic Breathwork Facilitator by Star Wolf. I am in air!

Air is the element of celebration, deep release, connection to the bigger picture, and the energy of the archetypes and myths. I have made it through the elements! Where I quickly receive the medicine of cosmic humor, *there is no end.*

Becoming aware of how I embody and journey through the elements has become a powerful navigation tool for my life. We all continue to move through the elements of transformation. Sometimes we are dancing, sometimes we are "kicking and screaming," as Star Wolf likes to say.

I, and now you, have shamanic language, the language of elemental alchemy. Knowing the map of elemental alchemy and where you are on the map allows your evolutionary transformation process to flow. A cosmic surprise of dancing the shamanic spiral path is synchronicity. Synchronicity and flow continue to show up as I transform with awareness and align my words and actions to my sacred purpose, just as it did on this cool autumn night under the waxing moon. It had been six years since I chose to jump into the fire. As we close our ceremony, I hear the voice that first spoke to me under the night sky in Tulum, *You are on your path.* I am remembering who I am, why I am here, and how to be in this world. *Thank you, Pachamama, for this dance, and thank you, Grandmother Moon, for shining light on my spiral path.*

SHAMANIC MEDICINE OFFERING

Gratitude! Being grateful. Throughout the day, make time to pause, take a deep breath, or even better, many deep breaths, and say out loud or to yourself what you are grateful for. This is the best medicine.

A personal power hour: Set aside at least an hour each day for you. During this time, unplug from all disturbances and allow yourself to be in whatever you have found that lights you up, brings you joy, relaxes, or energizes you. This is different for everyone and may be different on different days. Ideally, part of this time is physical movement. For me, this may be a combination of yoga, breathwork, and meditation.

What a power hour might include:

Meditation (I like Sam Harris' Wake Up app), drumming, playing a musical instrument, singing (great for opening the throat chakra), practicing breathwork (shamanic, kundalini, Wimhof, Ayurvedic, etc.), hot baths, cold plunges, writing, listening to music, dancing, yoga, gardening, walking, running, exercising, etc. Remember, it must light you up.

Once a week: Unplug for 4 to 24 hours

Turn off the cell phone, internet, and television. This is a time to be in nature as much as possible. When we unplug and immerse ourselves in nature, nature informs us. Long walks in nature with my beloved four-legged Molly are good medicine for me.

Create experiences of catharsis, ecstasis, and communitas. (Jamie Wheal-Stealing Fire)

Catharsis: We need cathartic releases to move stuck emotions through our energetic bodies. This can be in the form of crying, screaming, shaking, vomiting, laughing, or any way the body wants to move. Shamanic Breathwork can create a safe sacred container for cathartic release. Some other ways to experience catharsis can be through bodywork, making love, plant medicine ceremony, and authentic sharing from an open heart.

Ecstasis: We are meant to experience ecstasis in our life. Ecstasy, rapture, bliss, peace, and joy are part of our nature; this is our air. The experience of ecstasis can happen during Shamanic Breathwork. It can also occur while singing, dancing, drumming, praying, etc., especially when practiced as a community. Find ways in your life to experience your air!

Communitas: We need and long for community. For me, communitas is a conscious community that practices elemental alchemy and feels a profound response-ability to come together to heal the personal and the collective as within, so without. Our strength and sovereignty come from our shared experiences of catharsis and ecstasis.

Find or create your conscious community!

As Star Wolf likes to say, "Always stop for beauty, love, and magic."

In Peace and Joy,

Lisa Rochelle Rocha Asvestas Hawkmet

Lisa is a Shamanic Breathwork Facilitator, Shamanic Minister, founder of Third Eye Tribe Non-Profit, and steward of Spiral Dance Ranch. Third Eye Tribe's mission is to create a conscious community in South Texas and beyond. Lisa facilitates Shamanic Breathwork journeys, Shamanic Healing Initiatory Process (S.H.I.P.) retreat weekends, Women's circles and retreats, and sacred plant medicine ceremony in San Antonio, Texas, and in the canyons of Spiral Dance Ranch, a retreat center dedicated to healing humanity.

Consciously and unconsciously, Lisa's soul has guided her to seek out initiation. Her shamanic heart has led her to the Temples and Pyramids of Egypt; The Pyramids of Teotihuacan, Mexico, The Sacred Valley, and the Amazon jungles of Peru, Bali, Iceland, and the Blue Ridge Mountains of North Carolina.

Lisa is a seeker of knowledge and continues on her personal soul journey guided by teachers, ancestors, and spirit guides. Her teachers include Linda Starwolf, Kuauhtli Vasquez, the Temple of the Way of Light, the Shipibo healers of Peru, and Jamie Wheal. Lisa's Calling (Infinite Concern) is people experiencing peace and joy. She teaches from her heart all that has been shared with her, and she is passionate about creating a safe, sacred space for her community to feel seen, heard, and cared for. She is the mother of three (Dinero, Demi & Jonah) and has been a San Antonio-based restauranteur for over 20 years (The Cove).

www.thirdeyetribe.org

www.instagram.com/thirdeyetribetx/

www.facebook.com/thirdeyetribetx

CHAPTER 20

LIVING IN WHOLENESS
Uniting a Fractured Self

Keith Caplin

"Let go of who you think you're supposed to be; embrace who you are."

~Brené Brown

MY STORY

Tired, fatigued, frustrated, and unfulfilled were the feelings I was having. Feelings very uncommon for me to be experiencing. Typically, I'm a pretty upbeat and optimistic kind of guy. I found myself asking, *where are these feelings coming from? I'm eating well, I'm exercising and getting outside, I'm sleeping well, I am enjoying my work, the relationships with my friends and family all seem to be going well, so why am I feeling this way?* I thought through all the obvious things, but still, there were no answers; ugh. Normally, when faced with some challenges, I can "intellectualize" myself out of them, but not this time, so let's dig a little deeper. Even when I'm rationally working through a process, I'm keenly aware of my spiritual practices and looking at the bigger picture, and owning my part in the drama that is playing out. This time was different because there wasn't any drama. It was all about me and how I was feeling in my life. Creating time to sit and go a little deeper was needed. Some Shamanic Breathwork and time in nature were just what the doctor ordered to get to the root of what was ailing me.

Imagine seeing your life as a shattered mirror, each piece a reflection of you, but at the same time separate from the others. At that moment, the answer became quite clear as to where all the feelings were coming from. Every day with each encounter I had, I needed to decide which version of me was going to show up at that moment. At the time, I had many lives I was living simultaneously. I had my professional life as a high school Earth and Space Science and Biology teacher. I had my life that interacted with my family, I had the life of a gay man, and I had my life that connected with the world spiritually. Some of these "selves" crossed, but for the most part, they were separate beings. In that moment of me asking for some clarity, I saw all of the shards of my mirror float up and rearrange themselves into one whole complete mirror. In that whole mirror, I saw one image of myself, whole and complete. In the background of my reflection, I saw all the aspects of my life I'd unconsciously and consciously worked so hard to keep separate, happily coexisting in one life.

It became very clear what I was doing and the energy I was using to keep aspects of my life separate because I felt I needed to. Somewhere along my path, I decided that those parts of myself could not coexist and needed to be separate. I asked myself: *How can I show up in all aspects of my life completely as myself? How do I show up in a public high school science class as a spiritually-minded person and still teach good science? How do I engage with friends and family that do not have the same way of being in the world?* It all seemed so overwhelming and, in the same breath, so easy. Just 'show up' was the answer that boomed in my consciousness.

In a rush of thoughts and feelings, I was immediately struggling. In my mind, all sorts of questions were flying around. *How do I do it? What will it look like?* And the biggest of them all—*What if people don't accept me?* That was when the fear tsunami crashed the shores and almost swept me away, but then I remembered why I was on this journey in the first place, I didn't like how I was feeling, and I wanted to discover why. Well, I now had my "why," and I had a choice to make: stick with what I was doing and keep feeling the way I was feeling or do something different. The answer was clear but let me tell you, that fear of not being accepted was crippling.

So, I had my answer about the source of the feelings that started me on this journey in the first place. I was fractured, and I was spending so much energy keeping these "selves" separate that I was living in a state of perpetual depletion. In my head, all I kept hearing was: *How are you going to do this,* and *if you do, they will never accept you.* Baby steps, just take baby steps. I needed to take my own advice about being presented with a seemingly impossible task and just take it one step at a time. I just needed to take the first step toward the goal and then let momentum keep me moving.

Uniting a fractured self, let's do it. I took a weekend to go up to Sedona to spend some time among the red rocks to gain some clarity and grounding. I hiked out to one of my favorite spots that offered big views of the sweeping red rocks with a river of green cutting through them in a vast valley. *Nothing but opportunity lies in front of me,* I thought to myself. *The gains from uniting these parts would outweigh the fear that I'm feeling.* I kept telling myself this as I walked to my spot. With the sun on my back and the breeze flowing around me, I just surrendered to being shown how to do this. *Just be fully you always,* was what I heard quite clearly. Great, so now the hard part, how do I do that?

The main fracture I created was showing up in all aspects of my life as a spiritual being, allowing myself to fully engage in all areas of my life from that perspective as I knew it. Incorporating those practices in my professional life as well as my personal life because the one thing I knew for sure was that my job did feed my soul. However, I was not allowing myself to fully connect to my job because of my beliefs about what it should look like. So, what could I do to bridge that gap? How can I show up as my authentic self and walk with feet in both worlds? I teach high school science, which is truly the minor part of my job. Not only am I a teacher, but I also serve as a mentor, friend, counselor, role model, and so much more to the students I interact with.

I just decided to take the plunge. In my homeroom class, I started talking about meditation and mindfulness. I started doing what we began to call "meditation Monday," where I would do some form of meditation, be it a sound session with bowls and gongs to guided imagery, and I even brought in the form of breathwork. The students, after some resistance, really enjoyed it and looked forward to it. They would share stories of how they would do the practices at other times during the day to help them focus or relax, whether it was before a test or dealing with some issue at home. I started to openly talk about it with other staff members as well, which was very well received. Some of them even came to the regular sound healing sessions I facilitate for my private clients because they saw the benefits of the practice. It was happening!

Before I knew it all, that feeling of fatigue and frustration fell away without me even realizing it. It took me to stop and look to see where I was, and when I did, I realized I felt whole. All of the other fractures united just because I said "yes" to fully showing up in my life in all areas. The other fractures I was feeling were minor compared to the living in my spiritual wholeness, so when that one was addressed, the others just fell into place without me having to directly address them.

Being able to fully accept all aspects of who I am and allow myself the freedom to find a way to express that in all areas of my life was powerful. Years later, I still run into past students that thank me for what they learned from me. I often ask what it was they learned. Often the response from those past students is that they learned to listen to themselves and live their life because of how I showed up for them. What better validation could someone ask for? I often hear people say that they cannot be "spiritual" in their corporate world, and I can understand that statement because people often view what "being spiritual" means. I understand that you can't walk into a board meeting waving a burning bundle of sage; I mean, you need to know your audience, but my challenge would be to find those ways you can show up to live in wholeness in all areas of your life. This may take some creativity, but it has been my experience that it isn't about the "stuff," but more about how you show up—physically, mentally, emotionally, and spiritually—and are you willing to show up wholly with all parts to the party that is your life?

SHAMANIC MEDICINE OFFERING

So, you want to live in wholeness? All I can offer to you is what has worked for me. The first thing I needed to do was toss out what I thought living in wholeness looked like.

I discovered I was trying to live a life based on what other people told me wholeness looked like. I took on their idea as my own, which I later discovered led to some of the fracturings I experienced. What I needed to do was discover and decide what my living in wholeness would look like and then act in a way that would create that. Easier said than done.

In my work facilitating Vibrational Energetic Resets using different sounds, Shamanic Journeywork, and Shamanic Breathwork, the easy part is the session. What we do with the wisdom we gain is where the work begins. How do we integrate what we receive into our lives in a way that brings about the change we are seeking?

I'd like to share with you a practice I have found helpful for me. It can be used to help identify where fractures may have been created in your life, as well as areas of your life where you are not living in a way that supports your wholeness. I can provide a framework for basic practice, and my encouragement is that you take that framework and work it to make it yours. In my experience, a "tool" seems to work better when it is tweaked to better suit your specific needs. What I'm going to share would be the first step in creating a life where you honor yourself and begin the process of living in wholeness.

For this practice, you will need a drum and some type of incense or loose herb to burn to create a sacred space, as well as a journal to write down whatever may come up for you.

For me, I like to work in nature but find a place where you can sit undisturbed for a while. Remember that the point of this exercise is to get out of your thinking mind and allow yourself to sink into your heart space and permit yourself to feel what needs to be felt about where you may have created a fractured self. Set the intention to see where, how, and more importantly, why these fractures were created. Also, to help understand why you felt you needed to create them to survive. Create a container to hold the work you are going to be doing. This can be done by burning some sage or other aromatic plant, calling on directions, whatever that looks like for you. The point is to create a space where you feel protected and can let go and allow guidance to flow without judgment. Think of this as a journey to discover separate selves that you may have created. Play your drum and allow the beat to connect with your heartbeat as well as the heartbeat of the planet and even as far as the heartbeat of the Universe. Focus on your breathing. Deeply inhale and fully exhale. Repeat this process for a few cycles. Allow your mind to soften as you set the intention to see fractures that you may have created in your life. Call in any guidance from allies or spirit teachers in this quest and ask for them to show you what needs to be seen.

Find yourself just drifting into an altered space and allow the landscape to shift, transporting you to another place. Allow the images to just flow freely, without judgment or analysis. Notice how you are feeling. Sometimes the wisdom we seek does not show itself in images but instead makes itself known with our other senses. Fully engage in this space. Ask questions like "Where do I live a fractured life?" or "Why did I feel like I needed to create fractures?" However you ask, remember you are seeking where in your life that you may not be living in a fully authentic way. Try staying in this space, consciously engaged but still allowing things to flow freely, for 15 to 20 minutes. At the end of the session, take a moment to thank your helping spirits and the space for the wisdom and guidance shared with you. Allow yourself to drift back fully and completely to the current time and space with the full recall of what was shared. While still in this semi-meditative state of mind, take out your journal and allow for free writing of what was revealed to you. Take note of any images that stood out, any feelings that were present, any voices that you may have noticed that were not yours. The point is to just write unedited and without judgment. Also, be aware of any big "Aha" moments. All of these can help you to identify where you may have created fractured selves. The big question to ask after doing journaling, and you may want to go back to this after taking a step away, is, "Where in my life am I living in a way that is not in wholeness?"

Identifying where these fractures may exist is the first step in bringing them back into wholeness. This can be seen as the road map of the journey you are just beginning. Like any epic road trip, there is nothing but openness and possibilities that lie ahead. Even with the occasional speed bump or pothole that may show up, this epic journey will still move forward. The question you should ask is, "Do I want to be a driver or a passenger on this epic journey?"

Keith has always found himself to be a student by nature and a teacher at heart. The natural world has always been an inspiration to that learning. Finding and maintaining a balance between the worlds has always been important to Keith, and helping others find theirs is his passion. Keith is a high school science teacher and a certified wellness coach and fitness instructor. Keith is also a Shamanic Breathwork Facilitator and Shamanic Minister with Venus Rising Association for Transformation. He has been facilitating Vibrational/Sound Healing meditations and group Shamanic Journeys, Shamanic Breathwork, and Taking Circles throughout Phoenix for over 15 years. Keith believes in walking his talk and uses these practices and a variety of energy work in his personal development. Keith believes strongly in the power of community and strives to create a sacred space to develop in all of his sessions. Keith also knows that maintaining a balance between your spiritual, mental, and physical health is vital and facilitates spiritually centered hiking in the Phoenix area. Keith believes that living a spiritually connected life is achievable by everyone. He believes that if what you are doing in your everyday life is not feeding your soul, then look at doing things differently.

CHAPTER 21

EMBODIED CREATRIX

Magnetize Your Deepest Desires with Pleasure and Ease

Laura Wolf

Hello Gorgeous,

You are the most delicious, potent, amazing, creative Goddess walking this Earth. You are deeply woven with all of creation. You are creation itself, my love. There is nothing you need to do. Simply soften. As you drop the layers of patriarchal conditioning and the constant pressure to get stuff done, as you let go of controlling, directing, and striving, and as you learn to soften, open, and surrender, your magnificence and your creative power will blossom, magnetizing your deepest desires with pleasure and ease.

MY STORY

One chilly evening in November 2015, a few months after we moved in together, my fiancé came home and handed me his iPhone. Looking down at the phone, I saw a picture of him lying in a pile of red and orange autumn leaves with a beautiful young woman lying next to him, her long, shiny, red hair splayed out all around them. He had a dreamy, almost drunk look in his eyes. My voice shook as I quietly asked the question I already knew the answer to, "Are you in love with her?"

I made the next three months a living hell for myself as we continued cohabitating. I begged him to cut off contact with her, tried to shame and control him into going into therapy with me, and cried every day, praying that he would come to his senses. None of which worked, of course.

After he moved out, I lay on the floor in the middle of a Shamanic Breathwork journey, sobbing my guts out as tsunami waves of grief ravaged my body. I felt broken, ashamed, pathetic. *How did I create this*, I wondered? *What's wrong with me? If I can't keep a relationship together, what right do I have to teach, facilitate, or lead?* The loss of that relationship and everything it had meant rocked me to my core and deeply shook my belief in myself.

Not only was my heart in a million pieces as I lay there on the floor, but in my early 40's my body was already giving out on me. Every inch of my spine ached. My shoulders, neck, and jaw throbbed with tension. I had brain fog most days and couldn't think straight. And I was so exhausted I could barely get up off the floor. My body simply wouldn't let me.

In that Shamanic Breathwork journey, I called out to the Goddess, *Mother, help me, please! I can't go on this way.* Through Shamanic Breathwork, and many years of studying Goddess lore, I had gradually developed a deep and reliable relationship with the Divine Feminine as my primary source of guidance.

Yes, my daughter, the Goddess whispered to my soul. *You are right. You cannot go on this way. It's time to surrender, my darling. Just. Let. Go.*

I had been making my living as a Shamanic Breathwork Facilitator and coach in Kansas for several years at that point. I loved my work, but like many women called to a life of service, I pushed myself too hard. As a single mom and soul-driven entrepreneur dedicated to empowering others, I seldom stopped. I saw clients during the day while my son, Ryland, went to school. After school, we went to soccer and then did dinner, dishes, homework, bath, and read bedtime stories together. After Ryland went to bed, I took online classes to learn how to grow my soul-centered business. I often worked on my computer until midnight, and then I was too wired from staring at screens to go to sleep.

I felt anxious a lot of the time, got sick every couple of months, and my sex drive had all but vanished. I had too much stress and tension built up in my body to relax into lovemaking. I later learned that biologically speaking, it's much harder for women to feel turned on when we feel stressed and depleted.

In the aftermath of the breakup, I went to a naturopath who took one look at my bloodwork and said, "You're burnt out. You've been running on adrenaline for too long, and it's ravaging your body." She was right. I seriously needed to slow down and learn new ways of being and doing.

The day after that Shamanic Breathwork journey in which I called out to the Goddess for help, as if in answer to my prayer, a friend forwarded an email to me about a course on womb wisdom and the natural rhythms of women's bodies. I immediately knew I needed to sign up for that course. I spent the next several years studying feminine embodiment, womb wisdom, tantra, and the specific ways the female body is designed to channel energy differently than the male body.

Understanding Energy in the Feminine Body

Did you know that the feminine body is not designed to go and do all the time? I certainly didn't. It turns out that constant output of energy drains and exhausts women, and then we shut down and become brittle, anxious, depressed, sick, resentful, or "bitchy." It takes a toll on our sex drive, too. We can't fully receive abundance, love, intimacy, or surrender into deeply satisfying orgasms when we hold stress and armor in our bodies and constantly output our energy.

We live in a patriarchal culture that conditions us to work hard, over-schedule, push through, consume, and stay plugged in at all times. It promotes profit and productivity at all costs. It does not value rest, relaxation, rejuvenation, women's natural cycles, or women's bodies – except as they pertain to the sexual pleasure of men. Our American narrative has been telling us for 200 years: *If you work hard, you can accomplish anything. If you don't work hard, you are lazy and undeserving.* Many of us internalized that message as an inner drill sergeant living in our heads, constantly telling us that we aren't doing enough.

Contemporary empowered women tend to feel like we must do it all: career, relationship, kids, friends, working out, eating healthy, email, texts, social media, caring for aging parents, and trying to stay sane amidst all the negativity happening in this crazy world. The problem is that this lifestyle puts women into a state of adrenaline-driven depletion, overwhelm, and imbalance. We often function in a low-grade state of fight-or-flight without even realizing it.

When we keep ourselves in that constant output of energy, we fry our nervous systems, leading to adrenal shutdown, hormonal imbalances, chronic fatigue, joint pain, digestive problems, and a host of other auto-immune and inflammatory diseases. We end up feeling anxious, overwhelmed, depressed, depleted, disconnected, and too-tired-to-have-sex.

Does any of this feel familiar to you? If you've been working hard all your life to make shit happen and you're damn good at it, but you're getting sick and tired of living this way, you're in the perfect place to start learning about how to create from your feminine essence.

What do I mean by feminine essence? I'm talking about the expression of energy, not gender identity. Healthy feminine, or yin, expression of energy is soft, spacious, flowing, receptive, intuitive, emotional, and surrendered. Healthy masculine, or yang, expression of energy is penetrative, forward-moving, structured, solid, linear, directive, active, rational, and goal-oriented.

We all have feminine and masculine (yin and yang) energies and capacities within us regardless of gender identity or sexual preference. Neither expression of energy is good nor bad – they're just different. Ideally, we want to consciously choose which energy will best serve the present moment and easily shift gears to express different energy in a new moment. This does not imply that the feminine is not also powerful, intense, deep, and capable – she most certainly is! We are all everything, one with all of creation. I'm referring to the practical ability to access all parts of yourself at will, moment by moment – as opposed to the habitual, tense, anxious, armored ways that women often exist in our bodies to survive and achieve.

A woman operating primarily from her masculine capacities tends to live in her head a lot—always analyzing situations and thinking about what needs to get done—and has difficulty quieting her mind and enjoying the present moment. She holds excess buzzy energy and tension in her head, jaw, neck, shoulders, and back and often has a fair amount of protection around her heart and womb, which she may or may not be conscious of. Because of this unconscious shielding, she's sometimes perceived as distant, aloof, or unapproachable. She longs to feel more connected with others but also fears getting close to others.

She generally seems very confident and capable and exudes an energy of: *I can do it. I don't need help. I've got this* (and sometimes, *Get out of my way!)* Described as intimidating, intense, or a badass by colleagues and acquaintances, she's usually in charge of everyone and everything in her life. She secretly believes it's easier to do it herself because other people will mess it up anyway and frequently feels frustrated or disappointed in others for their low standards or sloppy work. She worries that if she stops working hard all the time, everything will fall apart, or she will not achieve her professional or financial goals.

This constant output of her energy causes her to feel energetically depleted over time. The demands she puts on herself and the accumulated tension in her body get in the way of her being able to feel relaxed and open to intimate connection. She would like to have more sex, but life is just so damn full all the time.

All that tension, stress, and striving makes a woman's body dense and contracted, preventing life, love, and happiness from freely flowing through her entire system. Your feminine body holds the keys to absolutely everything you desire to create. But creation can't move through you with ease if your body is tense and depleted. It's just physics. Creation has a harder time moving through a tight vessel.

In my women's mystery school, Embodied Creatrix, I teach about "feminestation," the art and practice of using feminine embodiment to magnetize your deepest desires with pleasure and ease instead of working hard all your life to make shit happen. I use the word 'shit' intentionally here, not just for dramatic effect. When you create from stress and hard work, you might succeed in achieving and acquiring in the outer, but the inner experience is pretty much a shit show. On the other hand, when women experience pleasure, our bodies naturally soften and open, and our energy becomes yummy, radiant, and magnetic.

An Embodied Creatrix is a woman who lives fully, comfortably, and passionately in her body and uses feminine creation principles of love, pleasure, and ease to create anything she desires. When you create from pleasure, you don't have to work so hard. Life comes to you instead of you having to hunt it down and kill it. The more pleasure and ease you channel through your body on a regular basis, the more of what you truly desire will naturally magnetize into your life with far less effort.

Pleasure also heals our bodies and our nervous systems by toning the vagus nerve. The vagus nerve is critical to your autonomic nervous system and impacts most of the major systems of the body, including regulating heart rate, respiration, digestion, urination, sweating, and your endocrine and muscular-skeletal systems. Stimulating your vagus nerve relaxes your parasympathetic nervous system, allowing energy to flow freely to all the major systems in your body. In other words, when you prioritize pleasure daily, you become a calmer, healthier, and happier person.

After the relationship breakup and body breakdown I experienced in 2015, I completely changed how I do life. For starters, I stopped working hard all the time to make things happen through the mighty will of my unconscious masculine. Instead, I prioritize pleasure and do simple practices every day that help me to soften into my feminine essence and embody the energy that matches my soul's true desires. I feel relaxed, energized, alive, and truly content most of the time. My libido came back! And I trust my essence to magnetize everything I need. Today I am grateful for the breakup and breakdown I had in my mid 40's that sent me on a journey to find healthier, happier, more satisfying ways of living, loving, parenting, and running my business. Based on my own experience, and the experience of women in my community, this is a far easier and far more enjoyable way to live!

SHAMANIC MEDICINE OFFERING

So how do you shift from working hard to make shit happen to magnetizing your deepest desires with pleasure and ease? As the Goddess whispered to me: *Just. Let. Go.* It all begins with softening your body, dropping your armor, and simply letting go. The practice below may seem so deceptively simple that you may think, *Yeah, right, Laura. How could this possibly change my life and magnetize my deepest desires?*

I hear you. And I ask you, *Are you doing it? Are you soft, open, and available? Or are you tense, anxious, and too-tired-to-have-sex too much of the time?* I lived the tense, anxious, exhausted way for nearly three decades until I learned how to soften and soften again, several times throughout my day. Dissolving layers of armoring takes time, practice, and lots of self-love.

HERE'S A LITTLE PRACTICE TO GET YOU STARTED: SOFTEN

To listen to a guided meditation of this practice, please visit

https://soundcloud.com/laurawolf-1/soften-feminine-embodiment-practice-with-laura-wolf

1. Close your eyes and begin to slow down your breathing.

2. Bring your awareness to your jaw and soften there just a little. Take some slow, deep inhales and as you exhale, say "Ahhhhhhhhh." Releasing energy with sound will help your body to relax.

3. Next, bring your awareness to your neck and shoulders and imagine gently dissolving any tension that's accumulated there.

4. When you're ready, bring your awareness to the front of your heart. Take some slow, full breaths into your heart, upper back, and along the bra line behind your heart. Gently soften any armoring you've built up around your heart.

5. Bring your awareness to your belly, pelvic floor muscles, and lower back. Notice where you are clenching and keep breathing and softening each area.

Sounds easy, right? It is, if you practice.

Softening might seem elusive or frustrating at first. You're probably holding way more tension than you were aware of. Uncomfortable feelings like anger, grief, shame, or panic may arise as you get more present with your body. All of this is perfectly normal when you're learning to soften your vessel. The good news is that the more often you practice softening, the easier it becomes to inhabit your body in a soft, juicy, open, yummy way as your new normal.

As you soften, dissolve, and let go, releasing years or perhaps lifetimes of patriarchal conditioning from your body, you begin to discover what you truly yearn for, which has been inside of you all along. What do you deeply long for, my love? Do you even know? Your feminine body knows. Here's a hint: it has nothing to do with anything out there. It's all inside of you already and has everything to do with how you are being, moment by moment. We all yearn for love, peace, joy, freedom to express our authentic selves, and ecstatic union with all that is. As you embody the energies you yearn for, you will automatically magnetize outer experiences beyond your wildest dreams.

I'm not going to lie to you. This practice is not a one-and-done or a magic pill. Just like the shamanic path, the feminine path requires a lifelong commitment to letting go of ego agendas and peeling back layers of patriarchal conditioning that keep trying to seduce you back into the fray, back into the constant pressure to go, and do, and be plugged into consumer devices at all times. Just as Star Wolf teaches in the Shamanic Healing Initiatory Process that life is a spiral, feminine embodiment is also a spiral path. With each turn of the spiral, we have the opportunity to embrace more and more of ourselves. We are infinite, after all.

So I invite you, sister, soften with me now. Let's begin the process of de-armoring your body and creating more spaciousness in your vessel so that you can magnetize your deepest desires. Practice softening every day for the next ten days. Then, when you're ready for the next steps for creating a pleasure-drenched life, go to my website, where you can download my free e-book, "Embody Your Feminine Essence."

I envision a world in which women feel relaxed, radiant, and deliciously alive in our bodies. A world in which we love ourselves unconditionally and see all other women on the planet as our sisters. I want you to know how to channel love and pleasure into every aspect of your life and know in every fiber of your being that you are completely one with all of creation. Ultimately, I want you to realize what an incredibly powerful Creatrix you are, that you can use your thoughts, emotions, vibration, and actions to create the life of your dreams.

I desire all of this because I believe that when women feel healthy, happy, vibrant, connected, and empowered, we create families, businesses, educational environments, food, financial systems, and social systems that serve the well-being of our planet and all her inhabitants. Your pleasure is not only good for you, my love; it's good for your kids, your partner, your clients, your community, and the world! Will you create this world with me?

Laura Wolf is Star Wolf's adopted spirit daughter and a Shamanic Breathwork Master Practitioner. A priestess, teacher, coach, and leader in the emerging paradigm of feminine embodiment, feminine empowerment, and feminine creation, Laura serves clients all over the world. Her work is embodied, energetic, empowering, practical, mystical, and life-changing. She works with body, breath, mind, emotions, energy, and spirit – because the alignment of all parts of you is required if you want to create the life of your dreams. When she's not teaching or coaching, you will find her communing with the forest, climbing waterfalls, frolicking in the ocean, dancing in her kitchen while making dinner, or traveling around the world to gorgeous tropical climates.

Founder of Shaman's Heart Sanctuary, the *WildWoman* retreats, and several live and online courses, Laura holds a Bachelor of Fine Arts in Theatre and Performance, a Master's degree in Shamanic Intuitional Practices, and a Doctorate of Ministry in Shamanic Psycho-Spiritual Studies. She has studied with many of the leading embodiment, intimacy, and consciousness teachers of our time: Linda Star Wolf, Dr. Joe Dispenza, Abraham-Hicks, Gay and Katie Hendricks, Claire Zammit and Katharine Woodward Thomas, Craig Hamilton, Jeff Foster, Matt Licata, Raphael Cushnir, Derek Rydall, Rikka Zimmerman, John Wineland, David Deida, Lisa Page, Dawn Cartwright, Lisa Citore, Sofia Sundari, Jumana Sophia, Mama Gena, Dr. Rima Bonario, Sierra Sullivan and Dakota Chanel.

To learn more about Laura Wolf and download her free e-book, "Embody Your Feminine Essence," visit her website: www.laurawolf.com

Check out lots of free feminine embodiment videos on her YouTube channel: https://www.youtube.com/watch?v=fqbfNnegzbc

Or connect with her on Facebook: https://www.facebook.com/laura.wolf.1276

and Instagram: https://www.instagram.com/laurawolf_embodiedcreatrix/

Chapter 22

FINDING PLEASURE

Shedding Layers of Generational Shame and Conditioning

Sara K. Aljneibi

MY STORY

It's summer 2001, I'm 14, and we're on a family vacation in Salalah, Oman. My stepmother has not hit me since we arrived; it has been about two weeks. I love when we are around family and other people; the chances of her beating me are less. I can relax and play when she's not around, but when she is, I'm constantly expecting those overbearing looks that freeze me in place and make me wonder, *what have I done wrong? Will I get punished in the next moment we are together alone?* I never truly understand what triggers her, to the point where I believe that everything I do is wrong. Whatever I do or not do comes with the likelihood of punishment. I tried relentlessly to be the good girl at all times. There is no room for mistakes.

I had just stepped into the bathroom to take a quick shower in the small apartment we stayed in during our time in Salalah. As soon as I begin to undress, my younger brother starts knocking on the door,

"Sara, when will you finish?"

"I just started, Ahmad. I won't take long."

After a few minutes, still covered in soap and shampoo, my stepmother knocks at the door and asks nicely,

"Sara, can you please hand me the shampoo?"

"Wait, I'm coming."

I had hardly rinsed my hair when I hastily grabbed for the shampoo, treading carefully on the now slippery floor covered in soap from my barely washed body. By the time I reached the door, shampoo had dripped down my face leaving me hardly able to open my eyes. I cracked the door open, put my left hand out to hand her the bottle. Instead of retrieving it, she pushes the door open and locks it behind her, thrashing me with a metal cloth hanger while repeating the phrase, "When we say open the door, you open the door immediately, do you understand me?"

My eyes are burning as I'm hugging myself to hide my vulnerable body while she is whipping the flesh on my back, arms and face. I cry silently to protect her, so whoever is in this apartment won't hear what's going on. I can sense her rage, but I cannot feel the pain. For some reason, this time, it's different. The beatings I frequently receive from her come discreetly, in secret, without warnings or lessons, and now with no physical sensations. I am numb.

A couple of days pass, and we have just come back from our day trip to the mountains. I walk up the stairs to our apartment on the third floor. I hear a scream, so I start running. There in the kitchen, my seven-year-old brother had just urinated on the floor, and apparently, my older sister reprimanded him, only to receive a loud slap on her face from his mother, our stepmother. I stood by the door observing my sister while she held her right cheek, stinging from the pain. I think it is the first time she's experienced this. To my surprise, she didn't take it silently. "You have no right to hit me. I will go tell my father." She shouted. She passed next to me while running downstairs to tell him what had happened.

I'm here excited and scared, almost in disbelief. Maybe there is hope that my 11 years of suffering may finally be exposed and come to an end. On a daily basis, I was being physically and emotionally abused by a woman who represented the mother figure to me. I had been threatened that I would certainly endure these punishments with greater frequency and severity if I told anyone about it. I came to learn from a young age that it's wrong to be vulnerable, share my pain with anyone or ask for help, so hiding my heart became my second nature. However, my sister had done what I could not, my entire life. She modeled power I'd never seen in the women around me. Fear should not hold me back. I can stand up for myself, and using my voice can be safe.

Few years back, during one of the Venus Rising's programs, I was asked to draw my life timeline highlighting major events. To my surprise, I had no memory of an entire portion of it. This was the moment I realized I was detached from my body sensations until the age of 17. I was saddened to acknowledge that it wasn't safe to be present in my body and as a cooping mechanism I was unconsciously numbing my feelings. I knew then it is my life's journey to reclaim the relationship with my body by defining the safety and boundaries within and without, to finally feel the pleasure of being alive.

Years passed, it's my last day in high school. Staring at my outfit for the evening, I feel so proud of the long black leather skirt I made. I'm going to wear it to meet my girlfriends from school at the ice rink on a private female-only day. It is finally time to dress up, dance, play, and have fun.

For the majority of Emiratis, it's not acceptable for men and women (after puberty) to hang out for fun together, even at family gatherings, unless they are close relatives.

It's 7:00 pm. I'm extremely happy. I get dressed a bit more than I usually do and put on my black leather skirt. It's tighter than what I usually wear. I wrap a black scarf with silver coins on my hips, similar to the ones belly dancers wear. I love the sound it makes every time I move; it will be so much fun dancing with this scarf. My hair is long, it reaches my knees, so it is easier to leave it loose.

Before putting my dark burgundy lipstick on, I run to my father to show him the skirt I made. "Uboya, look at what I'm wearing. Imagine I made this skirt from scratch." With a straight face, he says, "Yes, it's nice. Where are you going?"

"I'll go to the ice-rink with my girlfriends. I finally finished school for good!"

He didn't comment further.

Our driver at the time, an old, calm Pakistani man with a long white beard, dropped me off. It was a normal evening with my friends. We played, danced, and showed off our clothes. Around 10:30 pm, it was time for me to go home. I called the driver, who was already waiting outside. As I got into the car, he says, "Your father asked me to wait all evening and watch if you would leave. I told him, Sara is a very good girl she will never do something like this and see, you didn't leave."

Tears silently streamed down my face. I don't want him to feel bad for telling me, but the agony I'm feeling cannot be put into words. My whole body contracted, and I feel my throat blocking. The world seems darker.

I feel betrayed. If I cannot be trusted, then there must be something wrong with me! This was the first time I share my joy and excitement and be honest with him, and he didn't trust me! That's why I do things behind his back because he never allows me to do anything; see my friends outside of school, or even leave the house to the grocery store without a chaperone (Mahram)! It is better to just keep hiding and never share anything with him.

I feel terrified and even more distant from my father. I don't understand whether he intends to protect or suffocate me. I have never felt understood by anyone in my family. I always feel the need to hide and not show myself to anyone to protect myself from being judged. I feel constantly watched, but I was never truly seen. Now I know that being seen as a woman is not safe.

The sum of my experiences in a woman's body of pain, suppression, control, hiding, and dishonesty should have convinced me by the time I stepped into womanhood that freedom was not meant for me. However, deep inside, I've always been longing for more, longing to be wild and free. Dreaming of becoming an artist and exploring the world. Eventually, this desire became too loud to ignore. The primal need to hatch out of the egg grew bigger than the fears, conditioning, and restrictions I was facing.

My father believes when a woman leaves to live overseas she never comes back the same, so he is against it. Deep down, I feel he's afraid I would find myself, my pleasure and womanhood, and his little girl would never return. This didn't stop me from applying to art schools around the world for seven years, but nothing worked out because I never truly believed it was possible.

One day, sitting with my father in the garden, a voice inside me said, *open your heart to him.* I gathered my courage, "You know Uboya, I always had the desire to study art abroad." It was the first time sharing my desires out loud, connecting heart-to-heart with him, being vulnerable as a woman. He listened and encouraged me before quickly reminding me I could not leave alone. But somehow, something shifted. It felt as though my dream was closer and attainable now.

I finally gathered my strength and decided to choose myself instead of worrying about everyone else, and against my entire family's advice, I took action towards my dream. I was accepted into an art school, eventually quit my job, and started planning my departure. When everything was finalized, I announced the news. To my surprise, my father was calm and supportive of my dream, unlike he had been with my sisters. This changed the dynamic of our relationship. I realized that when I'm aligned with what is true to me, everything else falls into place.

Equipped with all the lessons I'd learned, I embarked on a self-discovery journey across four continents. This journey led me to Shamanic Breathwork, inner child work, and my career as an artist and embodiment coach. It seems my father's fear was true after all. I would never be the same again.

Few years back, during a Shamanic Breathwork journey, my father appears in one of my visions. Immediately my body goes into contraction and fear; *he cannot see me, he cannot be here!* I crawl like a child in fear, shaking and crying. I know I have to find my voice, gather my courage again, but there is nothing. No voice to even speak.

I'm feeling angry, a feeling I never permitted myself to acknowledge. I started punching and kicking the pillows around me while screaming and crying. I don't know why I'm angry. Maybe it's for all the years I was tamed and controlled. For all the years, I didn't know who I was, simply because I couldn't explore myself, or for all the years I'm trying to fit into a mold that didn't fit all of me, which, in reality, is not meant to fit any woman.

Screaming repeatedly in my native tongue of Arabic, "I will not sacrifice myself for you!"

The image changes. My father has a big smile, and his arms are wide open. "I'm so proud of you" he says. I cannot believe it! Is this the result of expressing myself and being honest? Both of us are open; we are connecting intimately, heart-to-heart, in a way I've never experienced before. I feel his unconditional love in a way I never felt before. His soul is giving me permission to live my life authentically, and I know in my heart that he will always be proud of me.

My relationship with both my stepmother and father went through many changes over the years and it is evolving as I am embodying my authentic self. My resentment and fear towards my father has been shifting to opening up, communicating my feelings to him, and standing up for myself no matter the consequences. With my stepmother, after upholding healthy boundaries in my life by voicing my needs and preferences, the dynamic of our relationship had shifted and morphed into a content, loving, and respectful relationship. None of this is easy, and as I continue to choose authenticity, love and make choices that honor me, they slowly are learning to lean in and bend their beliefs one at a time. Healing my co-dependency and being rooted in love and compassion were the key to healing and transforming my relationship with my family.

SHAMANIC MEDICINE OFFERING

SAFETY AROUND YOU

When creating safety around you, ask yourself these question:

- Do I have privacy in this space? ... not being observed or disturbed.
- Do I have enough space to move freely?
- Am I comfortable to express without holding myself back? ...crying, making sounds, loud music etc.
- Would anything else assist me in creating a pleasant atmosphere? dim lighting, specific music, certain scents...

SAFETY WiTHiП YOU

Start with taking deep breaths in. With your eyes closed, in every deep inhale, become aware of the tensions you hold in different parts of your body, between your eyebrows, jaw, neck, and shoulders. Relaxing and dropping in, moment to moment, with every exhale.

With complete presence and surrender, slowly putting your guard down, allowing your breath to flow in every inch of your body. Trusting your body, letting it take the lead, and giving yourself permission to take up space and express what is alive within you in every shape and form.

Giving yourself permission to stretch and move. Gently moving different parts of your body, moving from the inside out in a way that feels right only to you. Moving your feet, knees, legs, hips, spine, chest, shoulders, elbow, arms, hands, fingers, and head. It is not about the way you move; it is about the way you feel in every move. Letting your body guide your movements. Breathe into every stretch and explore how every part of your body feels.

Giving yourself permission to use your voice regardless of how it sounds, moaning, sighing, crying, laughing, screaming - however your body wants to express.

Breathe…

Going deeper within, observing what sensations are you feeling at this moment?

Is it cool, warm. Do you notice any tingling, tension, pain? Or maybe it's coming as a vision in colors like blue or red? or in an image such as a knot, a rock or an ocean? Try to drop into the bodily sensations to these visions. There is no right or wrong way to do this. Keep breathing deeply and trust what shows up for you.

Welcoming all ranges of emotions and being open to them with curiosity. Allowing them to flow with ease as pure bodily sensations without judgment, fear, guilt, or shame.

For instance, fear, to me, comes in heat waves rushing all over my body, leaving me freezing cold when every wave passes from my head to toe. Instead of talking myself out of it, analyzing and getting stuck in stories of why and I shouldn't be, I just allow these waves to pass through my body as pure sensations.

Emotions are energies in motion; when we allow them to flow with breath, movement, and presence, they transform into other sensations and energies.

After allowing the heatwaves and shaking with the freezing cold, a feeling of heaviness in my chest comes where I crawl and hug myself in tears. I cry out loud; my voice then turns into laughter covered with my sad and happy tears. Shortly after, my body opens up, and I lay on the ground, arms open; my breath is deeper and flows with ease. The sensations transformed now into lightness and tingling all over my body.

You see, if I judged the first sensation and talked myself out of it, I would've stayed in one state, which in the example I gave is fear. I wouldn't have allowed my body to process it and transform it into lightness and pure joy. I wouldn't have moved from contraction to expansion.

Sadly, the majority of us don't feel safe to feel or express our emotions freely, so we judge and control them as a cooping mechanism, and unconsciously store them in our system. Feeling heavy and most of the time stuck in our bodies and lives, which can manifest into physical illness over time.

I believe that everything within and around us is constantly moving, changing, and transforming. Trusting our body's intelligence and allowing the natural process to unfold is the pleasure of being alive.

To integrate your journey, I invite you to journal, draw or paint what came up for you. Always remember that your emotions, thoughts, sounds, movements and sensations are not who you are; they are only part of your rich and pleasurable human experience in this wild ride called life.

Sara K. Aljneibi is an artist, embodiment coach, Shamanic Breathwork Facilitator, embodied feminine flow teacher, Shamanic Minister, and co-founder of Ishtar Rising community. She is one of the first Emiratis coaching women on pleasure, love, and relationships using somatic therapy and transformational processes blending modern neurobiology and holistic healing with the ancient Shamanic and Tantric powerful teachings and wisdom.

She has made it her life mission to support women in the Middle East and beyond by creating safe spaces for them to come back to their bodies to allow the shedding of generational and collective shame, fear, and guilt. Guiding them to reclaim and explore their bodies with grounded and authentic expression to expand their capacity to love and healing. Offering holistic tools such as somatic therapy, breathwork, therapeutic movement and dance, self-love and shadow work, art therapy, inner child and trauma healing.

Her dream is to ignite the feminine essence through play, pleasure, and freedom to allow women to unfold in their own unique and beautiful ways. Unleashing the wild woman within, who is courageous to follow her desires, own her power & shadows and step into her life with grounded confidence, radiance, and magnetism.

Sara has dedicated the past 15 years to studying and teaching arts and healing arts across Europe, the United States, and the Middle East while working at one of the most prestigious museums in the world. She continues to offer embodiment retreats, one to one coaching, private and group (online and in-person) workshops internationally.

You can connect with Sara at:

www.embodiment-arts.com

Instagram and Facebook: @embodimentarts Embodiment Arts

www.ishtarising.com

Instagram and Facebook: @ishtarising Ishtar Rising

CHAPTER 23

HOWLING AT THE MOON. . . AND VENUS

Transformation through Yoga, Astrology, and Breathwork

Levi Banner, MA, E-RYT 500

MY STORY

I couldn't sleep that night. The moon was talking too loudly for me to shut out the sound any longer.

I stuck to the bed with sweat. It was a sweltering heat I hadn't felt before. I lie awake in the middle of the night with an eerie feeling of not knowing where or who I was anymore. I had just moved to Bali, an island in Indonesia.

I grew up in the Willamette Valley in Northern Oregon, a small, damp college town where it rains nine months out of the year. As a child, I patiently awaited snow in winter, feeling lucky when it sometimes came.

I was now discovering myself in the tropics, feeling the warm rain as it dropped down on my skin. Other than the drastic change in climate, something stronger urged me, pulling and lifting me out of my sleep.

I could feel the sweetness and warmth of my girlfriend next to me and tried not to wake her with my uncontrollable tossing and turning. As quiet as a rainless night in the middle of nowhere, I slid out of bed without waking her. I tiptoed down the spiral staircase like a burglar to the open-air living room, surrounded by see-through walls.

There I was, alone, downstairs, in a new country, in a two-story house with glass windows instead of walls that we just paid a five-year lease on. I sat at my desk feeling ungrounded excitement, perhaps associated with the fact I was now beginning a new life far from where I grew up and what I knew. Knowing only that it was a tropical island with some nice people on it, and not much more, I moved to Indonesia to start a life with my partner. I could almost taste the dragon fruit's seedy and purple insides as she described them to me before coming to this small island. I was uninformed about much else before coming.

A sense of relief poured through me like a water blessing to find out that this 'island of the gods' hosts a unique form of Hindu-inspired prayer, worship of water, and sees all nature as sacred. I was already accustomed to the more religious features due to my many years of yoga studies and recent travels through India merely months before this new chapter.

There was also another feeling churning in my stomach that night. Knots were tangling up as fear bubbled from my guts up through my mouth. Yuck. I suddenly screamed out.

"What do I do now?!"

I almost woke the slumbering woman upstairs who I felt so close to moments before, now a stranger in a strange land. Or was I the stranger here? I knew nothing about the local culture, language, or customs. All I knew is that I was on the opposite end of the planet feeling misplaced, lost, and scared, like a boy rather than a man well past his first Saturn return.

There was something more in this feeling—an explosive longing bursting out of me, keeping me up that night. I had to follow the feeling downstairs for answers. Then it dawned on me long before sunrise. Earlier that day, I tried something for the first time that was impacting my rest. I knew the moment I tasted it that it was for me.

Breathwork. Conscious, connected, breathwork.

Back in the mountainous valley of Oregon, I diligently practiced yogic breathing techniques in my daily yoga practice for many years. I grudgingly woke up to an alarm long before the sunrise and forced myself upstairs to the meditation room. My teacher and roommates sat and awaited the start of our practice cross-legged, circled around candles.

I felt the universal truths as the ancient texts were read aloud while sitting with a blanket tightly wrapped around me to keep in the sweet teachings and hold in the heat. The windows would open soon after, breaking us out of the comfort of ancient poetry into silence and bitter cold.

"Fresh energy is available to us now," said the teacher.

The breathing techniques awakened my senses, calmed me down, and centered my focus. I left each and every day feeling superhuman, with a spark for life and zest to engage in the day. It was worth it. Or was it?

Waiting patiently for years, longing to meet the masters of yogic breathing, I finally traveled through India just months before moving to Bali. Soon after, I found my pranayama guru who I would see yearly from then on. Though, earlier this day, the meditative qualities I was used to experiencing in the many hours sitting in sacred breath practice over the years were now in question.

As I walked past the flower-petal-lined walkway into the wellness studio, I could smell the fragrance not only of roses but also the incense wafting through the hall, luring me to the studio space. I was greeted by overly spiritually dressed individuals with huge smiles offering long hugs as they helped my lover and me to our mats.

There I lay feeling suspiciously at ease with overly helpful hosts of the sacred space, uncertain about the people dressed in white surrounding me. Our heads were towards the center of the room, which hosted a large mandala of flower petals. The room was serenaded with incense smoke. I could feel the fragrances in my bones giving me both a remembrance of something not of this life and a fresh perspective of a newfound way of being.

This must be a special occasion. There would never be this many flowers on the floor of a studio in Oregon, I thought. Feeling the fragrance permeate my body. I could almost taste the glorious smell of the flower altar like they were blooming inside the room. Or was that the taste of newly tried fruits that resonated in my mouth after lunch?

I laid down to breathe. I was confused as a new student. Breathwork is a cyclical, conscious, connected breath, much different than the slow, meditative version from yoga I was accustomed to. I thought I was some sort of "experienced" practitioner of breath as I arrived in Bali. Soon, through this experience, I felt like a baby, newly born, breathing for the first time.

When the music started and we began to breathe, I was sent off to another land. I journeyed back to see past traumas I experienced. I witnessed the cause of my habits and addictions and recognized unhealthy patterns, only to find deep healing, renewal, and rebirth into this new place I found myself in. Within what seemed like days, tears rolled down my face at times, puddling up on the floor beneath me. I experienced physical pain where my hands cramped up like crab claws reminding me of my Cancer moon and rising sign. I journeyed through weakness and into empowerment. As I did the technique, it was as if the breath itself was a great spirit whispering in my ears, telling me I must learn to do this work.

Through the simple breathing technique, the music, and the hands-on touch from the beautiful angels walking the room, I was carried away, back to heal my dark past, and carried ahead into a ripe new future. "I must find the masters of this!" I said. Breathwork was like a secret that had been kept from me all those cold mornings before dawn with the sharp wind biting my toes, huddled uncomfortably around candles, listening to ancient scriptures, and working hard to find a meditative state.

After waking that night from a failed attempt at sleep and snuggling my partner to dream of our new life together, I sat at my new desk. I opened my laptop with intense inspiration. I typed in the term "breathwork training."

As the slow internet connection loaded the chosen page, I couldn't help but feel the warm glow of the full moon that night, showering me with healing and soothing my lost soul. As I basked in the rays, I noticed something extraordinary in the sky, very close to the round ball of ferociously bright light.

I had recently discovered Shamanic Astrology when I traveled through India, a unique system of the stars. My mind was blown beyond belief learning this new approach to astrology after searching for the right system for so long.

I took up an interest in astrology when I was a curious, pot-smoking teenager. For better or worse, both habits were absorbed from my father. I would sit on the couch in his smoke-filled living room with eyes and ears wide open to catch any nuggets of wisdom he might throw my way. There, in conversation, he would sometimes complain about the moon or some planet, causing a negative reaction.

My childhood friends thought it was weird to discuss their astrology signs or other such things that fascinated me beyond belief. I felt I knew something deeper about my friends than anyone else as I learned their Moon signs. I committed further to yoga, and the astrology interest only grew with me into adulthood.

I felt sacred geometry aligning my body and soul with the heart of the earth as I learned this new system. This newfound relationship with astrology's original intent taught me about the intimate relationship between the sky and earth and our psyche.

Excited, I knew from my studies that the brightest thing other than the moon that night was the planet, Venus. Many cultures saw this planet as some form of the sacred feminine. The goddess herself was right there guiding me to my next steps in life.

I relied heavily on messages throughout my adult life. I learned at some point early on, perhaps from my mother, that the outer world speaks in messages and that spirit is woven through everything, speaking to us, telling our souls which way to go. Through my own intuition and connection with nature—the birds, flowers, and animals—I've been guided. Goosebumps spread down my arms many times, feeling like I was making the right choice, confirmed by the wind blowing on my skin or an affirmation written on a street sign or advertisement. Messages from the universe speak to you in nearly everything when you listen.

This was an omen, I thought. I had just learned why. I had just started to learn the deeper messages of the stars, and now they were singing me sweet songs. Though certainly not calming lullabies.

Venus returns to the same place, in the same type of cycle, and usually in the same sign, every eight years. Only weeks to my 32nd birthday, she was in nearly the same place when I was born. Called a Venus return in shamanic astrology.

Raining down from the Moon and Venus, magical light twinkled through my spine as I bore witness to this conjunction, out of my wall of windows directly over my laptop. I dropped my gaze to the computer screen. There, the website was now fully loaded.

In and out of my lungs, the same place as the heart space, the moon grew bright inside of me. There were chills down my whole body, a rush of deep knowing. Synchronicity. A cleansing feeling of release flowed through me as my heart opened wide as if the moon had just entered my breath after the profound new experience earlier that day.

On top of the website, a wolf was howling at a full moon almost identical to the one peeking out behind the screen of the laptop, straight out of the window wall. Me, the wolf howling, asking for answers. The top of the website read a very big "Venus Rising" with "Association for Transformation" just underneath. Venus, in all her glory, shining brightly next to the moon in front of me.

I was feeling like a wayfarer that traversed the seas for months before finding new land. It felt like coming home. A click that activated some ancient knowledge of the path my soul was on.

After spending some time looking through the website, I emailed and asked very simply to the teachers of this school, "Would you come to Bali and teach me Breathwork?" I think it was merely two days later I was on Skype with Star Wolf and her late husband, Brad Collins. Meeting my new teacher was soothing, comforting, and, well, confronting. I felt immediately at home with them as they clarified this new path I was on. A new life was emerging. My life was rebirthing.

I could almost smell the sage that Star Wolf smudged me with through the computer screen. During that first interaction, I felt as if I was in the living room with them in North Carolina. We recognized our obvious soul contracts and made immediate plans for Star Wolf to come out to Bali and share this magical modality. My whole body vibrated with resonance in that very first conversation where she told me in a charming southern accent:

"You know Levi; I think you're going to take this work all over the world."

Though only months after the plans were set in motion, the training was canceled. Brad left this life. Star Wolf would not come to Bali anytime soon. Instead, we would all mourn the passing of a great man.

I was deeply sad for the loss, though still felt the inspiration of my own new life and hope to learn new tools for transformation to share. I kept on teaching yoga and pranayama and gave astrology readings to hundreds of seekers passing through the magical land of Bali.

It was maybe a year or so later, and I couldn't wait any longer. I traveled back to the United States solely to study with Star Wolf and the staff of Venus Rising. With the pack of wolves still mourning from the papa wolf passing, I joined the very next training offered. We cried together. Learning to be a Shamanic Breathwork Facilitator was like everything I learned up to that point coming together.

I would bring Star Wolf back to Bali several times over the next few years. Fulfilling her prophecy of me, I would end up carrying this work into festivals all over the planet and breathing large classrooms full of students from all over the world each week. Learning to be a lead trainer in the school of Venus Rising, I felt like my life had purpose like I was guided every step of the way without always knowing it. Looking back, I know that each step was guided by Venus, by the moon, and by spirit.

SHAMANIC MEDICINE OFFERING

Yogic Breathwork and Meditation of Messages

Start by simply sitting cross-legged on a pillow or sitting in a chair with your feet on the floor. Feeling your sitting bones grounded like roots through your seat. Let the spine grow from the ground up to your crown.

Let your hips be like a flower, pot full of mineral-rich soil, fertile for roots to ground down through your seat—the spine like the stalk of your plant or the trunk of your tree. Let the arms and shoulders rest. The limbs of your body like branches, resting off to the side. To receive energy, have your palms facing up. To release energy, have your palms facing down on your lap or your knees.

The top of your head blossoms and opens like a flower towards the sun, towards the sky, towards spirit. Rest in this upright position.

Breathe deeply. Take a big inhale down into the belly, filling your trunk, letting the chest expand from there as well. Exhale, making a sound. Continue this a few more times. Inhale into the spaciousness you already have in your body, and release fully that which no longer serves you through the exhale.

You are now open for the Meditation of Messages.

With eyes closed gently, notice how you feel. Let your inner guidance tell you what's next. Let your inner guru inform you of the best approach to your life's tasks. Listen.

As you slowly open your eyes about halfway, with fuzzy vision, a soft gaze to the world, begin to feel your feelings fully as you let in the sights, sounds, and all senses. Notice as the outer world informs your inner world.

As you open your eyes fully, take in the full range of color, shapes, and objects that you see. Without too much judgment, notice what you see and how you feel. Take note of the very first things that catch your attention. Hear the birds chirping or the movement around you. Whatever it might be. Let that be your message. Let nature tell you.

You can now know what to do next. Where to go. Let nature be your guru. Let the universe guide you through every little thing around you. Take your time with this and fully accept whatever comes in first. Whatever message you receive is the right one. Try not to doubt.

Spirit speaks through all things. You can listen anytime. The breath is your guide. Your next step is always just a breath away.

To learn more about your own inner guidance, to train with me in Yoga, Astrology, Breathwork, or to get an astrology reading with me to find out about your own personal Venus return or the intent of your soul, please follow me or contact me here: https://www.instagram.com/levi.banner/

In love and magic,

~ Levi ~

With a warm smile, an energetic hug, and a sly sense of humor, **Levi Banner** draws you into his world – teaching the spiritual sciences for healing and transformation. Yoga, Breathwork, and Astrology comprise his trinity of mystical knowledge. He creates a safe, peaceful classroom space where students can learn and grow to their fullest potential. Levi's specialties are a strong, consistent vinyasa yoga practice, precious yet powerful pranayama practice, relaxing and healing restorative yoga, and divining deep astrological insights through the cosmic viewpoint.

Levi is a Shamanic Breathwork Master Practitioner. Mystery, transformation, and healing magically combine as he leads intensive shamanic breathwork journeys, helping participants reconnect to their highest selves. He strives to create a community of open-hearted difference makers with world-changing potential by gifting students with personal empowerment and self-healing.

Levi can be found traveling the shamanic path as he conducts workshops and immersions around the globe. In Yoga, Levi is rated E-RYT 500, the highest level of Yoga Alliance certification. His studies in India, Guatemala, Sedona, and Bali are taught techniques and ancient philosophies transmitted into his practice, gracing students with an unusually well-rounded experience and profound lifetime benefits.

Credentials:

- Specialties: Vinyasa Yoga, Restorative Yoga, Pranayama, Shamanic Breathwork, Shamanic Astrology.
- E-RYT 500 – Highest level of Yoga Alliance Certification.
- Shamanic Breathwork Master Practitioner and ordained Shamanic Minister by Venus Rising Association for Transformation.
- Certifications and training from 7 Centers Yoga Arts (Sedona, Arizona); SchoolYoga Institute – Advanced Yoga + Shamanic Studies (Lake Atitlan, Guatemala.)

- Certified pranayama teacher by Kaivalyadham Yoga Center in India by O.P. Tiwari.
- Advanced graduate of the Ashtanga Yoga Bali Research Center
- Studied Iyengar Restorative and Pranayama in an intentional community in Portland, Oregon, for three years.
- Fully certified and initiated shamanic astrologer from the Shamanic Astrology Mystery School.
- Bachelor's degree in Sacred Elemental Studies.
- Master's degree in Shamanic Intuitional Practices.

Contact: https://www.instagram.com/levi.banner/

https://www.facebook.com/levibanneryogaastrologybreathwork

Chapter 24

AWAKENING THE TRUE SELF
The Art of Making Love with Life

Crystal Dawn Morris

MY STORY

The spiritual awakening process is not a static goal that a person achieves. Rather, it is the continuous recognition that our true nature is awareness. This realization is available to those ready to discover the True Self. Below is a bit about my journey on the path of non-dual shamanic tantra and how I learned to make love with life.

In March of 2005, I drove to Sedona to visit a friend. As I descended into the valley, I went around a curve and was thunderstruck by the beauty before me. On the plateau above, the snow-covered San Francisco peaks sparkled; in the distance, the red rocks of Sedona glowed, and just ahead, the trees along the Verde River greeted me with their new spring leaves. At that moment, my heart expanded, filling me with joy. I heard Spirit telling me it was time to move to Sedona.

As I thought about moving to Sedona, my mind wasn't onboard. I had spent the past fifteen years creating a wonderful life in Sonoma County. I fell in love with the area as a teen, and when I finally moved to Sebastopol twenty years later, it felt like I had finally come home. I felt secure with the identity I created there; as a respected midwife, homeowner, and community builder. Up until my recent trip to Sedona, I felt sure I'd live in Occidental the rest of my life, on my ten acres of redwood trees. In retrospect, I see that this invitation from Spirit was a moment of power. It asked me to let go of the security I was seeking in the world of form and invited me to leap into the unknown.

Even though my mind had doubts, I took steps towards relocating to Sedona when I got back home. I figured it would take me at least a year to make the move. To my surprise, only five months later, I was sitting in my new house in Sedona, wondering how the redwoods of Occidental had transformed into the red rocks of Sedona. Everything happened so quickly, which I took as a sign of being aligned with Spirit. I didn't know what was next; then, it dawned on me that I was fifty years old, which seemed like a perfect time to take a year off.

I spent the next six months shifting my attention away from doing. Gradually, I discovered the joy that arose when I trusted the natural unfolding of life. I recognized that my mind was habitually trying to keep me safe in the past. Now, I was learning that safety is an inside job. I soon discovered the flow was always here guiding me, and it emerged from a place of clarity beyond the mind.

When spring came, I felt the flow inviting me to return to my tantra studies. Three years earlier, I began studying tantra with Margot Anand. I loved the first course I did, called "The Yin & Yang of Ecstasy." I then completed the first two levels of her Love & Ecstasy Training (LET). Due to moving to Sedona, I had postponed taking the LET 3. The timing was perfect, the next LET 3 was coming up in a few weeks, and there was a spot available. The transmission I received at the LET 3 renewed my interest in Tibetan Buddhism. I began spending a lot of time at the Buddhist Stupa, which was only a few blocks from my house, and I got involved with the local Buddhist temple.

By the fall, I was ready to dive deeper into tantra. I began a year-long Sky Dancing Tantra Teacher Training course, which required me to teach tantra classes and assist at LETs. I was excited to start offering tantra classes in Sedona. When I first moved to Sedona, I looked for a tantra community and couldn't find one. My intention was to use the classes as a way to create a local tantra community. In 2007, I began teaching tantra in Sedona. By the fall, I was a certified Sky Dancing Tantra Teacher. Soon after that, I launched my website, Tantra For Awakening.

Margot Anand encouraged me to speak at a sexuality conference, and that's how I got to know Baba Dez Nichols, the founder of the International School of Temple Arts (ISTA.) I presented at the ISTA Conference in Chicago in 2007 and again in Sedona in 2008. I joined the ISTA faculty in 2010 and became lead faculty in 2014.

I met Star Wolf and her husband Brad in 2010 while I was helping to organize an ISTA Conference in Sedona. They were at the conference to promote Star Wolf's new book, *Shamanic Breathwork*. Shamanism was my primary spiritual practice for over twenty years, and I was curious to learn how they combined shamanism with breathwork. I greeted them when they arrived, and I felt an immediate kinship with them both. Star Wolf was a fountain of energy and wisdom. I loved hearing her Kentucky twang as she spoke about Shamanic Breathwork. I asked Brad about their healing center in North Carolina. As he spoke, it became clear to me that he was the earth to her stars.

Brad's parents lived in Sedona, and he had arranged a Shamanic Breathwork event at his mother's church. He invited me to attend. A couple of days later, I arrived at the event. Star Wolf and Brad welcomed the group and gave us an overview of the Shamanic Breathwork process. Brad played a tune on his Native American flute. We entered into ceremonial time. I felt the spirits gathering around us. Star Wolf asked us to put on our eye cover and find a comfortable position to begin the journey. She played her flat drum and spoke aloud her intention for our transformation. The music started, the circular breathing began, and magic happened!

By the time the event ended, I knew Shamanic Breathwork (SBW) was something I wanted to learn, not only for my benefit but for the benefit of my clients and students. During my SBW journey, I received a vision of Star Wolf and Brad offering their certification, called SHIP, the Shamanic Healing Initiatory Process, in Sedona in a one-year format. Rather than the current two years. I stayed after to speak with them and helped them load up their van. I asked if they would consider manifesting the vision I received. They both smiled. Soon we agreed I would organize an event to see if there was enough interest to warrant creating this new program. In June, twenty healers gathered in Sedona, and by the end of the weekend, it was clear that an accelerated SHIP would launch there.

My SHIP was a wild ride along on the spiral path. One of the things that most stood out was when I was transforming my core wound of abandonment. On several occasions, Brad and Star Wolf laid next to me and held me with pure love as I moved through intense emotions. Those moments gave my nervous system a new reference point that allowed me to access my inner conscious parents. The SHIP prepared me for many things yet to come.

My mother moved to Sedona in March of 2010. She was a retired psychologist, a pioneer in clinical hypnosis, and a student of cosmology. In May of the next year, she was diagnosed with a goose egg-sized brain tumor. She needed brain surgery to diagnose the tumor, which was an aggressive form of brain cancer. After her release from the hospital, I moved her into my house to care for her. I wanted to support her in creating a conscious end-of-life process.

She died in my home on September 8, 2011, only four months after being diagnosed with a neo blastoma. The last week of the SHIP began the next day. A few hours after preparing my mother's body for cremation, I arrived at the venue. I felt fortunate to have Star Wolf, Brad, and my SBW community around me right after her death. Following her death, I was surprised by the intensity of the grief I experienced. I eventually recognized how hard it was for me to ask for and receive support. I gradually learned the power of vulnerability.

On Easter in 2012, I had a near-death experience. I fell out of my bed, unable to breathe. I looked down onto my body and, for a few moments, time stopped. Was I going to cross over or stay here? At that moment, I felt an intense desire to live! I was back in my body, my lungs filled with air, and I understood how precious life is and that we never know when our end will come. I was more committed than ever to wake up fully in this lifetime and excited for what was next.

Since then, my life's primary focus has been to recognize the non-dual nature of awareness as the True Self—to access it under all conditions and to release any remaining doubts I had about the nature of non-duality. It soon became apparent that to live an awakened life, I had to commit to making awareness the central focus, a journey that involved using Shamanic Breathwork, Tibetan meditation practices, tantric yoga, Saiva Tantra, and non-dual meditation as pointers to the Truth. Daily contemplation of *The Recognition Sutras* by Christopher Wallis also supports my clarity.

Awareness is both subtle and pervasive. Because it is always present, it fades into the background of our experience and mostly goes unnoticed. The world we live in is primarily concerned with what things look like and what we think about them. Therefore, to see beyond the limited view of duality can be a challenge because our culture constantly reinforces a dualistic point of view.

Change is the nature of reality. Having a dualistic view sets us up to believe that the source of happiness is outside the self, in the objective world. This creates the habits of grasping and aversion, which inevitably cause suffering. A non-dual view recognizes that there is only awareness at the core of being, and happiness comes from within. When we tap into our core, we feel joy; in Sanskrit, it's called "Ananda," often translated as 'bliss.' Ananda is the causeless joy that arises when we realize the True Self.

Another challenge interfering with realizing our true nature is chasing after peak experiences. This was something I struggled with for many years. Many peak experiences blessed me earlier in my life, but I got attached to them as destinations rather than seeing them as parts of the journey. When the peak experience ended, I felt confused and disappointed. Eventually, I noticed I was confusing a peak experience for the deeper truth it was pointing to. It's valuable to realize that peak experiences are gifts that may allow us to see beyond duality and remember our wholeness. They can also become barriers to awakening if we confuse them for truth. Alone, they are not enough to stabilize awareness. It takes daily practice for most people to fully steep in their True Self.

What helps me ground in awareness is shifting my attention inward, rather than looking outside myself for answers. I know spacious awareness is always available, and I rest there often. I savor these moments of connection. Please explore the practice below if you are ready to meet the True Self.

SHAMANIC MEDICINE OFFERING

Guidance for Awakening the True Self

With your eyes softly open, sit in a meditation posture that works for you. Take a few deep breaths and settle into this moment. Reflect on a recent experience when you were holding onto something you desired or felt an aversion to something you wanted to avoid. How did you feel at that moment? Both grasping and aversion tend to create a contraction in the body-mind.

Close your eyes. Shift the focus of attention inward, and rest in the core of your being. Notice what's there. Take a few deep breaths, become aware of your presence. Notice that presence is often associated with a sense of location. Presence may feel like it's located in the body or the mind. It may seem to be found in space or in time. Release any attachment you have to presence having a location. Once freed of place, presence naturally expands as the infinite light of awareness.

Experience limitless awareness. This is your true nature, the True Self. It naturally radiates a subtle vibration of joy, bliss, or Ananda. Surrender; be the vibration. Continue to expand, beyond the bliss, beyond the beyond. Beyond anything a mind can comprehend. Savor the experience of spacious awareness, and let it be the new reference point for what you essentially are. Inhale this realization into the core of your being. When you are ready, slowly return, taking your time as you transition back into the perception of ordinary reality. I recommend doing this practice daily.

Once you can easily connect with the True Self, you can do a simplified version as a micro-practice. I suggest setting an alarm on your phone to alert you several times a day. When alerted, stop and rest as awareness for 10-20 seconds. I did this micro-meditation for two years and now easily dip into the pool of awareness several times a day without the need for an external prompt.

As my connection with the True Self became more integrated, something wonderful revealed itself; I began to experience spontaneous moments of being at one with life. I call it "making love with life." I experience life as the beloved, and life force energy flowing through me creates experiences that pulsate with joy. I am awareness meeting itself.

I begin each day by connecting with the True Self, and the day then unfolds as I make love with life, no matter what it looks like. This creates a sense of well-being. When challenges arise, they are met with love and compassion and are processed until they can be met fully and merge back into awareness. Below is a practice that has helped me and others who felt ready to discover the joy of making love with life.

Making Love with Life and the Five Acts of God

The Five Acts of God come from the non-dual Saiva Tantra tradition of Kashmir. When I first learned about them, I immediately recognized them as an accessible way to introduce people to the art of making love with life. They are part of a lineage that is over one thousand years old. In this tradition, awareness is the ground of being, from which the one divine actor appears in countless forms. The first three acts are:

1. Creating an experience that emerges from awareness.
2. Sustaining the experience until it changes.
3. Dissolving or reabsorbing the experience back into awareness.

These first three acts unfold in a continuous cycle. When you are first exploring this practice, I suggest focusing on your subjective experiences. Sit quietly, take a deep breath and relax for a moment. Notice what is arising internally, be it a thought, a sensation, or an emotion (creating). Be present with it for as long as it lasts (sustaining). Watch as it disappears (dissolving). Where does it go? What is it reabsorbed into? This third step is the one that is the most overlooked. It is unfamiliar to most of us because we haven't been taught to value what is beyond form. So, give this third step extra attention. I encourage you to practice noticing these three acts daily until you recognize that you are awareness: the divine actor, the creator, sustainer, and dissolver of all that exists. Once this is integrated, you will always have ready access to the True Self.

The last two acts show you how what you are creating, sustaining, and dissolving are either concealing or revealing awareness as the one actor. The last two acts are:

4. Concealment. Ego separation. Forgetting the True Self. Contraction.

5. Revelation. Grace. Remembering the True Self. Expansion.

From a non-dual perspective, they are the sacred pulsation called *"Spanda"* in Sanskrit, from which everything emerges and into which eventually dissolves back. They are the continuous cycle of contraction or expansion. When this oscillation is recognized as an expression of awareness, we can allow everything to be as it is. When we cannot see this, we feel limited and separate and give our power to the appearances of duality.

For the past fifty years, I have been on an awakening journey of what has become Non-dual Shamanic Tantra. I am passionate about sharing what I've discovered with others: using Shamanic Breathwork and other practices to experience more love, freedom, and connection. This path requires radical honesty and deep self-reflection. Every experience is an opportunity for the True Self to be revealed and discover the joy of making love with life.

To learn more about these practices go to
https://www.youtube.com/user/CrystalSedona/videos

Crystal Dawn Morris is a spiritual midwife and non-dual shamanic tantra teacher who makes love with life in every moment. She has discovered powerful ways to resource infinite love and freedom and embody the True Self.

As a child, Crystal felt deeply connected to the unseen world around her. This eventually led her to study with the Foundation for Shamanic Studies, Venus Rising Institute, and the International School of Temple Arts (ISTA.) Crystal is a Certified Shamanic Breathwork Facilitator, Shamanic Minister, and a lead faculty member of ISTA. She has been a shamanic counselor since 1995.

At sixteen, Crystal experienced seven days of bliss, which arose when she realized she was one with everything. This knowing has been her guiding light. On the eighth morning, she was surprised when she opened her eyes and duality reappeared. At first, she felt confused, but life showed her the next steps on her path within a few weeks. After the birth of her sons, Crystal felt passionate about helping women experience childbirth as a spiritual initiation. She became a Certified Nurse-Midwife in 1988.

Crystal's introduction to tantra began with a spontaneous kundalini awakening that happened during lovemaking. Over the last 32 years, she has studied and practiced neo-tantra, Tibetan Buddhism, tantric yoga, Saiva Tantra as well as a variety of other meditation traditions. Crystal founded http://www.tantraforawakening.com/ in 2007 and began teaching tantra at that time. She is the mother of two sons and has five grandchildren. She lives in Sedona, Arizona.

Website: https://www.tantraforawakening.org/

Email: crystal@tantraforawakening.com

FaceBook: https://www.facebook.com/CrystalDMorris/

YouTube: https://www.youtube.com/user/CrystalSedona/videos

Instagram: https://www.instagram.com/crystaldawnmorris/

CHAPTER 25

SYMBIOTIC EVOLUTION
Co-Creating Sacred Work
with Your Beloved

Carley Mattimore & John Malan

OUR STORY

CARLEY

Sitting on our front porch with my beloved John Malan in early spring of 2005, he shared his excitement about discovering Shamanic Breathwork during a men's workshop he attended. The workshop was facilitated by Brad Collins (deceased beloved of Linda Star Wolf) of Venus Rising Association. John was passionate as he shared his experience; he was able to access the deep grief stored in his body from his father's death when John was three. For the first time, he had hope that he could change.

Uncharacteristically, John said, "Carley, I can see us doing this work together!"

As the sun streamed through the shadows of the trees, I reflected on this revelation. I went into disbelief. What was the Shamanic Breathwork process? It sounded foreign to me as a psychotherapist trained in the traditional methodology of psychological practices. How could laying on the floor and breathing to loud evocative music change one's life? How could my husband, who was an information systems professional, and I co-facilitate such work together?

Also, it wasn't my idea, so I scoffed a bit as I tried to regain some control of the disruption I was feeling in my psyche. Little did we know, we would be choosing a mutually beneficial excavation of our defensive patterns developed in childhood to evolve as a couple and share our sacred work in the world.

The air carried the promise and scent of new growth erupting from the dormant earth after a long winter, as the seed planted deep in our psyches was germinating. Over several years, that seed unconsciously informed us as we raised our five spirited daughters in a blended family. And with four of them teenagers at once! I was exhausted trying to hold it all together, maintaining the illusion I could keep everyone safe.

I tried hard to be a good mom and stepmom. I created a safe, loving home with family dinners, picnics, camping, games, yard work, and Friday pizza nights. I took lots of pictures and made family photo albums to document the narrative of our new family. Through family rituals, we attempted to form a cohesive story from the pain each of us felt. I tried hard to manage all the intensity of a stepfamily and to keep feelings contained. I wanted this ship to sail smoothly, denying our family's natural expression of grief.

To be a good partner was challenging as there was little room for my relationship with John, who was caught in his internal drama and not emotionally available, but neither was I. I felt overwhelmed trying to hold it all together.

Our family was born of grief. My first husband died in an automobile accident, leaving me to raise our two daughters (ages four and one). John was sharing custody of his two daughters, who experienced the pain of separation through a divorce. Not only did John's father die when he was three, but my father and 13-year-old sister also died in an automobile accident when I was 20. The lineage of this pain goes deep on both John's and my side of our family tree with parental abandonment through death and betrayal.

ȷOHꞰ

"Goddammit, you can't do that! What the hell is the matter with you? There is a right way and a wrong way to do everything, and this is wrong, wrong, wrong!" A man in his early 50s walks along the street, head down, talking to himself.

There are no cell phones yet, so this is not as ordinary as it seems now. For the most part, he keeps his voice low, but sometimes, as on this day, he shouts at someone who isn't there. He goes by on his way to work and on his way home, and he always has these angry conversations going through his mind and sometimes bursting out.

I can tell you this man is mortified by what he is doing. He's sure people are watching and judging him. He wants desperately to stop this painful, humiliating behavior, but he is incapable of doing so. I can tell you this because he was me.

It began in childhood and grew to become the dominant feature of my life. I want you to see the contrast between how I was and how I am now. The transformation began in December of 2005 when I experienced my first Shamanic Breathwork. I had never been to a personal growth workshop before and came to this one only because a friend invited me. When we each decided we didn't want to go, we went anyway as we didn't want to disappoint each other. So yes, codependence saved me.

My job was one of my "drugs of choice." I started as a computer programmer and rose through the ranks to become the director of a large IT department in a major hospital. The level of concentration my work required was so great that while I was working, I could free myself from the obsessive inner dialogues and chronic depression.

Indeed, I had many ways of numbing myself that I let go of as I began to heal. I went into recovery from alcoholism, stopped projecting my childhood trauma on my coworkers, began an active practice of gratitude, accepted that "what comes to me comes for me," and began to change.

CARLEY

John was the catalyst for the evolution of our relationship as he began the deep healing journey into his sacred wounds. He worked hard on recovering parts of himself hidden deep in his psyche from trauma in childhood. His emotional shamanic focus, combined with his vision of us facilitating this work together, worked symbiotic magic on our relationship.

We each influenced the other with every breath we took, creating change within our personal and shared system. Every action and word, shift and insight, cultivated a narrative of transformation for our relationship. John's deep healing within the shamanic world came out of every seam, crack, and marrow of his being. It caused both deep distress and excitement for my psyche.

We pushed, pulled, raged, and softened to uncover deep-seated patterns of thinking. Our conditioned responses, developed in our childhood, became personality traits and roles that we established to feel safe. The unraveling of our co-dependent nature was raw work, and learning how to be more compassionate and vulnerable with each other was essential for our marriage. It allowed us to go deeper in our love for each other.

JOHN

I had tried to change for decades and finally gave up. Therapy, alcohol, drugs, work, all of them gave me some temporary relief or numbness. None of them got at the desperate sense of helplessness or the compulsive, self-destructive behavior I was caught up in.

In my first breathwork, everything changed. I encountered my father, who died when I was three, and understood he had not meant to leave us. I saw myself as a spiritual being, something I had vehemently denied myself. For the duration of that breathwork, I was free of my neuroses and felt connected to something infinitely greater than myself for the first time. But the greatest gift from this breathwork was that it let me know that I could change.

Thus, it was that I told Carley I could see us doing this work together. I like to joke that she replied, "Who are you, and what have you done with my husband?" but what happened was much bigger than that. She heard me and took me seriously.

CARLEY

John dove into his process, unearthing mountains of repressed rage and grief. His psycho-spiritual work rocked our relationship, resulting in exhaustive discussions, dissociative reactions, and detachment. Our marriage, pushed to the limits by the effects of this alchemical change in our family system, was stressed. Yet, our commitment to each other and this process was unwavering. Each tangible shift in perspective served as the dangling carrot in front of us. We kept moving forward. This, and my soul's guidance, led me to the next right step for my personal and our collective shift.

The dive into my own inner work came when Venus Rising offered a month-long SHIP program. Encouraged by John, and against every grain of my being which said, "Do not do this work!" I signed up. I even showed up, albeit with a lot of resistance, as my ego shouted, "I'm just fine." My psychic wounds were still unconscious, hidden within my elaborate defense mechanisms, cultivated through a lineage of trauma. They expressed a "pull yourself up by the bootstraps" worldview.

Being the oldest of six children, I was keenly attuned to my emotionally unavailable mother's needs and our family's, both spoken and unspoken. She attempted to raise us in a much different manner than her parents raised her. Unfortunately, her good intentions were affected by the suppression of her pain and suffering. She buried her feelings deep in her body, putting them behind her, as if they were over and done with, never to return. She did not realize that trauma not processed will come out as unconscious behaviors.

I became hyper-vigilant in caring for others, modeling the strengths and weaknesses of my mother and father, including the suppression of my pain. In doing my transpersonal work through the Shamanic Healing Initiatory Process, I uncovered the deep trauma stored in my DNA.

This dense tar-like energy began to move out of my body, sluggish and heavy as it moved up my chakras and out the crown of my head. Each Shamanic Breathwork and energy session assisted in the passage through and out my body. This kundalini force ignited my sacred work, setting it aflame with renewed passion and purpose. I came home from my month-long SHIP in June of 2011 and told John we were going to start a congregation of Venus Rising and do this sacred process together. The vision he had six years prior was about to take form. In July of 2011, Aahara Spiritual Community of Venus Rising was officially born as a 501(c)(3) Congregation of Venus Rising.

John

Spiritually, I could not believe the Creator loved me because I did not believe myself worthy. This was also true of my relationship with Carley; we were close and affectionate, but part of me saw it as conditional. I couldn't allow myself to believe I was lovable. I did not love myself.

Battling my inner demons kept me in a co-dependent state. I played the role I'd had in my family of origin—being small, resentful, non-communicative, and depressed. My first breathwork put a crack in this armor, and the subsequent breathworks, therapy, and gradual process of opening to Carley shattered it.

I had been in many relationships before I met Carley, but none of them were strong enough to last through the kinds of changes that Carley and I went through. We are fundamentally different people now, and our relationship is stronger and richer than ever.

The work we do together is the most meaningful and satisfying of any I have done. I never imagined that my life could be what it has become. It wasn't quick, and it certainly wasn't always easy, but now I know I can change, and nothing will stop me.

CARLEY

As we contemplated what to call our new congregation, the universe led us to the Sanskrit word "Aahara" which means "to breathe." Breath connects us to the symbiotic relationship between us and trees, dependent on each other for our survival; we emit carbon dioxide through exhalation while trees emit oxygen through photosynthesis, a very shamanic exchange. It feels like divine intervention that John and I, through our commitment to each other, our community, and our roles as teachers and students of life, have evolved into shamanic guides supporting others through change.

This transformation is a continued tweaking of our relationship, finding a natural fit for each of us based on our unique gifts and sacred purpose. We navigate the cycles of change repeatedly. We take risks to release our co-dependency.

We moved up the spiral path and found balance in the rhythm of our teaching. We never gave up and found our niche in expressing our true nature. We created something greater between us—integration of the sacred masculine and feminine energy to be of service to others.

CARLEY AND JOHN

The birth of our congregation was a leap of faith toward our sacred purpose. We began this process through a series of events that led us onto the shamanic path. It cracked us both open, enabling us to go deep into our psycho-spiritual work. It led us to assume a leadership role in our community.

Shamanic Breathwork uncovered the truth of who we are through shamanic initiation. We learned that in doing our emotional work, we could make alchemy! We could transform our experiences into something more than the sum of our shared experiences.

We faced difficult and painful truths about ourselves and each other and dove into the well of holy longing to find ourselves so we could see each other. It is an ongoing process of recovery and discovery which requires us to be open and vulnerable and to accept responsibility for things we'd rather deny or project onto each other.

In the beginning, it was raw, heated, and unforgiving. Now that we've been doing it for years, it is sometimes easy and even funny, but always familiar and rewarding. We created a new matrix of relationship dynamics with each other.

This matrix is a new template for us to navigate strong feelings such as anger, shame, disappointment, and fear. It means meeting each other through the messiness of despair, hopelessness, and doubt. It is being vulnerable, apologizing, forgiving, and letting go. We must work hard on self-reflection and be honest with ourselves and each other compassionately.

It is not an easy process, but it is the only way to be authentic and truly present for each other. As we continue to grow and evolve, we can guide others into this metamorphic process to become agents of change for these challenging times. It is our sacred work.

SHAMANIC MEDICINE OFFERING

One of the most challenging aspects of a relationship is learning how to communicate. We have difficulty listening to each other and do not pay attention to what the other is saying. We fill in what we think we heard based on our experiences and perceptions at that moment.

Reading between the lines and responding to our partners from what we think they mean often leads to misunderstandings. It can generate feelings of not being seen or heard which can trigger defensive reactions or regression. We can react to what we think we heard and create a story around this perception. "He does not listen! He must not care." Or "She does not see me!" Not listening can lead to misunderstandings, defensive behaviors, and challenging conflicts.

We use a simple technique to help us create understanding between us, so we feel safe to go deeper into what we are feeling. This practice supports the notion that the whole is greater than the parts and is a symbiosis of our sacred work together. It is magic to listen deeply to each other with the ears of our hearts. The process of listening is essential. Lean in, open your heart, deepen your breath, soften your gaze, and use all your senses as you tune in to what your partner is communicating.

When they finish, which may be indicated by a pause and a deep breath, ask if you can reflect what was shared, using your voice to make sure you understand. Then ask if there is anything else that needs to be shared. Again, listen and reflect.

After this process, ask if they are ready to hear your experience and listen sincerely to what came up for you. Follow through with love and respect as you switch roles. Doorways can open as new pathways of understanding unfold through the healing practice of listening and reflecting. This exercise can bring about a shift in your relationship with your beloved.

In this process, a shift in energy between the two of you unfolds, and coherence expands with a deeper understanding of each other's truth. When this happens, it creates a greater depth of feeling between you. When we feel heard and understood, a shift can happen.

Here is a simplified outline of the process. When an argument intensifies between you and your partner, and you are stuck, take a step back and start over, using this technique:

- Decide who will go first. This person will describe their point of view in an assertive but not aggressive way. It is best to use the "I" language. For example: "I felt overwhelmed when…" or "I became defensive when…"

- The other will genuinely listen with the ears of their heart. The process of listening is essential: lean in, open your heart, make eye contact, nod, use all your senses, tune in to what they are saying openly.

- When the first speaker has finished, the listener asks if they can reflect what was shared in their own words to make sure they understand. Then they will ask if there is anything else that needs to be shared. Again, listen and reflect.

- Then switch roles as it is now the listener's turn to share. Follow through with the same love and respect in this process.

Doorways will open, and new pathways of understanding will unfold through the healing practice of listening and reflecting, supporting a shift in the relationship with your beloved.

Carley Mattimore and **John Malan** are the parents of five spirited adult daughters and grandparents of eight outrageous grandchildren. Their lives are rich in relationships with family, friends, and community. Together they support others in finding their own "inner authority" as independent beings so they too can support our interdependence with everything on the spiral path of life. They enjoy sharing the shamanic world with others personally and collectively.

Carley Mattimore, MS, LCPC, and John Malan are Shamanic Breathwork Master Practitioners, as well as Shamanic Ministers and co-founders of the Aahara Spiritual Community, an active 501(c)(3) non-profit congregation of Venus Rising, since 2011.

They offer psycho-spiritual workshops in the Heartland of the USA, including Dare' Dream Circles, The Shamanic Healing Initiatory Process (SHIP), and their signature program, The Shamanic Warriorship Path; a series of four initiations for a new paradigm of warrior energy.

They also offer transformational tours to Africa, guiding journeyers to sacred sites along the 31st meridian, the golden seam of the earth. They are both graduates of the White Lion Leadership Academy in Timbavati, South Africa.

Carley is co-author, along with Linda Star Wolf, of Sacred Messengers of Shamanic Africa: Land of ZepTepi. She is a shamanic midwife for our times, a shamanic psychotherapist with over 30 years of experience in working with children, adults, and families, as well as a therapeutic energy worker (healing touch practitioner and shamanic, Usui and Tibetan reiki master). Carley is writing her second book, the Shamanic Mystic Warrior. In addition, Carley co-facilitates a Global Shamanic Multi-Dimensional Mystery School with Judith Corvin-Blackburn, author of Activating Your 5D Frequency.

John is an explorer, mainly of his inner life but lately of the world at large as well. He wants very much to be a good, healthy man.

To learn more about us:

https://www.aaharaspiritualcommunity.org

https://www.carleymattimore.com

https://www.facebook.com/aaharaspiritualcommunity

https://www.facebook.com/SacredMessengersofShamanicAfrica

https://www.facebook.com/carley.mattimore/

https://www.youtube.com/channel/UCx-JuWpNNUcrvdr0ap-TNUQ

CHAPTER 26

STOP DIAGNOSING YOURSELF

Connect to Your Inner Shaman and Embrace Peace and Joy

Nita Gage, MA Doctor of Shamanic Psychospiritual Studies

MY STORY

Depression was my companion for most of my life until the age of 44. At that time, I stumbled into the arms of Star Wolf and participated in what became known as Shamanic Breathwork, where I found redemption.

I learned that it wasn't a clinical issue; instead, I had been diagnosing myself falsely and deepening my belief that something was terribly wrong with me, that I was sick and damaged.

I grew up on a Native American reservation, yet I'm not a Native American and do not have indigenous roots. It was here where I was surrounded by indigenous culture, spirituality, and ways of being. My earliest and most impactful memories are of being in tune with nature and the aliveness of the earth.

My neighbors of the Nez Pearce tribe were my closest friends, and their grandmother lived with them for half the year. She made me beaded buckskin moccasins and encouraged me, along with her granddaughters, to go with her on long walks in the desert and to pay attention to what the plants, animals, stones, and earth were showing us.

My earliest training in shamanic wisdom was my childhood, and it wasn't until many, many years later that I consciously reconnected to these deepest roots. Yet, there is no denying I was steeped in shamanic wisdom that has informed me my entire life.

At 18, I hit a deeper despair and began to consider suicide. I came later to understand that what I was calling depression was a disconnection from the earth that my soul longed for and couldn't live without.

My mother had a psychotic brother, Bub, which didn't help things. He snapped at the age of 24 and has been in a mental hospital since. When I had my meltdown at 18, they worried I was turning out like Uncle Bub, but instead of getting help, they retracted into fear and denial. I was on my own.

Stumbling through my late 20s with the birth of my first child, I floundered through serious postpartum depression; silently, I fantasized about suicide as my only escape from the unbearable emotional and mental pain I was experiencing.

Looking into the eyes of my precious and innocent baby at 26 kept me from ever seriously considering killing myself.

My twenties were spent living in London, England. During the 70s, I was involved with a group of renegade psychiatrists, the most famous of whom was R.D. Laing, who dared to suggest that insanity is a sane reaction to the alienation in families and society and that love is the healer.

"The main agent in uniting the patient, in allowing the pieces to come together and cohere, is the physician's love, a love that recognizes the patient's total being, and accepts it, with no strings attached." R.D Laing, *The Divided Self,* p. 165

I was drawn to his radical approach and came to see that Laing himself was a shaman, a magician.

The only rule in dwellings that very loosely resembled therapeutic communities headed by R. D Laing was "be authentic." It was as if it was etched over the doorway, as with the Delphi Oracle's command "know thyself." The authenticity mandate also meant deep raw, brutally honest connection to others that transcended social norms of behavior.

I often heard "you're not being authentic." as an indictment of my behavior or something I said.

I found myself mesmerized by living in a household where everyone questioned everyone else's motives for everything said or done or even thought. This was the path to enlightenment, or at least that is how I perceived it at the time.

The dwelling was actually a "squat," a house abandoned and subsequently occupied, illegally, by people who set up the community. There were no therapists or staff of any sort. Just people living together with the shared intent of discovering who we were. I was sharing a house with five to six other people and a few others at times. Some were there because it was an alternative to a mental hospital. Some of us because it was an alternative to loneliness and traditional family life. And some of us because it was as close as we could get to a politically active commune. A group of people working to find a better way to live than the false selves constructed from our nuclear families.

No one was diagnosed; even those coming straight from a psychiatric hospital were embraced and not vilified for their suffering. Instead of asking "what's wrong with you," people were asked, "what happened to you." Stories were listened to and validated, not judged and diagnosed.

We huddled around the fireplace with cups of strong tea and explored authenticity.

We studied psychoanalysis, yoga, rebirthing, eastern religion and shared our authentic selves in late-night conversations. The healing was in the holding of the community, the analysis, and the experiential sessions of rebirthing and breathwork.

After ten years and the home birth of my two sons, we moved back to California, and I found myself working in a psychiatric hospital with people in extreme states, in padded cells. I felt comfortable after my years in the Laing community. I saw people for the spirits they were, rather than the suffering they displayed. I connected to my inner shaman and traveled into their space no matter how extreme, and held space for them to find their way through.

In my late 30s, depression came screaming back with a vengeance. Like a scorned lover, depression caught up with me and promised to destroy me.

I had just left an abusive marriage. I fled the marriage with a suitcase, jobless and broke. My carefully constructed way of being in the world and my personality came unglued—deeply unglued. I tried in vain to hold it all together. Ignoring my mental, physical and emotional exhaustion, one day it dawned on me, *I am seriously depressed*. My ability to carry on with tenacity masked my deep-seated despair. The truth was, I was ashamed of being depressed. Despite my professional training, or perhaps because of it, I could not admit my disease and hid it like an alcoholic hides their drinking.

Suicidal ideation was my escape valve. There were days, even weeks, when all I could do was lay in bed all day and obsessively worry about how I was going to work and survive. In some odd attempt at comfort, I would remind myself that I could kill myself if it got too much worse. Knowing that was my "out," I found I could carry on another day.

I identified as a victim, but the twist was I felt like a heroic victim. "Oh, the things I have survived…" was my mantra. Running from self-loathing and despair fueled my mission of taking care of other people. My Mother Teresa complex kept me from feeling the deep longings of my soul. My strategy worked for a long, long time, and when it didn't work, I collapsed.

The deep exhaustion I experienced on every level of my being put an end to my ability to caretake others. I didn't know it at the time, but I was hitting, as they say in the 12-Step world, my co-dependent *bottom*. This is the moment when one's way of being in the world is no longer working.

Unable to work, I was forced to rely on the kindness of my friends. This was the greatest gift my depression brought me. Broken and hopeless, I found myself on the couches of a few good friends at different times over the next few years. I still owned my home, but I would stay with friends because I didn't feel safe being alone. My suicidal thoughts were beginning to be more pervasive.

One fateful day, I awoke, and something in me had shifted for the worse. There was a dead calm within me, and I felt anxiety-free and numb to my depression. I knew this was the time to end my life. Having some small presence of mind, I heard a voice in me say, "Okay, Nita, do you really want to die, or do you just want out of your life?"

In the moments that followed, I found myself speaking out to the universe, saying: "Today I am going to shop for a gun, and I will also go to a bookstore; if anyone is listening, help me find the right book first." Looking back, it sounds so silly—a book or a gun—but it was my moment of truth. Did I want to live? Part of me did.

Kmart is a great full-service store. Everything you need, including handguns, is there for the picking. I found myself at the gun counter discussing which gun to buy with the clerk.

"Women usually like this one," the clerk said, holding up a cute little pink thing.

A cute little pink thing didn't seem quite right for the task I had in mind, and even in my temporary psychosis of the day, I could see the humor.

I thanked him and even said, "I'll probably be back, but got to go to the bookstore first."

Walking into the bookstore in Yuma, Arizona, a very small rural town in the southwest, I was not expecting to find any book that would help me, but my soul knew better. The bookstore stocked best-selling novels and fish and game books mostly. I had been in the bookstore hundreds of times over the years, but I had never noticed anything that even resembled a self-help section.

That day, I walked in, almost trance-like. I looked straight ahead, and there, sitting on its own, was a book titled, *Awakening in Time*. I ran to the shelf, grabbed the book, and began to read it.

Awakening In Time, subtitled *From Codependency to Co-Creation*, by Jacquelyn Small, was the book that saved my life. And, there was that concept again, "codependency." What did that have to do with depression? I took it home, read it cover to cover, wept through most of it, laughed through some, and felt the life force coming back into my being.

When I finished it, I saw the author's phone number was in the book. I called her, and to my shock, Jackie answered the phone as though she was my best friend and waiting for my call. I blurted out my story, thanked her for saving my life, and was prepared to say goodbye and hang up when she said, "Nita, how are you now?"

She actually seemed to care, and I responded, "I want to live, but I am scared that I will stay depressed."

She told me about healing workshops and retreats she did, and I signed up on the spot, not knowing how I would get there or pay for it.

That is where I first met Star Wolf. We recognized a soul connection immediately and have been best friends ever since.

Star Wolf took me under her wing and trained me in Shamanic Breathwork and psycho-spiritual healing methods. After crawling on my knees to that first workshop, I was co-facilitating retreats with her for several years. Over the next 20 years, I worked with Star Wolf facilitating Venus Rising Workshops. I also led my own workshops utilizing Shamanic Breathwork in Healer Within Retreats for physicians and health care professionals on the island of Molokai. And for my third act in life, at 65, I became a teacher and coach for the Hoffman Institute. I turned my life around by becoming who I am and living my soul purpose.

Over and over in life, my soul, my essential self, knew and led me to where I needed to be. Despite the fear, I did follow my soul's urging, often through the darkness without knowing if I would ever see the light.

At 71, I live a joyous life in my home on Maui, loving my children and grandchildren and still loving my work as a coach and teacher.

SHAMANIC MEDICINE OFFERING

Changing who we are is a very popular activity these days—changing our bodies through surgery, changing our minds with psychedelics, changing our emotions with prescribed medications. The rush to change is usually motivated and guided by external influences that demand, cajole, and shame us into believing we are not enough, bad or wrong.

Change for personal transformation, joy, health, and well-being comes from an entirely opposite concept. *There is nothing wrong with you, and there is nothing to fix.*

The path to change is one of self-compassion and self-forgiveness. It is recognizing that you have deep unresolved hurts, unexpressed emotions, and underlying negative beliefs about yourself.

Acceptance and self-love as foundations for personal change are more sustainable and ultimately transformative than treating ourselves as a fix-it project.

We hide our pain because we are ashamed of it. We are taught to believe there is something wrong with us for suffering. "You are weak, pathetic, grow up, toughen up, get over yourself."

Or the modern shaming messages of: "You are not focusing on the positive, and you are attracting negative people, things, and places."

The real secret is that nothing is wrong with you. You are hurt and suffering from unhealed pain. You are not responsible for what happened to you in childhood. Yet, as an adult, you are responsible for healing and growing up emotionally to be accountable for your own joy and resilience.

Love is the healer: and self-love is the new primary care. You are your own first responder; you have the power to nurture and soothe yourself.

Practice self-love and root out the inner critical and judgmental voice within you.

Self-Love vs. Self-Critical Experience

Close your eyes, consider this statement: "I am lovable and good enough just as I am." Now listen for the critical voice within. Just listen. Notice the quality of that voice, often cynical, doubting, even abusive, maybe subtly questioning as though it's your wise counsel.

Open your eyes and write down what you heard. It's important to bring that voice out and into the light. Once you write it down, do something energetic with your body, put the paper on the floor, stomp on it, tear it up. Let yourself energetically set a boundary with that voice, "I won't listen to this any longer." Use your own words.

Now close your eyes again, take some longer, slower breaths, count of four. Place your hands on your heart, imagine breathing in and out through your heart, call to mind something you love to do or a place you love to be. Allow yourself to feel the goodness of the place and what you are doing. Now ask your essential self, your authentic self, your sometimes small but every present voice, for a supportive message or guidance about yourself.

Open your eyes again, and write what you heard, or felt, or sensed, journal from that self-loving voice, notice the quality of your inner self.

The practice is a step towards a compassionate appreciation of yourself, a practice that opens you to also be compassionate towards others.

Through self-love, we can be gentle with ourselves instead of harsh. Much research has been done to show that self-love and kindness are deep and sustainable motivators for change and learning.

At times we do need to get help; we need people and places that are nurturing and healing. Find healers who see everyone as a divine being. As you move through your struggles, and no matter how wounded or dysfunctional you feel or believe yourself to be, or others have told you to be (particularly if you have been diagnosed), make sure the healers you work with embrace and hold space, so you're able to drop into your deepest wounds and unhealed places. Only then will you emerge into your divine self.

Get away from your ordinary life, dive into the extraordinary, ditch your electronics, retreat and give yourself the time to heal and transform.

Through the practice of self-love and seeking experienced and loving facilitators, you will be able to find your deepest creativity, your vision for your life. There is nothing wrong with you, you took on strategies to survive, and you did! Now find out how to let go of limiting strategies and open to new and previously unimagined possibilities. Rather than live with self-diagnosis of anxiety and depression, you can learn to embrace yourself as a whole and vibrant human being.

Nita Gage, MA, DSPS, is a Hoffman teacher and coach. She has been leading transformational healing retreats for over 25 years, most recently with the Hoffman Institute. She is a certified Shamanic Breathwork Facilitator and Shamanic Minister with Venus Rising. She co-founded the NeuroImaginal Institute and created Healer Within Retreats working with physicians. She was executive director of the American Board of Holistic Medicine as well as clinical and executive positions in hospitals and treatment centers over the 40 years of her career. She trained in psychoanalysis with R.D. Laing in London from 1970 to 1980. Returning to the U.S., she pursued graduate degrees in clinical psychology and a doctorate in shamanic psychology. For many years, she worked in rural Arizona and Hawaii with diverse populations in addictions and mental health, initiating many innovation programs to address underserved populations. Growing up on a reservation in Arizona gave her a unique understanding of diversity. Nita has authored two books: Soul Whispering: The Art of Awakening Shamanic Consciousness with Linda Star Wolf and Women in Storage: How to Reimagine Your Life and articles and interviews about her personal story and her work.

Shamanic Breathwork with Venus Rising Association for Transformation gives people powerful transformational journeys of healing and self-discovery.

https://www.hoffmaninstitute.org

https://www.shamanicbreathwork.org

AFTERWORD

Linda Star Wolf

"I live my life in growing orbits
which move out over the things of the world.
Perhaps I can never achieve the last,
but that will be my attempt.

I am circling around God, around the ancient tower,
and I have been circling for a thousand years,
and I still don't know if I am a falcon, or a storm,
or a great song."

I Live My Life In Growing Orbits
by Rainer Maria Rilke (Translated by Robert Bly)

Dear Shamanic Soul Traveler,

Take a deep breath. . .exhale fully. . .and let go as you begin to open your beautiful heart and mind. Surrender to this precious fleeting moment outside of time and space and allow yourself to slowly feel the comforting presence of love supporting you as you embody who you really are.

Remember and recognize the truth of your being that you are the offspring of the Gods. You were born as a divine, elemental child of the universe. No more or no less than any of Great Spirit's other magnificent creations. I always like to say that we are all God's favorite child.

Now, say out loud these words in the old tongue of the Lakota Language, "O' Mitakuye Oyasin," which means we are all related. We are all relatives and part of the great web of life. Each one of us originated from the same mystical source. The powerful, elemental ancestors of Water, Earth, Fire, and Air are our great-great-grandparents, also known as the Ancient Egyptian Neteru Ancestors that gave birth to us all.

Yes! "We really are all God's favorite child." Yes! Nature really can transform us and work its magic of unconditional love in our lives.

By now, you have had the golden opportunity to take an intimate glimpse and journey into the multidimensional world of *Shamanic Breathwork, The Nature of Change*. My prayer is that you have gained a deeper understanding and respect for the healing power of your own breath and the transformative changes possible during the Shamanic Breathwork journey.

Our elemental bodies are mainly composed of water/blood, earth/flesh, fire/energy, and air/breath. When they become activated in a sacred manner through your sincere connection with Spirit, the supernatural energies of love and wisdom naturally flow from the heart of Great Mystery into our human hearts, and miracles become the new norm.

You have had the privilege of hearing personal, authentic, heartfelt, life-changing stories from some of Venus Rising's Shamanic Breathwork Facilitators and Shamanic Ministers. Many of these dedicated planetary change agents are actively focused on sharing their authentic soul's sacred purpose and "medicine" with our world.

Nature, in its supreme, archetypal, evolutionary state, continues to gift humankind with its mysterious, embedded wisdom of how to change. We are in the process of remembering that we are not separate from nature, and in fact, we are the new kids on the evolutionary block. The mineral, plant, and animal kingdoms and queendoms have evolved through millennia into their royal natural states, and human beings are waking up to claim their inherited shamanic evolution as well. Hopefully, the time is upon us to remember who we really are and that we are not born "in sin," but we are born "in blessing," and it's not too late. The time of great change is upon us. Can you hear the ancient ones calling to us in the winter winds, the crashing ocean waves, the erupting volcano's floes, the shaking shifting earth? Ready or not, big change is here. So let us take another deep breath as we step up and take our rightful sacred place in the nature of things as we realize that we are all indeed powerful forces of nature with our own sacred purpose to serve. Transformation is our birthright and our soul's destiny. It's time for a change.

THE SPIRAL PATH

There is a way of living
that follows the rhythms of nature
It will be your path, if only you slow down and listen
to the cyclical seasons that surround you
and discover how they live within you.

Nature grows and expands in spirals
what goes around comes around - just a bit more evolved
Do not forget that nature also lets go, falls to the ground
disintegrates and dissolves back into the darkness.
Not into eternity, but to rise again in a new form.

Darling, do you dare
to make a change and be totally bare
without holding any of the familiar strings
trusting that you truly need what life brings?

Allowing yourself to drop into the water
Resting, digesting, dreaming and forgetting

Dwelling in the depths of just being
like in the womb, nurtured, taken care of
Without an agenda, no plan or sense of direction
yet somehow preparing for a soul calling change.

Darling, do you dare
to simply stop and hibernate like a bear
without holding any of the familiar strings
so you may be nourished by life's water springs?

Later finding yourself stuck in the soil of earth
lost in your murky inner chambers - stinky but fertile
where you will meet your inner mother and father
feeling their absence or intense presence.
With agitation, wanting to find a way out of the pit.
Wondering if it's maybe better to give up and just sit?

Darling do you, dare
to admit where you lack proper self-care
without holding any of the familiar strings
even though sometimes the truth hurts and stings?

Walking straight into the flames of fire
feeling like a king without his fancy attire
naked and realizing your hidden corners are seen
Fear mixed with passion, forced to take action
pushing through, claiming your true power
Knowing that the only way out is to keep going.

Darling do you, dare
to see your shadow and tendency to compare
without holding any of the familiar strings
looking for each part of you that into hiding swings?

Suddenly finding yourself in spirit
with a deep inner knowing that the only way now
is to stop the struggles, give in and trust
Tasting the sweet sparkles of the mystery
the piercing love that resides in the unknown
feeling held, guided, knowing you belong.

Darling do you, dare
to surrender to life taking you anywhere
without holding any of the familiar strings
humbly hearing how gracefully the universe sings?

At last you will take in the fresh air
Not breathing for survival but for fully living
Harvesting the wisdom of your previous struggles
in hindsight understanding the meaning of the journey
Gaining compassion, ready to pay it forward
knowing your life has a sacred purpose.

Darling do you, dare
to stand up, shine and share
without holding any of the familiar strings
finally realizing that you got wings?

Áróra Helgadóttir
Shamanic Breathwork Master Practitioner

ACKNOWLEDGEMENTS

This book would not exist without the countless wisdom keepers who have kept the faith throughout the ages. I am deeply humbled with the many powerful lineages and masters I have had the privilege to learn from on my path. I want to give a special honoring to a few of the most influential persons and paths that have changed my life forever.

Mammy Jones and the garden, Seneca Wolf Clan Grandmother, Twylah Nitsch, Psychic Tarot Reader and cousin M.Jean Moore, AA Dr. Bob and Bill Wilson, Stanislov Grof (Holotropic Breathwork), Jacquelyn Small (Integrative Breathwork), Leonard Orr (Rebirthing Breathwork), Jeremiah Abrams (Jungian Shadow Work), Gabrielle Roth (5 Rhythms), Marion Woodman, Ram Dass, Brad Collins, Mom, Dad, and Casey.

My heart is overflowing with gratitude to all the beautiful Shamanic Breathwork co-authors in this book. Nita Gage and Judy Redhawk, thank you for your constant steadfastness and faith in me throughout the years.

Thank you Lindi Dye, Crystal Allen, and Kitty Kremzar for all of the support with our creatures, our Loveland home, and the Venus Rising Elemental Temples.

Gratitude to all of our Venus Rising core staff, past and present.

Special thanks to Kathy Morrison for your ongoing support for all VR programs and especially for your dedication to sharing 30 Shamanic Questions with others.

This book would not have happened without Atlantis Wolf's encouragement, and Laura Di Franco's fearlessness.

Beloved Nikólaus, you are the wind beneath my wings, the thief of my heart. Your brilliance is brighter than any star I have ever known.

December 5, 2021 *(Grandmother Twylah's Birthday!!)*

Linda Star Wolf

Davide De Angelis is an award-winning Designer and Visionary Artist. He is also a Master Tarot Reader, Teacher and Facilitator. In his personal life he is a wild percussionist, powerful didgeridoo player and jump rope fanatic. He has worked with some of the most innovative companies and leaders in the world, including Apple, Virgin, Sony, and for seven years with the iconic David Bowie, creating album art, fine art and a diverse range of innovative projects. Davide is the creator of the Starman Tarot, an international bestseller, that has radically reimagined the tarot and its ability to reveal the miraculous beauty and deep wonder of life. Bowie described Davide's creative work as "potent visual alchemy" and called him 'The Visual Alchemist'. He has been fascinated and involved in the field of human potential for more than 30 years and has spent over a decade training with Shamans and Energy Masters from both East and West. Inspired by adventure and a passion for learning, Davide has travelled extensively, engaging with the art, cosmologies and mystery traditions of many diverse cultures. Throughout the years he has taught a plethora of systems including self-enquiry, yoga and sound healing. For the past five years his Creative Alchemy seminars and masterclasses have been teaching the art of living fully expressed and opening to the vital spirit of creativity. Central to everything is his desire to inspire, explore and astonish.

OTHER RESOURCES

Along with all of the resources received from each of the co-authors within this book, you can also visit Venus Rising's website for further resources on Shamanic Breathwork, Star Wolf, and Venus Rising.

✿ Contact Star Wolf & Venus Rising ✿
venusrising@shamanicbreathwork.org

✿ Shamanic Breathwork Up-Coming Events ✿
https://www.shamanicbreathwork.org/events

✿ Locate a Shamanic Practitioner Near You ✿
https://www.shamanicbreathwork.org/find-a-shamanic-practitioner

✿ Learn about being Ordained as a Shamanic Minister ✿
https://www.shamanicbreathwork.org/shamanic-ministry

✿ Learn about Certification as a Shamanic Breathwork Facilitator ✿
https://www.shamanicbreathwork.org/shamanic-breathwork

✿ Learn about earning a Degree with Venus Rising University ✿
https://www.shamanicbreathwork.org/about-venus-rising-university

We would also like to take a moment to recognize a dear friend and famous award-winning musician, Michael Brant DeMaria. His music can be found around the world. Michael graciously grants permission for Venus Rising to use his music in many of our Shamanic Breathwork ceremonies. If you are in search of shamanic music to breathe, journey, and transform with, we highly recommend his original music.

✿ Michael Brant DeMaria ✿
https://michaeldemaria.com

OTHER PUBLICATIONS BY LINDA STAR WOLF

Shamanic Mysteries of Peru: The Heart Wisdom of the High Andes

— by Linda Star Wolf & Vera Lopez, Published by Inner Traditions / Bear & Company, 2020.

Sacred Messengers of Shamanic Africa: Teachings from Zep Tepi, the *Land of First Time*

— by Linda Star Wolf & Carley Mattimore, Published by Inner Traditions / Bear & Company, 2018.

Soul Whispering: The Art of Awakening Shamanic Consciousness

— by Linda Star Wolf & Nita Gage, Published by Inner Traditions / Bear & Company, 2017.

Sacred Medicine: Shamanic Teachers of the Instar Medicine Wheel

— by Linda Star Wolf & Anna Cariad-Barrett, Published by Inner Traditions / Bear & Company, 2013.

The Spirit of the Wolf

— by Linda Star Wolf & Casey Piscitelli, published by Sterling, Inc, Oct 2012.

Visionary Shamanism: Activating the Imaginal Cells of the Human Energy Field

— by Linda Star Wolf & Anne Dillon, Published by Inner Traditions / Bear & Company, 2011.

Shamanic Egyptian Astrology: Your Planetary Relationship to the Gods

— by Linda Star Wolf & Ruby Falconer, Published by Inner Traditions / Bear & Company, 2010.

Shamanic Breathwork: Journeying Beyond the Limits of the Self

— by Linda Star Wolf, Published by Inner Traditions / Bear & Company, 2009.

The Anubis Oracle: A Journey Into the Shamanic Mysteries of Egypt

— by Nicki Scully & Linda Star Wolf, Published by Inner Traditions / Bear & Company, 2008.

Shamanic Mysteries of Egypt: Awakening the Healing Power of the Heart

— by Nicki Scully & Linda Star Wolf, Published by Inner Traditions / Bear & Company, 2007.

The 30 Shamanic Questions for Humanity: From Ego Agenda to Soul Purpose,

— by Linda Star Wolf, Self-Published, 2005.

You can view all of Star Wolf's publications and other offerings here:

https://www.shamanicbreathwork.org/venus-rising-shop

VENUS RISING
UNIVERSITY

In August 2010, Star Wolf's dream of a Shamanic Psycho-Spiritual University was realized when the University of North Carolina recognized Venus Rising University (VRU) as part of its educational system. As far as we know, VRU is still the only Shamanic Psycho-Spiritual University in the world.

Venus Rising University is a unique, non-traditional university that offers Bachelor, Master, and Doctorate degrees in Shamanic Psycho-Spiritual studies. The foundation of all VRU degrees is the Shamanic Healing Initiatory Process (SHIP).

As a non-traditional university, students receive credit for Life Experience. The programs are self-designed. Our curriculum is structured to promote and accelerate personal transformation and embodied leadership. At Venus Rising University, students have the opportunity to change not only their lives but also change the world through their spiritual evolution and activism. A goal of VRU is to support students in remembering who they really are and awakening to their souls' purposes. Shamanic Psycho-Spiritual Studies provides a challenging and exciting perspective on how to embody a spiritual career that has a heart and gives meaning and purpose to students' lives. VRU supports individualism and diversity actively experienced through the healing power of community. Our graduates are the leaders and way-showers for future generations. Many can of which are found as Co-Authors in this book!

As a graduate of VRU, whatever you choose to do in the world will be infused with the love and wisdom you have opened up to during your time with Venus Rising University.

https://www.shamanicbreathwork.org/about-venus-rising-university

ONE BREATH
ONE TRIBE • ONE LOVE

VENUS RISING ASSOCIATION FOR TRANSFORMATION

www.shamanicbreathwork.org

Made in USA - Kendallville, IN
35505_9781954047501
03.18.2022 1012